Revised 2nd Edition

SEDONA HIKES

by

Richard & Sherry Mangum

HEXAGON PRESS
FLAGSTAFF, ARIZONA

BOOKS BY HEXAGON PRESS

FLAGSTAFF HIKES
105 Day Hikes Around Flagstaff, Arizona
224 pages, 8 pages of color photographs
$14.95
FLAGSTAFF HISTORIC WALK
A Stroll Through Old Downtown
64 pages, Dozens of photographs historical & modern
$6.95
FLAGSTAFF ALBUM
Flagstaff' First 50 Years in Photographs
64 pages, 135 historical photographs
$9.95

NONLIABILITY STATEMENT

While we have expended considerable effort to guarantee accuracy and have personally taken every one of these hikes, errors in field notes, transcription and typesetting can occur. Changes also occur on the land and some descriptions that were accurate when written may be inaccurate when you read this book. One storm, for example, can block a road, or the Forest Service can change a trail. In addition to the problems of accuracy, there is the problem of injury. It is always possible that hikers may sustain harm while on a hike. The authors, publishers and all those associated with this book, directly or indirectly, disclaim any liability for accidents, injuries, damages or losses whatsoever that may occur to anyone using this book. The responsibility for good health and safety while hiking is that of the user.

Produced by Northland Graphics, Flagstaff, AZ, on recycled paper
Cover Design by Joan Carstensen, Northland Graphics
Cover Photo by Sherry G. Mangum

TABLE OF CONTENTS

ABOUT THE AUTHORS

Dick was born in Flagstaff and has lived there all his life. When his family acquired a second home in Back O' Beyond, south of Sedona, in 1951, he began his love affair with the Sedona area. He learned that by driving 25 miles (the distance between Flagstaff and Sedona) the hiking enthusiast can hike year around: in cool Flagstaff in the summer and warm Sedona in the winter, and in either place in between.

After graduating from Flagstaff High School in 1954, he became a lawyer. He practiced law in Flagstaff for 15 years, then became a Superior Court Judge for Coconino County in 1976, retiring in 1993 to devote full time to hiking and writing.

Sherry has lived in Flagstaff since she was seven years old. The daughter of hiking parents, she has enjoyed getting into the outdoors from the time she was a toddler. She loves the scenic beauties of Sedona.

She also inherited a love of photography from her parents, who are both professional photographers. She has refined her skills to produce the photographs you will see in this book. Adept at all aspects of photography, she prefers landscapes. Her work has been published in books and periodicals since 1978. Sherry likes to work with a Nikon F4.

TIPS ON SEDONA HIKING

ACCESS

Many of these hikes can be reached on paved roads. For those hikes on unpaved roads, you need to pay attention to conditions. Some of the roads become slippery and impassable when they are wet. Some, such as the upper part of Schnebly Hill Road, are officially closed during the winter by locked gates.

ROCK CLIMBING

We do not provide any rock climbing information in this book. If you want to go rock climbing, you are on your own. Much of the rock around Sedona is sandstone, a notoriously unstable rock.

THORNS

It seems sometimes that every plant along the hiking paths in the Sedona area has thorns, spines or sharp-edged leaves. Pay attention. Learn to identify the fanged plants and avoid them.

VARMINTS

Sedona is in a life zone favorable to rattlesnakes. Even so, we have only seen one on all our hikes and he was just warning us from several feet away. There are also some scorpions and black widow spiders in the area, though we have never seen either. Pests like mosquitoes are scarce. There are no chiggers nor swarming insects like black flies. Our advice about varmints is: be watchful but not paranoid.

WATER

Do not count on finding water anywhere. Take your water with you. In Sedona's hot dry climate you will need plenty of it.

WEATHER

Sedona is in a high desert location, at an altitude of about 4,000 feet. Its finest weather is from October to May. During the summer it can be quite hot, with many days over 100 degrees F. Some of the strenuous hikes can be exhausting in this kind of heat, so be prepared.

How to Use This Book

Alphabetical arrangement. The 121 hikes in this book are arranged from A-Z.

Index. The index starts at page 252. It groups the hikes by geographical area and by special features.

Layout. The text describing a hike and the map of the hike are on facing pages so that you can take in everything at once.

Maps. The maps are not to scale but their proportions are generally correct. The main purpose of the maps is to get you to the trailhead. The maps show mileage point-to-point. The text gives cumulative mileage.

Larger scale maps. For the big picture, buy a Forest Service map or *Experience Sedona.*

Bold type. When you see a trail name in bold type it means that the hike is described in this book.

Ratings. We show hikes rated as easy, moderate and hard. We are middle-aged hikers in normal condition, not highly conditioned athletes who never tire. Hikers should adjust our ratings for their own fitness level. The hike-in-a-box on each map may best show how hard a hike is.

Mileage. Driving distance was measured from the Sedona Y, located at the junction of Highways 89A and 179. All hikes start from this point. Milepost locations are also shown on the maps (as MP) on highways that have them. Hike mileage was measured by a pedometer.

Access roads. To reach many of these hikes, you will have to travel unpaved roads, some of them rough. Our Tercel has 4-wheel drive but not much clearance. Our access ratings were based on how well the Tercel handled the roads. Some drives require a high clearance vehicle.

Safety. We avoid taking risks on hikes. None of these hikes requires technical climbing.

Wilderness Areas. The Sedona area is blessed by having many of its hiking places included within federally designated Wilderness Areas. This is great for the hiker. Please read the Rules of the Trail on page 256.

 Cairns. These are stacks of rocks used as trail markers. Some are officially placed, while others are made by hikers.

Mileposts. Major Arizona highways are marked every mile by a sign about three feet high on the right side of the road.

MILE
3
7
5

Location Map

LEGEND

Paved Road ▬▬▬▬

Unpaved Road ▬▬▬▬

The map starts with Row B and Column 2 so that places beyond the map can be indicated in the articles

OAK CREEK CANYON RECREATION SITES

Oak Creek Vista
16.0 mi.

NOTE: All campgrounds require a user fee

Pine Flat
59 Spaces   12.8 mi.

Cave Spring
78 Spaces   11.8 mi.

89

Bootlegger
10 Spaces   9.0 mi.

Banjo Bill
8 Spaces   8.3 mi.

Halfway   8.0 mi.

Slide Rock   7.2 mi.

6.4 mi.   Manzanita
           19 Spaces

Encinoso

5.3 mi.

2.5 mi.   Grasshopper Point
           Swim Only

89

89

Sedona Y

179

Picnic Sites
Campgrounds

CHANGES FOR THIS EDITION

Changes to trails still in the book

Little Horse Trail: new trailhead; **Old Jim Thompson Road**: a new subdivision has changed the access road where the hike began; **Old Schnebly Hill Road**: this has been incorporated into the new Schnebly Hill Trail; **Schuerman Mountain**: construction of a new high school wiped out the old trailhead; **Thomas Point**: new parking area; **West Fork**: new parking area and trailhead.

Hikes we removed from the book:

Briant Canyon: now included as part of the Little Horse Trail; **Cathedral Rock from Verde Valley School**: now posted with No Trespassing signs; **Coyote Ridge Trail**: the officials at Red Rock State Park consider this to be only a connector; **Frye Wash Trail**: never built; **Munds Mountain South**: difficult and dangerous; **Oak Creek Vista**: we decided to keep all hikes in this book below the Mogollon Rim; **Rattlesnake Ridge**: too short; **Thompson's Ladder**: access closed.

New hikes for this edition:

Cathedral Rock: from Red Rock Crossing; **Flume Road Trail**: an adventure in the Verde River area; **Harding Mountain**: a hidden treasure in upper Oak Creek Canyon; **Javelina Trail**: new trail at Red Rock State Park; **Long Canyon Trail #63**: from the bank of Wet Beaver Creek to the top of the Mogollon Rim; **Verde Hot Springs:** long scenic drive to a hike with many features; **Schnebly Hill Trail:** from the Schnebly Hill Road to Munds Mountain; **Wild Horse Connector**: equestrian access from Jacks Canyon to the Hot Loop Trail; **Yavapai Ridge Trail**: another new trail at Red Rock State Park.

Mountain Bikes:

In the first edition of the book, we sought to help mountain bikers by giving information about trails suitable for biking. We did not intend a full blown bike book, but some readers took it that way and were disappointed. A rider's range is so much greater than a hiker's that a good hiking trail description may be of little value to a biker. So, for this edition, we have removed bikes and are sticking with the subject we know best: hiking.

We have re-checked our mileage figures by driving access roads and re-doing hikes, looking for changes and checking for accuracy. We were embarrassed to find errors, and hope we have corrected all of them. Our goal is perfection. Our greatest joy is meeting someone on the trail who looks at us, lights up, and says, "Oh, you're the people who wrote the book!" a copy of which is sticking out of their pack. We hope that we will meet *you* on the trail someday.

A. B. YOUNG TRAIL #100

General Information
Location Map B5
Munds Park and Wilson Mt. USGS Maps
Coconino Forest Service Map

Driving Distance One Way: 8.8 miles *14.0 km* (Time 20 minutes)
Access Road: All cars, Paved all the way
Hiking Distance One Way: 1.6 miles *2.56 km* (Time 80 minutes)
How Strenuous: Hard
Features: Views

NUTSHELL: This is a steep trail up the west wall of Upper Oak Creek Canyon near Bootlegger Campground, 8.8 miles *14.0 km* north of Sedona.

DIRECTIONS:
From the Sedona Y Go:
        North on Highway 89A for 8.8 miles *14.0 km* (MP 383). There is no official parking area for the trail. Sometimes you can park in the Bootlegger campground, but don't count on it. Look for a place on the shoulder of the highway.

TRAILHEAD: Walk through Bootlegger Campground, where you will see a trail going down to the creek. You must wade the creek or try to hop across it on boulders. There is a marked trailhead on the other shore, for this is a maintained trail; its sign reads, "A B Young #100."

DESCRIPTION: Once you get across the creek you will see an old road running parallel to the creek. This old road was formerly the main road through Oak Creek Canyon and it is not what you want. Your trail goes uphill.
        The trail is a broad one at the beginning. It started its life as a cattle trail, but it was improved during the 1930s with CCC labor, so it is better engineered than many of the old cattle trails that are now hiking trails. It was widened and the grades were moderated so it is not as vertical as it was originally.
        An interesting thing about the hike is that you experience three conspicuous life zones. Down at the creek, there is the lush riparian life zone. As you begin to climb, you get into a high desert life zone. At the top, you are in a pine forest. Once you rise above the trees at creekside, you are on an exposed face with no shade. This can be a very hot hike in the summer though it is in the cool upper canyon.

The hike is steep, so although the trail is a good one, it is a hard climb. You get some fine views as you go. At the top, you will notice that the trail continues. For the purposes of this book, we have ended the trail at the top, but you can continue southwest about 1.25 miles *2.4 km* to a fire lookout tower. If this tower is occupied, the ranger may be willing to have you come up and share the tremendous views. The tower is the East Pocket Fire Lookout Tower, as this part of the rim is called East Pocket.

From many vantage points both above and below the A. B. Young Trail you can see it zigzagging up the face of the west canyon wall. It makes sharp diagonal turns at the end of each zag and is so obviously a passageway cut into the face of the canyon wall that some people mistake it for Highway 89A when they see it from a distance.

A. B. YOUNG TRAIL #100

N
W ◆ E
S

To Top of Rim

Altitude	6800
5100	
Feet: 1700 Miles: 1.6	Hard

To Fire Tower

Altitude	7196
5100	
Feet: 2096 Miles: 2.85	Hard

1.25 mi.

1.6 mi.

Oak Creek

89

Bootlegger Campground

Ⓟ
MP383

89

8.8 mi.

Sedona Y

89   179

WILDERNESS
R'Rock-Secret Mt

Driving Distance One Way, Miles: 8.8
Hiking Distance One Way, Miles: 1.6 (1.25 mi. optional)

AIRPORT HILL VORTEX

General Information
Location Map E4
Sedona USGS Map
Coconino Forest Service Map

Driving Distance One Way: 1.3 miles *2.1 km* (Time 10 minutes)
Access Road: All cars, Paved all the way
Hiking Distance One Way: 0.5 miles *0.8 km* (Time 30 minutes)
How Strenuous: Easy
Features: Vortex Spot

NUTSHELL: This is the easiest and most accessible Sedona Vortex spot.

DIRECTIONS:
From the Sedona Y Go:
Southwest on Highway 89A for 1 mile, to Airport Road. Turn left onto Airport Road and drive uphill to a spot that is 1.3 miles *2.1 km* from the Y. Here you will see a wide apron on the right side of the road. Park there.

TRAILHEAD: Unmarked, but you will see a path across the road to your left.

DESCRIPTION: There are a couple of access points to the vortex spot on the Airport Road. This is the easier one.
After walking 0.1 miles *0.16 km*, you will reach a saddle where the trail forks up to the right, and down to the left. If you want to go directly to the place generally regarded as *the* vortex spot, go downhill to the left, where you will come to a flat spot on a ledge. There is usually a medicine wheel made of stones here. This trail goes on for about 0.5 miles *0.8 km*, descending and getting fainter as it goes. It terminates at an interesting old stone water tank, and is probably not worth hiking beyond the vortex spot unless you just want to stretch your legs.
After experiencing what you can at the vortex spot, climb back up and take the path to the top of the knoll. It is easy to climb and is a great viewpoint. You will see another knoll to the south, with a path connecting it to the knoll on which you are standing. It's fun to go over there and explore too.
The other vortex spots in this book are shown on page 254.
People want to know what will happen at a Vortex. Books have been written about Sedona's vortexes (vortices?) and you will find these books in Sedona stores. Experts claim that each vortex spot is different:

some have negative energy, some positive; some are male, some are female; some are magnetic, some electric, and on and on. People come from great distances to visit these power spots and some are taken to the vortexes on guided tours. We have been at a couple of the spots when tours came along. Our preference is to enjoy these places quietly and in solitude.

Each person will have a unique experience, ranging from negative to neutral to positive. Some people have a really cosmic experience, while others feel nothing. The best advice we can give is to let yourself be open.

Because this vortex is so easy to reach, it is often crowded, which may detract from the spiritual feeling you are seeking at a vortex. Our personal favorite vortex spot is at Boynton Canyon, but to each his own.

From the farthest south knoll you can see a distinct trail running horizontally across the face of Airport Mesa and there is clear access to it from the knoll. We have hiked this trail. It started out promisingly but then dwindled down to nothing in about a half mile.

AIRPORT HILL VORTEX

4900	Altitude
	4800
Feet: 100 Miles: 0.5	Easy

Sedona Y

1.0 mi.

89   89

MP 373.1

89   0.3 mi.

179

Airport Road

0.5 mi.

Driving Distance One Way, Miles: 1.3
Hiking Distance One Way, 0.5 mi.

ALLENS BEND #111

General Information
Location Map D5
Munds Park USGS Map
Coconino Forest Service Map

Driving Distance One Way: 2.3 miles *3.7 km* (Time 10 minutes)
Access Road: All cars, Paved all the way
Hiking Distance One Way: 0.5 miles *0.8 km* (Time 30 minutes)
How Strenuous: Easy
Features: Creekside walk, Small Indian ruin

NUTSHELL: This trail, located 2.3 miles *3.7 km* north of Sedona, provides an easy, yet delightful creekside ramble.

DIRECTIONS:
From the Sedona Y Go:
    North on Highway 89A 2.3 Miles *3.7 km* (MP 376.5) to the Grasshopper Point Recreation Area. Park at the lot on Highway 89A or drive to the bottom lot.

TRAILHEAD: Rusty sign at north end of creek-level parking lot.

DESCRIPTION: The picnic area is open only during the summer season, roughly May 1-November 1. If it is open, you can drive down a paved road to a loop parking lot that has capacity for a couple of dozen cars. It also has a toilet. If the gate is closed, then you can park in the upper lot, next to the highway. It's about 0.33 miles *0.5 km* to walk to the trailhead from there.
    The trail does not go down toward Oak Creek. Instead, it hugs the west wall of the canyon. The trail is easy. For about the first 0.15 miles *0.25 km*, it moves along a redrock ledge. In some spots stones have been mortared into place to pave the trail and to make steps. You walk along the base of a 100 foot tall red cliff, which is undercut and is very interesting. The cliff is not nearly so towering as many in the Sedona area, but it has its own charm and is more human sized and intimate. The creek is to your right (east) at all times, anywhere from 20 to 100 yards away.
    At 0.19 miles *0.3 km* you reach a fork. The main trail is the left fork. The right one goes to the creek, to a scenic spot that is well worth a short detour. The trail is shaded all the way and the creek—if by nothing other than its sound—offers refreshment.
    Just beyond this fork take a look to your left and you will see what appears to be a small Indian ruin in a shallow cave.

The vegetation along the trail is agreeable, a forest of sycamores, cypress, juniper and shrubbery.

At 0.41 miles *0.66 km* you reach another fork. You are almost at the end of the trail here. To your left you will see an abandoned stone building and some rock walls and a flat area. This is an old campground. The building was a public toilet. If you take the left fork, you will go uphill and join Highway 89A at the **Casner Canyon** trailhead. If you go right, you will end at a nice scenic place on the creek.

The Allens Bend Trail is a sleeper. Many hikers who prefer to hike in remote country away from crowds might feel it unworthy of a look when they find out where it is located. We prefer the back country but every trail has its charm and its contribution to make. This is a pretty trail that is accessible any time of year, unlike some of the wild backcountry hikes, the trailheads of which can't be reached when the roads are muddy. Allens Bend is also valuable as a hike that goes right along the creekbank.

ALLENS BEND #111

Altitude

4400 —————————

Feet: 100 Miles: 0.5	Easy

N
W ✦ E
S

MP 376.5   89

2.3 mi.

89

Sedona Y

89

179

0.5 mi.

P

Grasshopper Point Recreation Area

Oak Creek

Driving Distance One Way, Miles: 2.3 mi.
Hiking Distance One Way, Miles: 0.5

ANGEL FALLS

General Information
Location Map D4
Wilson Mountain USGS Map
Coconino Forest Service Map

Driving Distance One Way: 1.5 miles *2.4 km* (Time 10 minutes)
Access Road: All cars, Last 0.4 miles *0.65 km* is unpaved
Hiking Distance One Way: 2.5 miles *4.0 km* (Time 90 minutes)
How Strenuous: Moderate
Features: Waterfall

NUTSHELL: You start this hike on a maintained trail then bushwhack along a streambed to reach a box canyon where two waterfalls are located.

DIRECTIONS:
From the Sedona Y Go:
 North on Highway on 89A (toward Flagstaff) for 0.30 miles to Jordan Road, which is in the middle of uptown Sedona. Turn left (north) and take Jordan Road to its end, where the paving stops. Keep going on the unpaved road. Your goal is the former Shooting Range. At 1.1 miles *1.8 km*, you will intersect a private road. Turn left here. You will reach the Shooting Range gate at 1.5 miles *2.4 km*. Park outside.

TRAILHEAD: Start this hike at the Brins Mesa Trailhead.

DESCRIPTION: On the other side of the gate you will find a rusty sign reading **Brins Mesa #119**. Follow this trail. The first 1.25 miles *2.0 km* of the trail follow a closed jeep road, where the trail is wide and easy. It takes you to the foot of Brins Mesa.
 Stay at the bottom of the mesa and follow an old road to your right. It disappears in about 0.2 miles *0.32 km*. From there a footpath is marked by cairns, following along the base of Brins Mesa. The trail goes onto a redrock ledge, and here the cairns become tricky. Some lead you directly toward Brins Mesa while others take you downhill, into a side canyon. The down-hill cairns into the canyon mark the trail that you are to take.
 The trail goes into a small wash that runs parallel to Mormon Canyon. You must come out of the wash and move across country for about 0.1 mile *0.16 km*, and then enter Mormon Canyon, which is much bigger.
 From that point, you work your way upstream (left). There is an irony here: if there is water in the streambed, you may not be able to hike it. If there is no water, you can hike it, but there will be no water coming over

Angel Falls.

Walking the stream is hard, but a payoff comes when you get to the end of the canyon. It stops in a spectacular box against the flank of Wilson Mountain, where Angel Falls is located. This place feels truly remote and is fun to explore. You can work your way up into the box, where there are some fascinating redrock ledges and sculptures.

Wilson Mountain is the tallest mountain in the Sedona area and its land mass is huge. There are two good hikes to the top of Wilson: **Wilson Mountain North** and **Wilson Mountain South**, but this is one of the rare hikes that takes you to the base of the mountain. **The Old Jim Thompson Road** is another, although it is at a higher level than the Angel Falls hike.

Generally we have tried to focus our attention in this book on established trails. However where there is a special hike that can only be reached by bushwhacking, we include it—such as Angel Falls.

ANGEL FALLS

Altitude	4700
4500	
Feet: 200 Miles: 2.5	Mod.

Brins Mesa Trail

N
W ← → E
S

2.5 mi.

Old Shooting Range

Brins Mesa Trailhead

Ⓟ

WILDERNESS
R'Rock-Secret Mt

1.2 mi.

Jordan Road

Sedona Y   0.3 mi.

89   89

179

Driving Distance One Way, Miles: 1.5
Hiking Distance One Way, Miles: 2.5

APACHE FIRE TRAIL

General Information
Location Map F3
Sedona USGS Map
Coconino Forest Service Map

Drive Distance One Way: 8.8 miles *14.1 km* (Time 15 minutes)
Access Road: All vehicles, All paved
Hiking Distance, Complete Loop: 1.7 miles 2.7 *km* (Time 1.0 hours)
How Strenuous: Moderate
Features: Oak Creek, Red Rock State Park, Views

NUTSHELL: This moderate trail is located in Red Rock State Park 8.8 miles *14.1 km* southwest of Sedona. It takes you to the top of the hill on which the exotically named House of Apache Fire is located.

DIRECTIONS:
From the Sedona Y Go:
　　　　Southwest on Highway 89A (toward Cottonwood) for a distance of 5.5 miles *8.8 km* (MP 368.6) to the Lower Red Rock Loop Road. Turn left on the Lower Red Rock Loop Road and follow it to the 8.5 miles *13.6 km* point, where you will see the entry to Red Rock State Park. Turn right into the park. You will come to a toll booth where an admission is charged. From that point, drive to the Visitor Center and park there, at 8.8 miles *14.1 km*.

TRAILHEAD: This is a marked and maintained trail, part of the network of trails in the park. Go through the Visitor Center. Though the center is not marked as the trailhead for this hike, it is the starting point.

DESCRIPTION: Enjoy the Visitor Center and then walk through it, turning right on the paved trail. At 0.08 miles *0.13 km* you will come to the first trail junction. Here the **Smoke Trail** forks to the right, where Sentinel Crossing is located. Go straight here. The sign at this junction shows your destination as *"Kingfisher Crossing, House of Apache Fire."*
　　　　Soon after this you will reach another junction. Turn right here, to Kingfisher Crossing, which is a major bridge across the creek. You will see the House of Apache Fire on a hilltop, a pueblo style house of native rock.
　　　　When you cross the bridge you will reach another trail junction, where the **Kisva** and **Eagles' Nest** trails go right. You will go left there and shortly thereafter will be at the base of the knoll on which the house is located. You will see a driveway going uphill to your right to get to the house. To your left is a short flight of redrock steps and a sign for the Apache Fire

Trail. This is the place where the Apache Fire Trail starts.

Walk up the steps and you will find yourself on a nice gentle trail heading south, away from the park and into undeveloped country. This part of the trail is a welcome getaway from the developed area. The trail makes a big loop. Just before the trail begins climbing out of the creek bed, the **Javelina Trail** takes off to your left. From here you begin to turn north and climb the knoll.

At the top of the knoll you will be at eye level with the House of Apache Fire and you will have a good view of this interesting structure. A bench has been thoughtfully placed at about the one mile point. It is a good place to sit and enjoy the views. Just beyond the bench the **Coyote Ridge Trail** forks left.

From this point the trail comes down the knoll and intersects the Kisva Trail. Turn right here and return to the Visitor Center.

APACHE MAID TRAIL #15

General Information
Location Map G6
Casner Butte and Apache Maid USGS Maps
Coconino Forest Service Map

Driving Distance One Way: 17.2 miles *27.6 km* (Time 30 minutes)
Access Road: All cars, Last 0.3 miles *0.48 km* gravel, in good condition
Hiking Distance One Way: 3.75 miles *6.0 km* (Time 2 hours)
How Strenuous: Hard
Features: Views of Wet Beaver Creek Country, Rock Art

NUTSHELL: You hike the Bell Trail for two miles, then branch off to climb Casner Butte, 17 miles south of Sedona.

DIRECTIONS:
From the Sedona Y Go:
      South on Highway 179 (toward Phoenix) for 14.7 Miles *23.5 km* (MP 298.9), to the I-17 intersection. Go straight here rather than getting on I-17. Follow paved road FR 618 until you see a sign for Beaver Creek Ranger Station and trailheads at 16.9 miles *27.1 km*. Turn left. Parking is at 17.2 miles *27.6 km*.

TRAILHEAD: Signed and marked at the parking lot.

DESCRIPTION: From the trailhead, you take the Bell Trail. It goes upcanyon along Wet Beaver Creek, sometimes near it, sometimes away from it, but always following its path. Even when you are not near the creek, you can hear water running, a pleasant sound in desert country. The water-way is lined with tall sycamores and cottonwoods.
      As you look up the canyon, you see a flank of the Mogollon Rim, a giant uplift running across Arizona and New Mexico. The rim marks the southern boundary of the Colorado Plateau. Its base is the northern bound-ary of the Sonoran Desert; so it is a highly significant land feature.
      The trail is an old jeep road, broad and easy to walk. As you go along the trail, note the canyon walls: they contain the same redrock as in Sedona in the lower layers but the top is covered with a thick cap of lava. If it weren't for that top layer of hard rock, this country would be just as erod-ed and colorful as Sedona.
      At about 0.6 miles *1.0 km*, look for a large boulder on the left side of the trail. On the side facing away from you is some rock art.
      At the 2.0 mile *3.2 km* point you will hit a fork where the Apache

Maid Trail, #15, branches to the left and climbs Casner Butte. This is a steep climb, rising about 1000 feet in 1.75 miles *2.8 km*. You will be rewarded by good views at the top, but the trail itself is uninteresting. We suggest stopping at the top.

The trail goes on to the head of Wet Beaver Creek, and is the point of departure for the rugged types who hike Wet Beaver Creek from top to bottom, a multi-day trip, definitely not an undertaking for day hikers.

The Apache Maid Trail was built as a cattle trail, not as a scenic path. Sedona ranchers would graze their animals in the lower warm country in winter and then take them to the high county on top of the rim for summer. Apache Maid is the name of a mountain on top of the rim where one of the largest ranches of its day was located. There is a lookout tower on top of Apache Maid. You can drive all the way there. Take the Stoneman Lake Exit off I-17, then FRs 213, 229 and 602.

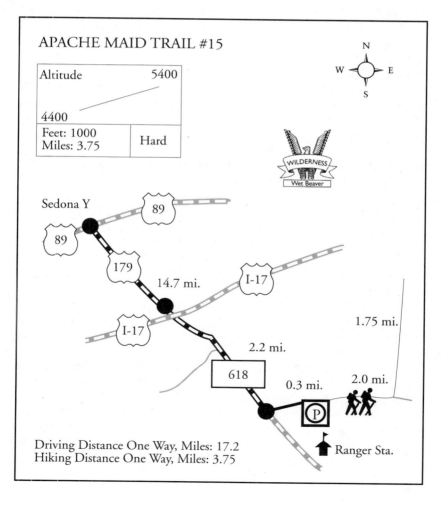

APACHE MAID TRAIL #15

Altitude	5400
4400	
Feet: 1000 Miles: 3.75	Hard

N
W   E
S

WILDERNESS
Wet Beaver

Sedona Y

89

89

179

14.7 mi.

I-17

I-17

1.75 mi.

2.2 mi.

618

0.3 mi.

2.0 mi.

P

Ranger Sta.

Driving Distance One Way, Miles: 17.2
Hiking Distance One Way, Miles: 3.75

BATTLEMENT MESA

General Information
Location Map E5
Sedona USGS Map
Coconino Forest Service Map

Driving Distance One Way: 2.0 miles *3.2 km* (Time 10 minutes)
Access Road: All cars, Paved all the way
Hiking Distance One Way: 1.5 Miles *2.4 km* (Time 60 minutes)
How Strenuous: Moderate
Features: Devil's Dining Room (sinkhole), Views

NUTSHELL: This trail is located in Sedona's "backyard" at the south end of Marg's Draw. It requires a moderate climb among interesting rocks

DIRECTIONS:
From the Sedona Y Go:
South on Highway 179 (toward Phoenix) for 1.4 miles *2.3 km* (MP 312.1) to Morgan Road in the Broken Arrow Subdivision. Turn left (east) on Morgan Road and follow it to its end, at 2.0 miles *3.2 km*, where you park just beyond the cattle guard.

TRAILHEAD: This is an unmarked, unmaintained trail. Walk the road, FR 179F, to Devil's Dining Room, where this trail begins.

DESCRIPTION: At the cattle guard you will see a sign indicating a "Trail Walk-through." Ignore it and walk right down the middle of the road.

This road is used by the jeep tours that abound in Sedona and you are likely to meet some of them on this hike in good weather. They act as if they own the road, and in a certain sense they do, as they have a maintenance agreement for it with the Forest Service.

At 0.26 miles *0.42 km* turn right, going up on a red sandstone ledge. The jeeps go up there to thrill the dudes, so the trail is easy to follow. You stay on the lower part of the ledge and walk across it, where the dirt road resumes.

At 0.34 miles *0.6 km* go to the right on a sunken road. This will lead you to the Devil's Dining Room at 0.42 miles *0.7 km*. At the site, you will come out into a small clearing where you will see a line of boulders and a barbed wire fence. These surround the sinkhole. Behind the sinkhole is a hill. You will see a path going up this hill. Take this path. It is your trail.

At 0.65 miles *1.0 km*, you will come out onto a redrock ledge. Walk along it toward the saddle you can see on the skyline. In a little over one hundred feet you will see a trail marked by cairns to the left. It is the trail you want.

Climb it to the saddle, where you will get great views to the north toward Sedona and to the south toward Poco Diablo. The **Twin Buttes** Trail takes off to the left from here, but you want to go up to the right, toward the "castle" rock formation on top of Battlement Mesa. Once there, you can explore, working your way around the mesa if you choose. It's a fascinating place.

Battlement Mesa is one of those sites that has a deceptive appearance. From the ground you have the impression that it is flat and bare on top and that you would be able to walk around it as if you were on a football field. Not so. The top is rugged and broken by fissures and declivities so that you have to pick your way around. In spite of this, it is possible to circle the top if you want to make the effort.

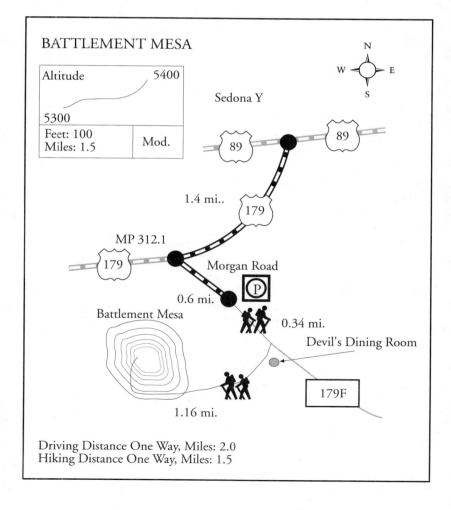

BATTLEMENT MESA

N
W E
S

Altitude   5400

5300
Feet: 100
Miles: 1.5   Mod.

Sedona Y

89   89

1.4 mi..

179

MP 312.1

179   Morgan Road
P

0.6 mi.   0.34 mi.

Battlement Mesa   Devil's Dining Room

179F

1.16 mi.

Driving Distance One Way, Miles: 2.0
Hiking Distance One Way, Miles: 1.5

BEAR MOUNTAIN #54

General Information
Location Map C2
Wilson Mountain USGS Map
Coconino Forest Service Map

Driving Distance One Way: 8.9 miles *14.3 km* (Time 20 minutes)
Access Road: All cars, Last 1.2 miles *2.0 km* dirt, in good condition
Hiking Distance One Way: 2.2 miles *3.5 km* (Time 90 minutes)
How Strenuous: Hard, Very steep
Features: View

NUTSHELL: Climbing this prominent mountain 8.9 miles *14.3 km* northwest of Sedona is a challenge, but the views from the top are superb.

DIRECTIONS:
From the Sedona Y Go:
    Southwest on Highway 89A (toward Cottonwood) for 3.2 miles *5.2 km* (MP 371) to Dry Creek Road. Go right on Dry Creek Road to the 6.1 mile *9.8 km* point, where Dry Creek Road joins the Long Canyon Road, both paved. Turn left here, on FR 152C, and go to the 7.7 mile *12.4 km point*, where it joins the Boynton Canyon Road.
    Turn left here on the Boynton Pass Road, FR 152C. The paving soon ends, to be replaced by a good dirt road. Stop at the 8.9 mile *14.3 km* point, just before a cattle guard. The parking area is on the right.

TRAILHEAD: The Bear Mt. Trail shares its parking space with the **Doe Mt. Trail**, and you will see signs for both trails there. Crawl through the "window frame" in the fence to begin the Bear Mt. Trail, #54.

DESCRIPTION: The first 0.25 miles *0.4 km* of the hike are across what seems to be flat land to the base of the mountain. In fact, the land is badly eroded and there are many gulches. You have to cross three of them. The trail is marked by cairns. Be sure to follow them, because this is cattle country, and wherever the cattle wander in this dry soil they leave what appears to be a trail but is really an aimless meander.
    Bear Mountain will surprise you. As you climb, you keep thinking that you have reached the top. Actually, you will encounter five steppes or terraces. You are climbing steeply almost all the way. The good news is that the beautiful views begin with the first steppe. The higher you go, the more of a panorama you get and the better the views are.
    At 2.2 miles *3.5 km*, you reach the base of steppe number five, the

true top. It's a good stopping place. We quit here, but the trail goes on, making what appears to be a hard climb over slickrock.

The bulk of the mountain is on steppe four. The surface here is eroded along crossbedding lines and a tiny amount of soil has formed in the cracks. Sparse vegetation grows in this soil, making the grasses and other plants form lines and rows that match the seams in the stone. In the right light, this causes fascinating patterns.

The top could well be called *Bare* Mountain rather than Bear Mountain, for there is precious little growing on it.

Friends tell us that from **Capitol Butte** you are supposed to be able to see a bear in the contours of the top of Bear Mountain. We have tried this from several viewpoints but were never able to see the bear. That's the way it is with these figures: sometimes you can see them and sometimes you can't, no matter how hard you try. According to our sources, the bear is lying down and it is his round ears that really make the formation.

BEAR MOUNTAIN #54

Altitude	6100
5000	
Feet: 1100 Miles: 2.2	Hard

2.2 mi.

Boynton Canyon Road

Long Canyon Road

1.6 mi.

1.2 mi.

152C

2.9 mi.

WILDERNESS
R'Rock-Secret Mt

152C

Dry Creek Road

3.2 mi.

Sedona Y

89

89

MP 371

179

N
W E
S

Driving Distance One Way, Miles: 8.9
Hiking Distance One Way, Miles: 2.2

BEAR SIGN TRAIL #59

General Information
Location Map C4
Loy Butte and Wilson Mountain USGS Maps
Coconino Forest Service Map

Driving Distance One Way: 9.6 miles *15.4 km* (Time 45 minutes)
Access Road: Last 4.4 miles *7.0 km* medium unpaved
Hiking Distance One Way: 3.25 miles *5.2 km* (Time 90 minutes)
How Strenuous: Moderate
Features: Secluded canyon, Beautiful redrocks

NUTSHELL: Located 9.6 miles *15.4 km* north of Sedona, this is a wilderness hike that follows a streambed to the base of the Mogollon Rim.

DIRECTIONS:
From the Sedona Y Go:
Southwest on Highway 89A (toward Cottonwood) for 3.2 miles *5.2 km* (MP 371) to Dry Creek Road. Turn right on Dry Creek Road (FR 152C) and proceed to the 5.2 mile *8.4 km* point. Turn right on FR 152, the Vultee Arch Road, and follow it to the 9.6 mile *15.4 km* point. Here there is a parking loop, with the **Vultee Arch** Trailhead at the tip. Curve around and head back, and you will see the parking for the Bear Sign and **Dry Creek** trails to your right, just a few yards beyond.

TRAILHEAD: At parking area. There is a rusty sign: Dry Creek #52.

DESCRIPTION: You will walk across a little arroyo and around the toe of a hill for about 0.1 miles *0.16 km*, where you will encounter Dry Creek. At the entry point, the canyon cut by Dry Creek is rather shallow and wide. Turn right and follow the trail up the creek, which usually *is* dry, northerly. If any appreciable amount of water is running in the creek, you might want to postpone this hike until the creek is dry, for the trail crosses the creek at least a dozen times.

As you walk, the trail climbs, but this is gradual and you are barely conscious of it.

At 0.63 miles *1.0 km*, you reach a point where the creek forks at a reef. The left-hand channel is the Bear Sign Trail, and the right fork is the **Dry Creek Trail**. There is a rusty sign in the left channel marked "Bear Sign #59."

From this point, the canyon deepens and you are treated to the sight of giant redrock buttes on both sides of the creek. As you proceed, you will notice a change in the flora, as the rise in altitude changes the life zones.

The trail ends where it intersects a channel running east and west. We are informed that this channel can be hiked. To the east, it would connect with Dry Creek Trail. Maps show that you could do a loop, going up the Bear Sign Trail and coming back via the Dry Creek Pack Trail, but we have not tried this.

Both the Bear Sign Trail and its neighboring Dry Creek Trail take you far away from habitation, and are nice if you want to get away into pristine country. Both trails head toward the Mogollon Rim and bump right against the base of it. The beauty of such trails is that even though they take you into wild and primitive country they are not dangerous. Stay in the canyons that define these trails and you won't get lost.

We haven't seen bears in Bear Sign, but it is bear country. Experts estimate that there are about four thousand bears in Arizona.

BEAR SIGN TRAIL #59

Altitude 5500

5000

Feet: 500
Miles: 3.25
Mod.

3.25 mi.

Vultee Arch Tr.

4.4 mi.

152

2.0 mi.

152C

Dry Creek Road

Sedona Y

3.2 mi.

89

89

MP 371

179

WILDERNESS
R'Rock-Secret Mt

Driving Distance One Way, Miles: 9.6
Hiking Distance One Way, Miles: 3.25

BEAVERHEAD

General Information
Location Map G5
Casner Butte and Lake Montezuma USGS Maps
Coconino Forest Service Map

Driving Distance One Way: 11.2 miles *18.0 km* (Time 20 minutes)
Access Road: All paved
Hiking Distance One Way: 1.1 miles *1.8 km* (Time 45 minutes)
How Strenuous: Moderate
Features: Historic road, Views

NUTSHELL: Located 11.2 miles *18.0 km* south of Sedona, this hike climbs 1000 feet to the top of the Mogollon Rim along an ancient Hopi trail that was converted into a wagon road in the 1870s.

DIRECTIONS:
From the Sedona Y Go:
    South on Highway 179 (toward Phoenix) for a distance of 11.2 miles *18.0 km* (MP 302.2) where you will see a gravel driveway to your left. Turn in on it and park by the gate in the barbed wire fence.

TRAILHEAD: You will follow the old road from the gate.

DESCRIPTION: From the unlocked gate where you parked, walk up the dirt road a distance of 0.1 miles *0.16 km*. There you will see a road to your right that has been blocked by a dirt berm. Walk over the berm and you will pick up the old road. You follow it uphill.
    At the start of the hike, take a moment to look at your objective. High above, you will see a ridge with a long section of jagged cliffs. This is not an isolated ridge but a part of the Mogollon Rim. You are about to walk a short stretch of The Palatkwapi Trail, used by the Hopi Indians for more than 1200 years. The trail starts at the Hopi mesas and ends at Camp Verde (with a branch to Jerome). The challenge to the pathfinders as they came off the high country was to find a gentle way down from the top of the Mogollon Rim to the Verde Valley. The route went from the Hopi mesas to Sunset Crossing (Winslow), Chavez Pass, Stoneman Lake, and Rattlesnake Canyon to the top of the Rim. As you walk along this trail, you can admire the choice that the ancients made. Except for being rocky, the way is excellent.
    Spanish explorers followed the trail in the late 1500s, then army scouts in the 1860s and then, when the army undertook to subdue hostile

Indians, the old trail was improved as a wagon road linking Fort Apache and Camp Verde. Once established by the military, private operators became interested in the road and ran a stage line over it between 1876-1882. Until the Schnebly Hill Road was built in Sedona in 1902, the Beaverhead Road was the only road Sedona residents had to get to Flagstaff in a wagon.

The road is easy to follow and the area has a pleasant feel. You soon climb high enough to get good views of the scenic surrounding country. At 0.75 miles *1.2 km* you will reach the beginning of an incredibly rocky passage. Many a wagon wheel must have broken here.

At 0.85 miles *1.4 km* you will reach the first top. In this area the old road looks almost like a trench, as it is deeply lined by the stones that were rolled to the sides. At 1.1 miles *1.8 km* you will be at the true top, where there are great views. The road veers away from the cliffs and continues its long journey northward (it is 145 miles long) from here over drab country.

BEAVERHEAD

Altitude	5400
4400	
Feet: 1000 Miles: 1.1	Mod.

N
W E
S

Sedona Y
89
89
179
11.2 mi.
1.1 mi.
MP 302.2
179
Mogollon Rim

Driving Distance One Way, Miles: 11.2
Hiking Distance One Way, Miles: 1.1

BELL TRAIL #13

General Information
Location Map G6
Apache Maid and Casner Butte USGS Maps
Coconino Forest Service Map

Driving Distance One Way: 17.2 miles *27.6 km* (Time 30 minutes)
Access Road: All cars, Last 0.3 miles *0.48 km* gravel, in good condition
Hiking Distance One Way: 4.0 miles *6.4 km* (Time 2 hours)
How Strenuous: Moderate
Features: Permanent Stream, Rock Art

NUTSHELL: This trail follows the course of Wet Beaver Creek, 17.2 miles *27.6 km* southwest of Sedona. The trail is broad and easy, with many attractions.

DIRECTIONS:
From the Sedona Y Go:
South on Highway 179 (toward Phoenix) for 14.7 Miles *23.5 km* (MP 298.9), to the I-17 intersection. Go straight here rather than getting on I-17. Follow paved road FR 618 until you see a sign for Beaver Creek Ranger Station and trailheads at 16.9 miles *27.1 km.* Turn left. Parking is at 17.2 miles *27.6 km.*

TRAILHEAD: Well marked with signs at the parking area.

DESCRIPTION: From the trailhead, the trail goes up canyon along Wet Beaver Creek. The trail is broad and easy to walk. It was built by a cattle rancher named Earl Bell in 1932, as a means for taking his cattle to the top of the Mogollon Rim in the spring.
At about 0.6 miles *1.0 km*, look for a large boulder on the left side of the trail. On the side that faces away from you are a number of interesting petroglyphs.
At 1.5 miles *2.4 km* you will find the **Casner Mt. South Trail** to your left.
At the 2.0 mile *3.2 km* point you will hit a fork where the **Apache Maid Trail, #15** branches to the left and climbs Casner Butte.
Just beyond this fork you will find a signboard containing a map and discussion of the geology, plant and animal life of the area. The life is richer than you might think. Just beyond the billboard is a trail going off to the right, down to the water. This is the **Weir Trail.** It is only 0.5 miles *0.8 km* long.

the right, down to the water. This is the **Weir Trail.** It is only 0.5 miles *0.8 km* long.

Bell Crossing is 2.0 miles *3.2 km* up the canyon from the signboard. There the trail narrows and crosses the creek. Along the creekside from the crossing are delightful places for a picnic. We recommend that you go upstream about 100 yards to check out a large pool known as The Crack.

From the crossing, the trail goes 2.5 miles *4.0 km* on up to the top of The Rim. The full hike is scenic, but is much longer and harder. We recommend stopping at the crossing for most day hikers.

Earl Bell was a wealthy Easterner who fell in love with the Beaver Creek area when he was a guest at one of the dude ranches that flourished there from the 1920s through the 1940s. Such places as the Soda Spring Ranch and Rancho Roca Roja had a national reputation and became winter retreats for the wealthy.

BELL ROCK

VORTEX

General Information
Location Map F5
Sedona USGS Map
Coconino Forest Service Map

Driving Distance One Way: 5.2 miles *8.4 km* (Time 15 minutes)
Access Road: All cars, All paved
Hiking Distance One Way: 1.0 mile *1.6 km* (Time 45 minutes)
How Strenuous: Moderate
Features: Vortex Spot, Views

NUTSHELL: This landmark south of Sedona is one of the famed Vortex Spots. There is no defined trail. You explore as you wish.

DIRECTIONS:
From the Sedona Y Go:
South on Highway 179 (toward Phoenix) a distance of 5.2 miles *8.4 km*.(MP 308.4). You will see parking areas on the opposite side of the road.

TRAILHEAD: Not a marked trail, but hundreds of visitors have worn an easy-to-see path up to the rock. At the rock there are some cairns.

DESCRIPTION: As you near the rock, there are many trails. Don't be concerned about these. Just pick out one that strikes your fancy. All of them go to the rock. Once you are there, you may or may not see cairns marking trails going up onto the rock. If you see none, just pick a likely access and ascend. You are on your own.

You probably will encounter medicine wheels or other outlines on the rock made by New Agers. We know of no particular spot that is regarded as *the* vortex spot on Bell Rock. Different people get different responses. Other vortex spots covered in this book are shown in the Index, page 254.

The redrock around Sedona was laid down in layers and has weathered in such a way that it has created ledges that are almost like stairsteps. This is especially true on Bell Rock, with its conical slopes. What you will do on this hike is look for likely ways to go up. Even the timid hiker should be able to get quite close to the top in comfort. Going to the top is dangerous. As you wind your way around the rock, you are treated to great views.

The early settlers in the area were hard pressed to come up with names for all of the rock formations around Sedona. There is controversy over the correct names for some of them. Nobody ever disagreed about Bell Rock, however. It *looks* like a bell. This is a very popular place because it is so well known and easy to reach, and is on the road to Phoenix. So, you won't have a wilderness experience here, but it is a lot of fun, and you may even get a significant experience from the vortex power.

Bell Rock is often a busy site and it doesn't look very big. For those who like solitary places, its aspect is off-putting when you see people of all stripes, including whining infants and disrespectful teenagers assaying its slopes. A funny thing happens when you get to the rock, however. It suddenly seems much bigger than it looked from afar. You can pick out a way that no one else is using and before you know it, you are having an enjoyable peaceful experience in spite of the busy atmosphere. Give it a try in spite of the crowds.

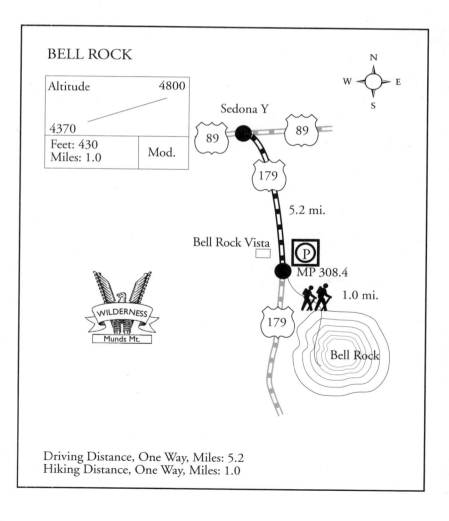

BELL ROCK

Altitude	4800
4370	
Feet: 430 Miles: 1.0	Mod.

Sedona Y

89   89

179

5.2 mi.

Bell Rock Vista

P MP 308.4

1.0 mi.

WILDERNESS
Munds Mt.

179

Bell Rock

Driving Distance, One Way, Miles: 5.2
Hiking Distance, One Way, Miles: 1.0

BLACK MOUNTAIN

General Information
Location Map C1
Clarkdale, Loy Butte,
Page Springs and Sycamore Basin USGS Maps
Coconino Forest Service Map

Driving Distance One Way: 27.6 miles *44.2 km* (Time 45 minutes)
Access Road: High clearance vehicles, Last 2.1 miles *3.4 km* rough
Hiking Distance One Way: 2.25 miles *3.6 km* (Time 90 minutes)
How Strenuous: Moderate
Features: Views

NUTSHELL: Located 27.6 miles *44.2 km* southwest of Sedona, Black Mt. borders Sycamore Canyon. This hike follows a road to the top.

DIRECTIONS:
From the Sedona Y Go:
Southwest on Highway 89A (toward Cottonwood) a distance of 16.0 miles *25.6 km* (MP 358) to FR 761, the unpaved Bill Gray Road. Turn right and take FR 761 to the 25.5 miles *41 km* point, its junction with FR 258A, Buckboard Road. Go right here, staying on FR 761. At 26.2 miles *42 km*, you will see a road to your left marked FR 761A. Turn left onto this road. Up to this point, the road has been good, but now it gets quite rough. A high clearance vehicle with sturdy tires is recommended, and only when the road is dry. At 27.6 miles *44.2 km*, you reach a Y fork, with FR 761A going right and FR 761C going left. Park and walk FR 761C, the road going uphill left. We would not drive any vehicle we ever owned up FR 761C.

TRAILHEAD: Walk the road, FR 761C.

DESCRIPTION: The road and the surroundings are rather bleak. There isn't much of interest near at hand. However, you are treated to some great views.

You will see some signs of yesteryear's flagstone quarrying here and there along the road. This is great country for javelina, and you may see some of them. We were treated to the sight of a whole family of javelina on the road ahead of us peacefully grazing. Then they caught our scent and disappeared. It is amazing how they can melt into the brush in an instant.

You will reach the top at 1.25 miles *2.0 km*, and may be surprised to find that the top is larger than you'd have thought. The top is a juniper-piñon pine life zone. There are no cliffs along the rim to furnish natural viewpoints, as the sides are rounded.

At about 2.0 miles *3.2 km*, the road forks where there is a steel fence post. The left fork takes you to the south, onto the bulk of the mountain, where the road ends in about a quarter mile. The fork to the right takes you to the north. We recommend taking it. You can bushwhack to the edge of the mountain in a quarter mile for colorful views into Sycamore Canyon.

This is not a premier hiking trail, but makes an interesting mountain bike ride. The road is plenty good for that. The grades are not bad. The problem with driving it is the danger of getting high centered, which would not be a problem for a mountain bike.

Black Mountain looks black when the sun is high but in the evening when the light is low you can see that it is just about as red as it is black. The red strata occur in the lower parts of the mountain.

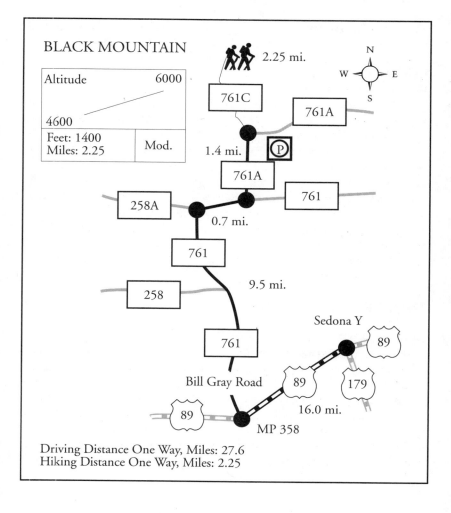

BLACK MOUNTAIN

Altitude 6000
4600
Feet: 1400
Miles: 2.25 Mod.

2.25 mi.

N
W — E
S

761C
761A
1.4 mi.
761A
258A
761
0.7 mi.
761
258
9.5 mi.

Sedona Y
761
89
Bill Gray Road
89
179
16.0 mi.
89
MP 358

Driving Distance One Way, Miles: 27.6
Hiking Distance One Way, Miles: 2.25

BLACK MT. MYSTERY HOUSE

General Information
Location Map C1
Clarkdale, Loy Butte,
Page Springs and Sycamore Basin USGS Maps
Coconino Forest Service Map

Driving Distance One Way: 30.3 miles *48.5 km* (Time 60 minutes)
Access Road: High clearance vehicles, Last 4.1 miles *6.6 km* awful
Hiking Distance One Way: 0.4 miles *0.65 km* (Time 20 minutes)
How Strenuous: Moderate
Features: Strange abandoned house in remote area, Views

NUTSHELL: After a rough drive, you hike an old road to a strange abandoned house high on Black Mountain, where you have tremendous views.

DIRECTIONS:
From the Sedona Y Go:
> Southwest on Highway 89A (toward Cottonwood) a distance of 16.0 miles *25.6 km* (MP 358) to FR 761, the unpaved Bill Gray Road. Turn right and take FR 761 to the 25.5 miles *41 km* point, its junction with FR 258A, Buckboard Road. Go right here, staying on FR 761. At 26.2 miles *42 km*, you will see a road to your left marked FR 761A. Turn left onto this road. Up to this point, the road has been good, but now it gets quite rough. A high clearance vehicle with sturdy tires is recommended, and only when the road is dry. At 27.6 miles *44.2 km*, you reach a Y fork, with FR 761A going right and FR 761C going left. Drive FR 761A, to the right. This is a very rough but spectacular road. At the 30.3 mile *48.5 km* point you will reach the remains of a barbed wire fence. You can drive farther, but it's a killer. Park at the fence.

TRAILHEAD: Walk the old road.

DESCRIPTION: We became aware of the mystery house one day when we were hiking the **Casner Mountain South Trail.** We looked over at Black Mountain and saw the sun glinting off of something. We checked it with our field glasses and were astonished to see the spooky remains of an old house. After a lot of map work and trial and error, we figured out how to get there.
> When you get to the site, you will find the ruins of a fairly modern house. It is situated uniquely, with a million dollar view, but also a million miles from anywhere. It was a split level, the front being about 60 feet long, with view windows all along it.

We have puzzled over the mystery of the house. The boards used in the walls came from World War II ammunition boxes, so our best guess is that it was built between 1946 and 1948, when such boxes were plentiful as war surplus items.

From the flagstone rubble that is seen all around the premises, we would guess that whoever built the house operated a flagstone quarry here. Under the influence of Frank Lloyd Wright designs, it was popular in the late 40s and early 50s to use brick sized pieces of flagstone as a building material. The 1955 addition to the Coconino County Courthouse in Flagstaff is an example of this. The fashion died out at the end of the 50s, so maybe the quarry was abandoned then. It seems obvious that at times there was a sizable quarry operation here. You can see where almost a whole cliff face was cut away if you walk the road to its end.

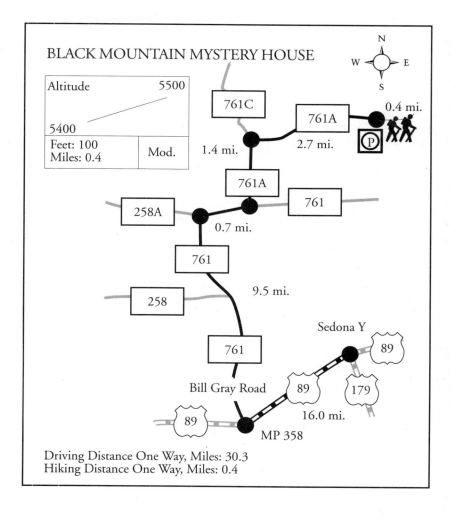

BLACK MOUNTAIN MYSTERY HOUSE

N
W ✦ E
S

Altitude 5500

5400

Feet: 100
Miles: 0.4

Mod.

761C

761A

0.4 mi.

P

1.4 mi.

2.7 mi.

761A

258A

761

0.7 mi.

761

258

9.5 mi.

Sedona Y

761

89

Bill Gray Road

89

179

16.0 mi.

89

MP 358

Driving Distance One Way, Miles: 30.3
Hiking Distance One Way, Miles: 0.4

BLODGETT BASIN

General Information
Location Map G6
Walker Mtn. USGS Map
Coconino Forest Service Map

Driving Distance One Way: 28.7 miles *46 km* (Time 1 hour)
Access Road: All cars, Last 14.0 miles *23 km* good dirt road
Hiking Distance One Way: 2.0 miles *3.2 km* (Time 1.5 hours)
How Strenuous: Hard
Features: Views

NUTSHELL: This trail runs from a point high on the Mogollon Rim to the bottom of the chasm of West Clear Creek, a 2000 foot drop in 2.0 miles.

DIRECTIONS:
From the Sedona Y Go:
         South on Highway 179 (toward Phoenix) for 14.7 miles *24 km*, to the I-17 Interchange. Instead of going onto I-17, go underneath it onto the paved road. At 15.2 miles *25 km*, you will come to a junction. The right fork goes to Montezuma Castle. Take the left fork (FR 618), toward Beaver Creek Ranger Station. It is paved for a couple of miles. Several minor roads branch off FR 618, but it is always obvious that it is the main one. Follow FR 618 to the 24.5 mile *40 km* point, where you will see a dirt road branching left, marked "Cedar Flat." Take this left road, and you will soon see a sign identifying it as FR 214, which takes you to the top of the Mogollon Rim, about a 2000 foot climb. There are some great views along the way. At the 28.7 mile point *46 km*, high up on the road, you will see the sign for the Blodgett Basin Trail to your right through a fence with tall gate posts. Pull in and park by a number of circular rusty water troughs.

TRAILHEAD: You will see cairns marking the trail as it goes downhill from the parking area.

DESCRIPTION: There is very little shade on this trail and you will be dangerously exposed to the sun. It can get very hot. We recommend that you do not even try this hike in full summer. If you do, please be prepared with lots of water, hats, sunscreen, etc.
         From the place where you park, you can see the huge chasm of West Clear Creek before you. You will wind around the sides of several hills as you work your way down to the bottom, enjoying good views, particularly of Wingfield Mesa and later the trees lining the bottom of West Clear

Creek Canyon. Though the gorge of West Clear Creek is clearly before you, you never come to a lip from where you can look directly down into the main canyon; instead, you will come into it by means of a side canyon.

At the end of the trail, you will intersect the **West Clear Creek Trail #17** (also known as the Bull Pen Trail), on a shelf some distance from the creek. It's about 0.20 miles *0.32 km* down to the water; turn right and you will come to the parking area at the Bull Pen trailhead, from where it's a short hop to the creek.

We definitely recommend using two cars on this hike. Park the first car in the West Clear Creek Campground at the West Clear Creek #17 trail-head. You reach this by following FR 618 south 2.0 miles *3.2 km* from its intersection with FR 214, then turning left (east) on FR 215 and going 3.0 miles *4.8 km* to the campground. Take the second car to the top as described herein.

BLODGETT BASIN TRAIL

Sedona Y

89   89

179

14.7 mi.

I-17

I-17

Bridge

5600	Altitude
	3600
Feet: 2000 Miles: 2.0	Hard

WILDERNESS

W. Clear Creek

618

9.8 mi.

4.2 mi.

214

618   214

2.0 mi.

Driving Distance One Way, Miles: 28.7
Hiking Distance One Way, Miles: 2.0

BOYNTON CANYON #47

VORTEX

General Information
Location Map C3
Wilson Mountain USGS Map
Coconino Forest Service Map

Driving Distance One Way: 8.0 miles *13 km* (Time 20 minutes)
Access Road: All cars, All paved
Hiking Distance One Way: 3.25 miles *5.2 km* (Time 90 minutes)
How Strenuous: Moderate
Features: Indian Ruins, Vortex

NUTSHELL: This wonderful canyon is located just 8.0 miles *13 km* north-west of uptown Sedona, and is easily reached by paved roads. Its beauty is unsurpassed. **A personal favorite.**

DIRECTIONS:
From the Sedona Y Go:
Southwest on Highway 89A (toward Cottonwood) a distance of 3.2 miles *5.0 km* (MP 371), to Dry Creek Road, where you take a right turn onto Dry Creek Road (FR 152C). Follow it to the 6.1 *10 km* mile point, where it joins Long Canyon Road. Take a left here, staying on FR 152C. At the 7.7 mile *12.4 km* point, you reach another junction. Go right. At 8.0 miles *13 km*, just before the gatehouse to the Enchantment Resort, you will see a parking area to the right. Park there. There is also a small parking area on the left side of the road.

TRAILHEAD: It is marked at the parking area.

DESCRIPTION: This trail is gentle and wide. For the first mile it over-looks the Enchantment Resort. The trail winds along the east face of the canyon, hugging the towering ruin-dotted red cliffs so as to skirt the resort property. At the 0.85 mile *1.4 km* point you will see a path going off to your right. This leads uphill to Indian ruins in two caves, and is well worth a detour. It takes a bit of scrambling and climbing to get up to the ruins, but even if you don't climb to them, it is worth going over to the face of the cliff on which they are located for a look. This is a detour of about 0.25 miles *0.4 km* each way.

Just beyond this point the trail turns away from the cliffs and fol-lows along the canyon floor. It is much wider and easier to walk from this point on.

At 1.0 miles *1.6 km* you will cross a shallow wash, beyond which the vegetation changes. As you go up canyon, the altitude increases and it is cooler.

At about 3.0 miles *4.8 km*, the trail pinches down suddenly as the canyon narrows. This is a good stopping place. However, you can bushwhack another 0.25 mile *0.4 km* and see the head of Boynton, which is a box canyon against the side of Secret Mountain. The streambed forks here. Take the right fork and you will soon see a primitive path, which is almost a tunnel through the lush growth at stream level. You will emerge into the box, ringed with towering cliffs.

Boynton Canyon is considered to be one of the Sedona Vortex spots. We have been to all of them, and this is the only one that really gives us any special feeling. The red cliffs here can really be spectacular. We love them at about four o'clock in the afternoon on a winter's day. There is something about the angle and clarity of the light resonating on the beautiful red rocks that is really special at such times.

BOYNTON CANYON #47

Altitude	5200
4700	
Feet: 500 Miles: 3.25	Mod.

3.25 mi.

N
W ← ◇ → E
S

Enchantment

0.3 mi.

Boynton Canyon Road

Ⓟ

Long Canyon Road

1.6 mi.

152C

2.9 mi.

WILDERNESS
R'Rock-Secret Mt

152C

Dry Creek Road

3.2 mi.

Sedona Y

89

89

MP 371

179

Driving Distance One Way, Miles: 8.0
Hiking Distance One Way, Miles: 3.25

BOYNTON SPIRES

VORTEX

General Information
Location Map C3
Wilson Mountain USGS Map
Coconino Forest Service Map

Driving Distance One Way: 8.0 miles *13 km* (Time 20 minutes)
Access Road: All cars, All paved
Hiking Distance One Way: 0.25 miles *0.4 km* (Time 30 minutes)
How Strenuous: Moderate
Features: Vortex, Interesting rock formations, Views

NUTSHELL: Located next door to the popular Boynton Canyon hike, this shortly takes you to a vortex spot and a scenic viewpoint.

DIRECTIONS:
From the Sedona Y Go:
Southwest on Highway 89A (toward Cottonwood) a distance of 3.2 miles *5.0 km* (MP 371), to Dry Creek Road, where you take a right turn onto Dry Creek Road (FR 152C). Follow it to the 6.1 *10 km* mile point, where it joins Long Canyon Road. Take a left here, staying on FR 152C. At the 7.7 mile *12.4 km* point, you reach another junction. Go right. At 8.0 miles *13 km*, just before the gatehouse to the Enchantment Resort, you will see a parking area to the right. Park there. There is also a small parking area on the left side of the road.

TRAILHEAD: It is marked at the parking area.

DESCRIPTION: From the trail sign at the parking lot, take a look to your right, where you will see two spires on the toe of a ridge. The saddle between these spires on the back side of the ridge is your target.
Begin walking down the main trail. In about 220 feet (90 paces before a small pole bridge) you will see side trails branching to your right. The challenge of this hike is to pick the right one. The bad news is that the trail is not marked, not even with cairns. The good news is that if you keep your eye on the target and follow the trails that look like they go there, you will succeed.
The trail climbs uphill and winds around the toe of the ridge. Boynton Canyon is regarded as a Sedona Vortex Center and some psychics think the vortex point is located below the back of the toe. We found a little crystal shrine there. Another theory holds that the spires are points on the Vortex, one female the other male.

Once you are around the toe you have your choice of paths up to the saddle. All are obvious. The saddle is a nice vantage point from which to see down onto the Enchantment resort on the left and **Mescal Mountain** and the approach to **Long Canyon** on the right.

From there you will see a trail over to the taller spire. It requires a brief, relatively safe bit of climbing to get to the spire's base. Fit hikers should have little trouble with it. To that point you will have hiked 0.25 miles *0.4 km.*

Some maps show a cliff dwelling farther along the butte at its base. There are some primitive trails along the base, some of them aimless game trails. We went to the half mile point, where there is a shallow alcove with a low line of stones covered by a fallen boulder. There are graffiti on the cliff walls here, one of which is *EHP 1901.* This was probably done by Elmer Purtymun, a Sedona pioneer. See the **Purtymun Trail** for a bit of information about the Purtymun family.

BOYNTON SPIRES

Altitude	4900
4700	

| Feet: 200 | Mod. |
| Miles: 0.25 | |

Enchantment

N
W — E
S

0.25 mi.

Boynton Cyn. Rd.

0.3 mi.

Long Canyon Road

1.6 mi.

152C

WILDERNESS
R'Rock-Secret Mt

2.9 mi.

152C

Dry Creek Road

3.2 mi. Sedona Y

89

89

89

MP 371

179

Driving Distance One Way, Miles: 8.0
Hiking Distance One Way, Miles: 0.25

BRINS MESA EAST #119

General Information
Location Map D4
Wilson Mountain USGS Map
Coconino Forest Service Map

Driving Distance One Way: 1.5 miles *2.4 km* (Time 10 minutes)
Access Road: All cars, Last 0.40 miles *0.65 km* gravel, in medium condition
Hiking Distance One Way: 2.75 miles *4.0 km* (Time 1.5 hours)
How Strenuous: Moderate
Features: Easy to reach, Good views

NUTSHELL: You hike a maintained trail to the top of Brins Mesa, then you go across country to a stunning rock formation on the lip of the mesa next to Wilson Mountain.

DIRECTIONS:
From the Y in Sedona, Go:
North on Highway on 89A (toward Flagstaff) for 0.30 miles *0.48 km* to Jordan Road, which is in the middle of uptown Sedona. Turn left (north) and take Jordan Road to its end, where the paving stops. Keep going on the unpaved road. Your goal is the former Shooting Range. At 1.1 miles *1.8 km*, you will intersect a private road. Turn left here. You will reach the Shooting Range gate at 1.5 miles *2.4 km*. Park outside.

TRAILHEAD: Start this hike at the Brins Mesa Trailhead.

DESCRIPTION: The **Brins Mesa East** Trailhead is on the other side of the gate. Follow this trail. It is wide and crosses over rolling hills on a moderate incline, taking you to the foot of Brins Mesa in 1.25 miles *2.0 km*. The next half mile climbs the mesa. It is fairly steep and moderately strenuous, a 500 foot climb. When you begin the climb, look behind you. As you rise, you will get better and better views.

When you top out on the mesa, you will be treated to great views. The trail continues across the mesa to the west, where it intersects a trail coming up from the **Soldier Pass Trail** and then goes all the way to the **Brins Mesa West** trailhead on the Vultee Arch Road. However, we are suggesting a different hike. This is to turn right at the mesa top and go north along the rim of the mesa. There is an ill-defined trail there, but it is easy to find your way by just following the rim. You will go a mile *1.6 km* to the end of the mesa.

About half way along, there is a great vantage point where a bare redrock cliff juts out like the prow of a ship. There are beautiful sights from here. But the best is yet to come. At the very end of the mesa, there is an eroded redrock turret that is easily climbed. The sculptures and carvings in the redrock are a true delight to the eye. There is a deep crevice between the end of the mesa and gigantic Wilson Mountain. This is one of the best sitting and gazing points in all Sedona, one of our all-time favorite spots in the redrock country.

From this point, you will have the best possible place to watch **Angel Falls** and its unnamed neighbor waterfall when they are running. There is a problem with this waterfall viewing, and that is that if it is wet enough for the falls to be running, it probably will be quite muddy on the mesa.

When the mesa is muddy, hiking there is miserable. There is no way to avoid the sticky, heavy mud.

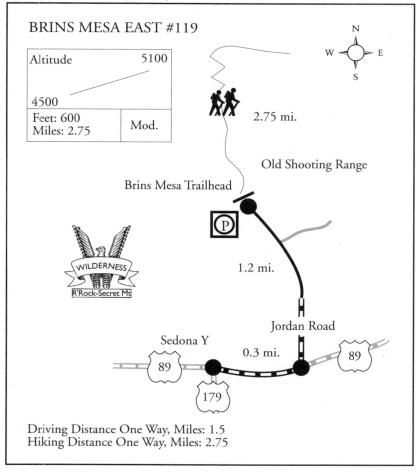

BRINS MESA EAST #119

Altitude	5100
4500	
Feet: 600 Miles: 2.75	Mod.

2.75 mi.

Old Shooting Range

Brins Mesa Trailhead

1.2 mi.

Jordan Road

Sedona Y

0.3 mi.

89

89

179

Driving Distance One Way, Miles: 1.5
Hiking Distance One Way, Miles: 2.75

BRINS MESA WEST #119

General Information
Location Map D4
Wilson Mountain USGS Map
Coconino Forest Service Map

Driving Distance One Way: 7.7 miles *12.4 km* (Time 30 minutes)
Access Road: Dirt road last 2.5 miles *4.0 km*, Any car with reasonable clearance
Hiking Distance One Way: 2.5 miles *4.0 km* (Time 75 minutes)
How Strenuous: Moderate
Features: Views

NUTSHELL: Brins Mesa overlooks uptown Sedona, giving fine views of the south face of Wilson Mountain and the Dry Creek drainage to the west.

DIRECTIONS:
From the Sedona Y Go:
Southwest on Highway 89A (toward Cottonwood) for 3.2 miles *5.2 km* (MP 371) to Dry Creek Road. Turn right on Dry Creek Road (FR 152C) and proceed to the 5.2 mile *8.4 km* point. Turn right on FR 152, the Vultee Arch Road, and follow it to the 7.7 mile *12.4 km* point. Pull off to the right into the big parking area and park.

TRAILHEAD: There is a rusty sign marking the trailhead at the parking area reading, "Brins Mesa #119."

DESCRIPTION: FR 152 is rough, but improvements to the road since the first edition of this book have made the road accessible to all cars except low riders.
The trail seems to be a combination of an old jeep road and stock path. It crosses a streambed ten times. Usually this is dry, and is no problem. If it is carrying much water, wait for another day. At the 1.0 mile *1.6 km* point you climb out of the streambed. You then begin to climb to the top of the mesa. This is a fairly gradual climb, because this side (the west side) of Brins Mesa slopes, forming an inclined plane, which makes for easy access. At 2.0 miles *3.2 km* you are near the top, out on the mesa, where you begin to have some fine views. You can look to your right into Soldier Pass, at **Coffee Pot Rock**. Straight ahead you look at Sedona. To your left you see Wilson Mountain. Behind you are views of the Dry Creek area.
The mesa top is quite flat and broad. There are some junipers growing there but in many places the mesa is rather bare. It was good grazing land

for cattle, though it isn't big enough to support many of them. The mesa itself is not particularly interesting but it provides a fine viewpoint.

You walk all the way across the mesa and peer down a fairly steep drop into the area of Mormon Canyon and Jordan Road, which is the **Brins Mesa East Trail** access. You can work these two hikes as a two-car shuttle, parking a car at each trailhead. The Brins Mesa West hike has a more gradual climb, is less scenic at the beginning and has more difficult access than the Brins Mesa East hike.

Brins Mesa is a large, interesting place. It forms a low barrier between Sedona and the Dry Creek backcountry. The legend is that in the old ranching days a brindle steer managed to avoid roundup and went wild on the mesa. Cowboys who tried to capture him became so frustrated by his escapes that they finally shot him. Their nickname for the critter was Brins or Brinds because of his brindle coloration, hence the name Brins Mesa.

BRINS MESA WEST #119

Altitude	5000
4600	
Feet: 400 Miles: 2.5	Mod.

2.5 mi.

152

2.0 mi.

152C

Dry Creek Road

2.5 mi.

Sedona Y

3.2 mi.

89

89

MP 371

179

Driving Distance One Way, Miles: 7.7
Hiking Distance One Way, Miles: 2.5

BROWN HOUSE CANYON

General Information
Location Map C5
Wilson Mt. USGS Map
Coconino Forest Service Map

Driving Distance One Way: 6.9 miles *11.1 km* (Time 15 minutes)
Access Road: All cars, All paved
Hiking Distance One Way: 0.3 miles *0.5 km* (Time 20 minutes)
How Strenuous: Moderate
Features: Scenic canyon, Slide Rock State Park

NUTSHELL: While the hordes enjoy the creekside pleasures at Slide Rock State Park, you can enjoy this little-known scenic canyon hike there.

DIRECTIONS:
From The Y in Sedona Go:
North on Highway 89A (toward Flagstaff) a distance of 6.9 miles *11.1 km* (MP 381.1) to the entrance to Slide Rock State Park. The park is well marked and signed and you will have no trouble finding it. Park in the main parking lot as near the brown house (ticket office) as you can.

TRAILHEAD: This trail is not signed or maintained. You will see the trail leading west from the picnic tables at the Ponderosa Picnic Area, immediately west of the brown house.

DESCRIPTION: You will have to pay an entrance fee to get into this state park ($3.00 per car in 1994). The brown house is used by the Park Department as its headquarters, and is where you buy entrance tickets. This hike goes up the canyon behind the house. Walk up to the Ponderosa Picnic Area (signed) and you will see the trail going west of the picnic tables.

Those who are familiar with the landscape around Sedona are amazed to find out how different things are in the upper canyon. The altitude at Slide Rock is about 5100 feet and you are going into a shaded moist canyon. As a result, you will find a dense alpine forest of pine, oak and maple. Near the entrance to the canyon blackberry bushes grow profusely.

The trail is one of those now-you-see-it, now-you-don't affairs, but you can't go wrong because the canyon is narrow and you just keep following the main channel to the canyon's end. There is a small streamed in the canyon and the trail crosses it several times.

As you begin the hike, your attention is on the trees, but as you go higher, you begin to see interesting redrock formations on either side of you.

You get rather mysterious peekaboo glimpses of these through the thick foliage. At about the quarter mile point you come into sight of immense white and gray cliffs.

The canyon ends in a box and you cannot get right to the base of the cliffs without some serious bushwhacking as the place is so overgrown. The trail plays out on a ridge some distance from the cliffs, a remote silent place surrounded by towering cliffs.

This is a good hike for a summer day, cool and delicious.

The area where Slide Rock State Park is located was once an apple orchard owned and operated by the Pendley family. It was the Pendleys who built the long irrigation flume that allowed their orchards to succeed where others had failed. Many apple trees are still on the grounds. One of the main old orchards was cut down in 1991 and new trees were planted, as the old ones had lost their vigor. There are many signs placed around Slide Rock Park showing points of interest.

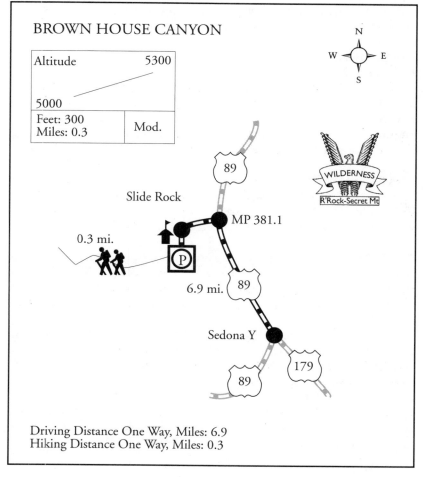

BROWN HOUSE CANYON

Altitude	5300
5000	

Feet: 300 Miles: 0.3	Mod.

N
W — E
S

89

Slide Rock

WILDERNESS
R'Rock-Secret Mt

MP 381.1

0.3 mi.

P

6.9 mi. 89

Sedona Y

179

89

Driving Distance One Way, Miles: 6.9
Hiking Distance One Way, Miles: 0.3

CAPITOL BUTTE

General Information
Location Map D4
Wilson Mt. USGS Map
Coconino Forest Service Map

Driving Distance One Way: 5.2 miles *8.4 km* (Time 15 minutes)
Access Road: All cars, All paved
Hiking Distance One Way: 0.5 miles *0.8 km* (Time 30 minutes)
How Strenuous: Moderate
Features: Views

NUTSHELL: Capitol Butte is one of the main Sedona landmarks, and the town partly wraps around it. This hike takes you to the top of a ridge radiating from the west face of the butte for fine views out over scenic country.

DIRECTIONS:
From the Sedona Y Go:
Southwest on Highway 89A (toward Cottonwood) for a distance of 3.2 miles *5.2 km* (MP 371) to the Dry Creek Road, FR 152C. Turn right onto Dry Creek Road and follow it to the 5.2 mile *8.4 km* point, where FR 152 branches off to the right. The road is paved to this point. Pull onto FR 152 just far enough to find a parking place and park.

TRAILHEAD: This trail is not marked, but the trailhead is easily found. From where you park, you will see a large metal sign frame, about 8 feet high. Walk up the road about 75 paces from it and look to your right, where you will see a ditch and a blocked dirt road. This is the trailhead.

DESCRIPTION: Walk up the old road a few yards, where you will meet another trail. Go right. At 0.15 miles *0.24 km*, the trail forks. The left fork is an old jeep road, and takes you on the **Chinup** hike. Take the right fork instead. It will lead you down into a little wash and then back up the other side.

At 0.18 miles *0.3 km*, you will have partly climbed a ridge. Here the main trail, a horse path leading to stables on Dry Creek Road, goes straight ahead, at the same level. You will find a fainter trail going uphill, toward the top of the ridge. This is the trail you want.

After a short, stiff climb, you will find yourself on the ridge top at 0.4 miles *0.66 km*. Though the top is covered with vegetation, it is not dense and it is easy to walk through it. Go to your right (west), to the clear edge of the ridge, where you can see down onto Dry Creek Road. This is a nice view, though you are looking down at a lot of homes in subdivisions.

After this, work your way east toward the cliffs that top the butte. High above you is the formation called Lizard Head. Seen from the right angle, it fully lives up to its name. Look to your left (north) in the middle distance and you will see an urn-shaped balanced rock on the skyline.

We bushwhacked around this ridge, did a bit of climbing up the redrock, and felt that we had had a nice outing. While we were there we noticed a hiker coming down from a saddle at the top. He might have even been able to get to the base of Lizard Head from the saddle. As it was late, we were unable to see whether this adventurer had a trail or was just picking his way. You might want to do some exploring here if steep climbing is your fancy.

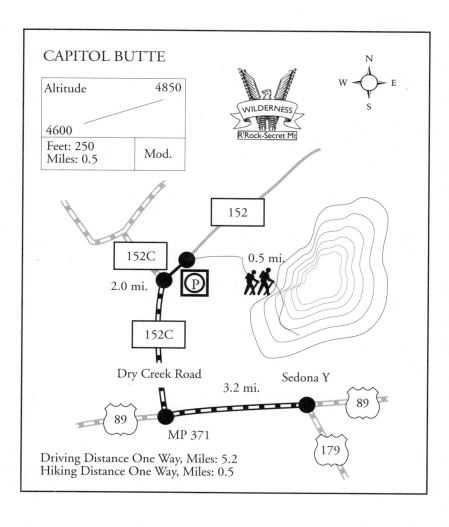

CARROLL CANYON

General Information
Location Map E4
Sedona USGS Map
Coconino Forest Service Map

Driving Distance One Way: 6.2 miles *10.0 km* (Time 20 minutes)
Access Road: All cars, All paved
Hiking Distance One Way: 1.25 miles *2.0 km* (Time 40 minutes)
How Strenuous: Easy
Features: Arch

NUTSHELL: This canyon, located 6.2 miles *10.0 km* southwest of Sedona, runs just south of Airport Hill. An easy walk, it features a "pocket-sized" arch.

DIRECTIONS:
From the Sedona Y Go:
      Southwest on Highway 89A (toward Cottonwood) a distance of 4.2 miles *6.7 km* (MP 368.9) to the Upper Red Rock Loop Road. Turn left and follow the Loop to the 6.0 mile *9.8 km* point, where you turn left, heading toward Red Rock Crossing on a dirt road. At 6.2 miles *10.0 km*, you will come to a bridge. Park just beyond the bridge.

TRAILHEAD: No marked trail. You walk up the floor of the canyon.

DESCRIPTION: The bridge that you reach at the 6.2 mile point *10.0 km* spans Carroll Canyon, so park anywhere near it. There is space for a couple of cars just beyond the bridge.
      Get out and walk into the wash and hike upstream. There are many places where the stream has cut down to a redrock shelf, where it is almost like walking on pavement. In other places, you must do a bit of boulder hopping. In about 0.25 miles *0.64 km*, you will be out of sight of habitation, although you will hear lots of airplane activity because the big hill to your right is Airport Hill.
      As you go, the canyon gets deeper and more interesting. At about 0.6 miles *1.0 km*, you reach an area where the canyon rises steeply and has carved out a series of terraces. You can keep climbing upstream over these ledges.
      Many pools have formed in declivities in the rock and some appear to be deep enough to hold water year around.
      At 0.9 miles *1.5 km*, you reach a place where the words "Arch

Spring" have been carved into a rock near a pool. The lettering looks old fashioned and may have been carved there many years ago when the spring was active. It seems inactive now, or perhaps it is active only during the time of snow melt. The arch is at ground level—just about big enough for your cocker spaniel to squeeze through.

Although the canyon goes all the way to Sedona (it crosses under Highway 89-A at Coffee Pot Rock Road), the scenic part of the canyon ends at 1.25 miles *2.0 km*. Beyond there, the channel flattens and due to the nearness of "civilization" becomes littered with trash.

Carroll Canyon is named after the Carroll family, which homesteaded in Sedona in its earliest days. The Carrolls occupied a tract of land on what is now the Red Rock Loop Road. Exhausted by their hardscrabble existence, they sold the land to Henry Schuerman, a hard working German immigrant of many talents. Schuerman was able to develop the property successfully and his descendants lived there for many years.

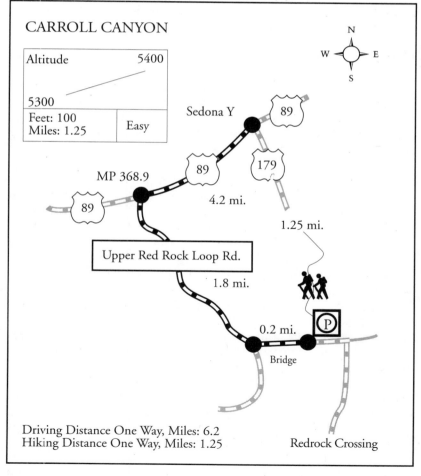

CARROLL CANYON

Altitude	5400
5300	
Feet: 100 Miles: 1.25	Easy

Sedona Y

89

179

MP 368.9

89

89

4.2 mi.

1.25 mi.

Upper Red Rock Loop Rd.

1.8 mi.

0.2 mi.

Bridge

Driving Distance One Way, Miles: 6.2
Hiking Distance One Way, Miles: 1.25

Redrock Crossing

CASNER CANYON NORTH #11

General Information
Location Map D5
Munds Park USGS Map
Coconino Forest Service Map

Driving Distance One Way: 2.6 miles *4.2 km* (Time 10 minutes)
Access Road: All cars, All paved
Hiking Distance One Way: 2.0 miles *3.2 km* (Time 75 minutes)
How Strenuous: Hard
Features: Views

NUTSHELL: Located just north of Sedona, this trail takes you across Oak Creek, then up Casner Canyon to a point on the Schnebly Hill Road just north of Schnebly Hill Vista.

DIRECTIONS:
From the Sedona Y Go:
        North on Highway 89A (toward Flagstaff) a distance of 2.6 miles *4.2 km* (MP 376.8) where you park at the mouth of a closed road.

TRAILHEAD: Walk down the old road a few feet and you will see a rusty sign reading, "Casner Canyon #11" where the trail goes downhill left.

DESCRIPTION: Follow the path down to Oak Creek. You have to wade across the creek here. We like to bring a towel along to dry our feet when we get to the other side. This is not a hike you would want to do while wearing wet tennies. A good method is to pack a pair of Tevas or other sandals, as walking the creek is tricky. Use the sandals for crossing the creek, then dry your feet and switch back to your hiking shoes on the other shore. You don't want to fall in. Count on wading, because even though there may be stepping stones, our experience is that they are unreliable.
        Once you are across the water and have dry shoes on, you will see Casner Canyon. You head right up the canyon on its right (south) side. Soon the trail lifts out of the canyon and climbs the north wall of the canyon, meaning that you are on a southern exposure. There is no shade and you are fully exposed to sun. Don't do this hike on a hot day.
        From the point where you rise above the crowns of the trees growing in the bottom of the canyon, the trail just goes to the top in a very businesslike way. It cuts a straight diagonal line from the bottom of the canyon to the top of Schnebly Hill. There is no scenery along the trail. In fact, it is quite drab. You do climb to the point where you get sweeping views.

You reach the top at a place that is close to the Schnebly Hill Vista, going through a gate in a barbed wire fence; so one way to do this hike is to use the two-car switch, parking one at Schnebly Hill Vista and the other at the Casner Canyon Trailhead. The easy way to do the hike is to start at the top, from Schnebly Hill. It is easy to recognize the start of the trail there by looking for the gate in the fence.

When you stand at the Schnebly Hill Vista you can see the Casner Canyon Trail. Sometimes, when the light is just right, it looks like a road and you wonder what on earth it can be, because no car could drive straight up the mountain as the trail goes. The trail was built by the Casner ranching operation as a livestock trail in the late 1890s.

The Casner family left its name in several areas: **Casner Mountain,** northwest of Sedona, the **Casner Canyon South** Trail in the Wet Beaver Creek Country, Casner Canyon Draw near Woody Mountain and others.

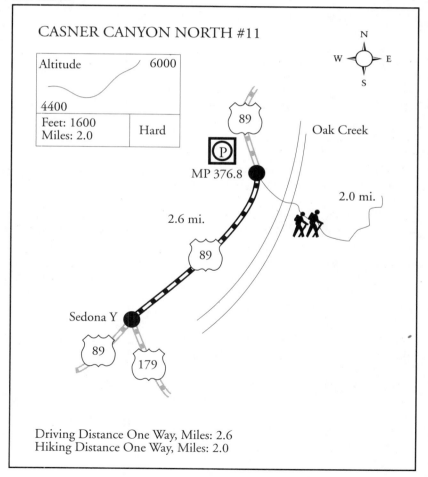

CASNER CANYON NORTH #11

Altitude   6000

4400

Feet: 1600
Miles: 2.0   Hard

89

Oak Creek

MP 376.8

2.6 mi.

2.0 mi.

Sedona Y

89   179

Driving Distance One Way, Miles: 2.6
Hiking Distance One Way, Miles: 2.0

CASNER CANYON SOUTH

General Information
Location Map G6
Casner Butte USGS Map
Coconino Forest Service Map

Driving Distance One Way: 17.2 miles *27.6 km* (Time 30 minutes)
Access Road: All cars, Last 0.3 miles *0.48 km* gravel, in good condition
Hiking Distance One Way: 2.0 miles *3.2 km* (Time 1.25 hours)
How Strenuous: Moderate
Features: Permanent Stream, Rock Art, Views

NUTSHELL: This trail follows the Bell Trail along the banks of Wet Beaver Creek and then branches off to climb to the top of a mesa.

DIRECTIONS:
From the Sedona Y Go:
South on Highway 179 (toward Phoenix) for 14.7 Miles *23.5 km* (MP 298.9), to the I-17 intersection. Go straight here rather than getting on I-17. Follow paved road FR 618 until you see a sign for Beaver Creek Ranger Station and trailheads at 16.9 miles *27.1 km*. Turn left. Parking is at 17.2 miles *27.6 km*.

TRAILHEAD: Several hiking trails here share a common trailhead that is well marked with signs at the parking area.

DESCRIPTION: From the trailhead, the **Bell Trail** goes up canyon along Wet Beaver Creek. The trail is an old road, broad and easy to walk. It was built by cattle rancher Earl Bell in 1932, as a means for taking his cattle to the top of The Mogollon Rim in the spring.

At about 0.6 miles *1.0 km*, look for a large boulder on the left side of the trail. On the side that faces away from you are a number of interesting petroglyphs.

The Forest Service's parking lot sign indicates that the Casner Canyon Trail is 1.5 miles *2.5 km* from the trailhead. When you make the hike, you will see a small sign for the trail to your left just before the Bell Trail dips down into a gully.

The trail goes up the south wall of Casner Canyon in a straight line, not zigzagging as many trails do. It is not terribly strenuous, though it does climb 1000 feet in 0.70 miles *1.2 km*. Along the way you are treated to some good views and some shows of colorful redrock.

The top of the mesa is covered by a hundred foot thick layer of lava, which is typical of all the mesas in this area. In most places there are sheer cliffs at these mesa rims. This trail takes advantage of a gap in the caprock and emerges at the top without requiring any rock climbing. On the top the trail just ends at a cairn at a point 2.0 miles from the beginning.

We suggest that you turn left and walk to the edge of the mesa overlooking Beaver Creek (about 0.20 miles *0.32 km*) for some excellent views of the creek and the Verde Valley. Hikers along the Bell Trail will wonder how you got there.

The Casner family was very active in the livestock business and left its name in several locations. In this book you will find the **Casner Mountain South** and **Casner Canyon North** hikes in addition to this hike.

CASNER CANYON SOUTH

N
W ← → E
S

Altitude	5200
4200	
Feet: 1000 Miles: 2.0	Mod.

WILDERNESS
Wet Beaver

Sedona Y

89

89

179   14.7 mi.   I-17

I-17

0.7 mi.

618

1.3 mi.

0.3 mi.

2.2 mi.

P

Ranger Sta.

Driving Distance One Way, Miles: 17.2
Hiking Distance One Way, Miles: 2.0

CASNER MOUNTAIN SOUTH #8

General Information
Location Map C1
Loy Butte and Clarkdale USGS Maps
Coconino Forest Service Map

Driving Distance One Way: 19.6 miles *32.4 km* (Time 30 minutes)
Access Road: All cars, Last 10.0 miles *16 km* good dirt road
Hiking Distance One Way: 2.0 miles *3.2 km* (Time 1.5 hours)
How Strenuous: Hard
Features: Views

NUTSHELL: This hike takes you to the top of a mountain overlooking Sycamore Canyon and the Sedona back country.

DIRECTIONS:
From The Y in Sedona Go:
Southwest on Highway 89A (toward Cottonwood) a distance of 9.6 miles *15.4 km* (MP 364.5) to the Red Canyon Road. Turn right on Red Canyon Road, also known as FR 525, and follow it to the 12.4 mile *20 km* point where FR 525C branches to the left. Turn left on FR 525C and stay on it to the 15.6 mile *25 km* point, the next major junction. Here FR 761, the Bill Gray Road, goes to the left. Stay on FR 525C, the right fork, and follow it to the 19.6 mile *31.4 km* point, where you will see a trail sign marked "Casner Mtn. #8." There is a parking spot big enough for one car at the trailhead.

TRAILHEAD: The trailhead is marked with a sign. The trail follows the power line up the south face of Casner Mountain, and you can see clearly from the start of the hike where the trail goes.

DESCRIPTION: Casner Mountain is bare of shade trees except for a few junipers and the trail takes you up its south face. Because of that, you are in full sunlight with no shade, so take a hat and plenty of water and don't try this hike on a hot day. The trail follows along a jeep road created for the construction of the power line. You will climb about 0.4 miles *0.65 km* to join the power line, then hike across a gradually rising shelf. From there you will begin the steepest ascent. Look over to your right (east) and you will see the rounded red butte known as **Robber's Roost.**
The payoff for this hike is the viewing. Casner is a tall mountain and is situated so that you can see into some beautiful country. To the south you see the Black Hills and Jerome. To the east you will see many Sedona

landmarks and parts of the town. As you climb higher you will begin to see the red towers of Sycamore Pass to your left (west).

From the end of the shelf, the trail goes straight up the mountain to about the halfway point, where the pitch becomes quite steep, and from there the trail serpentines. At the 1.6 mile *2.6 km* point you come to a sharp switchback at the west edge of the mountain where you break over a shoulder so that you can suddenly see into the whole of Sycamore Canyon. It is a vast and soul-stirring view, worth the trip all by itself.

From this point you will make the final push and stop at the top, at the highest point. Though Casner Mountain looks like a free-standing mountain when you start the hike, it is attached to the Mogollon Rim by Buck Ridge. The power line runs across this ridge and you can continue hiking the power line road for four miles to the rim. This hike from Casner's summit to the rim is in our *Flagstaff Hikes* book as **Casner Mountain North.**

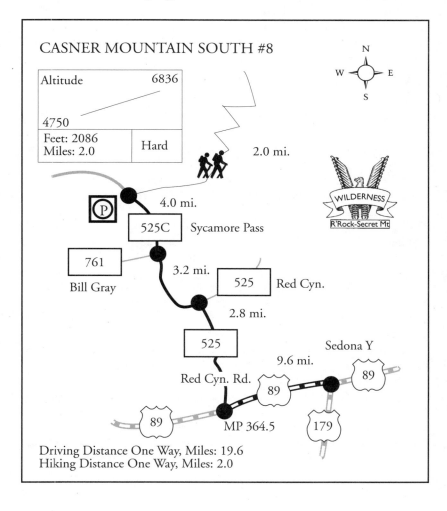

CASNER MOUNTAIN SOUTH #8

N
W — E
S

Altitude	6836
4750	
Feet: 2086 Miles: 2.0	Hard

2.0 mi.

WILDERNESS
R'Rock-Secret Mt

4.0 mi.

525C   Sycamore Pass

761
Bill Gray

3.2 mi.

525   Red Cyn.

2.8 mi.

525

Sedona Y

9.6 mi.

89   89

Red Cyn. Rd.   89

179

MP 364.5

Driving Distance One Way, Miles: 19.6
Hiking Distance One Way, Miles: 2.0

CATHEDRAL RIDGE

General Information
Location Map F4
Sedona USGS Map
Coconino Forest Service Map

Driving Distance One Way: 4.1 miles *6.6 km* (Time 15 minutes)
Access Road: All cars, All paved
Hiking Distance One Way: 1.5 miles *2.4 km* (Time 60 minutes)
How Strenuous: Moderate
Features: Views

NUTSHELL: Located 4.1 miles *6.6 km* south of Sedona, this interesting ridge connects Cathedral Rock and Little Park Heights. You hike a closed road to the base of the ridge and then make a moderately strenuous climb to the top, from where you have interesting exploring and great views.

DIRECTIONS:
From the Sedona Y Go
        South on Highway 179 a distance of 4.1 miles *6.6 km* (MP 309.4) to a point where a dirt road to the left (east) is visible at the city limits sign. Turn left onto the dirt road and park there on the little loop.

TRAILHEAD: This is not a marked trail. You walk across Highway 179, where you will find an old closed road. Then you walk the road.

DESCRIPTION: You will see a marker at the start of this road indicating that it has been closed. Here and there you will see places where the roadbed has been torn up to discourage vehicles from using it. Because it was once a road, it is wide and makes for easy walking.
        The first leg of the hike is confusing because there are a number of false trails. You will walk over a little hill crest and then go down into a creekbed. The road is a bit hard to follow as you come down the hill to the streambed, as there is a berm of dirt across the road, and a false road takes off to the left, where it ends in an old materials pit. If you have any doubt about the trail, head for the creek bottom. There is only one road on the other side, and from that point the way is obvious.
        The trail takes you over gently rolling land, climbing gradually until you come into a basin at the foot of Cathedral Ridge. Behind you are fine views of the Chapel of the Holy Cross. The road ends here, becoming a footpath. Where the path comes to a T intersection near the foot of the ridge, take the left fork (south). There is only one way to get to the top from here,

so look carefully for cairns and tracks.

The trail climbs up the ridge, gradually at first and then becoming steeper. It is less than a half mile to the top. You will first come out onto a redrock ledge over one hundred feet thick, forming some beautiful cliffs. It is fun to explore along this ledge, enjoying the many interesting eroded rock sculptures and formations.

Once you have had your fill of the ledge, you hike up to the next level. This requires another short steep climb. Then there is a final push to the top level, where you have your choice of going either north toward **Cathedral Rock** or south toward **Little Park Heights**, or both. If you do any exploring, then you can add another half mile or more to the 1.5 miles *2.4 km* we have shown as the mileage for this hike.

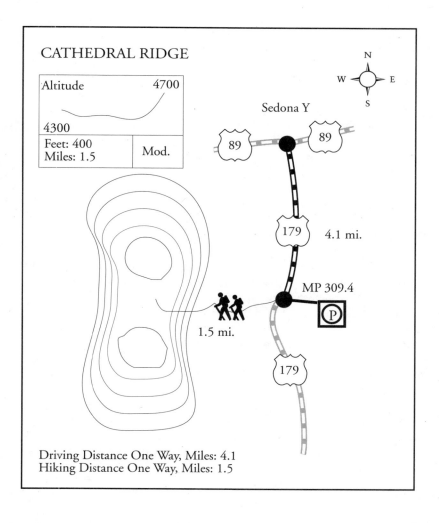

CATHEDRAL RIDGE

Altitude	4700

4300

Feet: 400 Miles: 1.5	Mod.

Sedona Y

89   89

179   4.1 mi.

MP 309.4

Ⓟ

1.5 mi.

179

Driving Distance One Way, Miles: 4.1
Hiking Distance One Way, Miles: 1.5

CATHEDRAL ROCK

VORTEX

General Information
Location Map E4
Sedona USGS Map
Coconino Forest Service Map

Driving Distance One Way: 7.1 miles *11.4 km* (Time 20 minutes)
Access Road: All cars, All paved
Hiking Distance One Way: 1.5 miles *2.4 km* (Time 40 minutes)
How Strenuous: Hard
Features: Views, Vortex Site

NUTSHELL: You drive to Redrock Crossing, a picnic area, then walk across Oak Creek to hike to the base of Cathedral Rock's west face, from where you can climb to its high cliffs.

DIRECTIONS:
From the Sedona Y Go:
        Southwest on Highway 89A (toward Cottonwood) a distance of 4.2 miles *6.8 km* (MP 368.9) to the Upper Red Rock Loop Road. Turn left and follow the Loop to the 6.1 mile *9.8 km* point, where you turn left, heading toward Red Rock Crossing on a paved road. Follow the paved road to Red Rock Crossing, a total of 7.1 miles *11.4 km.*

TRAILHEAD: No marked trailhead.

DESCRIPTION: From the parking area, walk south, toward Oak Creek. As you near its bank you will see a trail to your left (east). It is a concrete walk for a short distance. When the sidewalk curves to your left, away from the creek, continue walking upstream along the creek bank. You will notice the Chavez Ranch, established by early Sedona pioneers, to your left with its a water wheel, an unusual sight in dry Arizona.
        When you come to the irrigation control box, which is built out of concrete block, it is time to go across the creek. The box sticks out into the stream and creates a narrow place where there is sometimes a line of rocks that you can hop. Just above the box is a wide shallow redrock ledge, a good place to wade.
        Once you are across, keep working your way south, away from the water. You will hit a small side stream which you must also cross. Once you have crossed the side stream, keep going south until you run up against a low redrock cliff. Here you will find the main hiking path. It is wide and sandy and unmistakable.

Turn left (east). As you walk along here, you will see Cathedral Rock ahead of you, in a V-shape, with two smaller spires flanked by much bigger ones. At two-thirds of a mile from the beginning, you will find a gate. Go through the gate.

From the gate, you will walk along the bank and then the bottom of a wash for a short distance. The trail you want to follow soon lifts out of the wash to your left and climbs up the far side of the valley going up to the V in Cathedral Rock. Look carefully here, because you may be confused by a horse trail that follows the wash all the way out and goes to the Verde Valley School Road. There are cairns marking the true way.

From the point where you leave the wash, you climb to the top of some slick rock knobs, along a path that is fairly steep but not too hard. From that point the trail continues, but requires some scrambling and climbing to get to the base of the highest cliffs. There are wonderful views all along the way from the first heights.

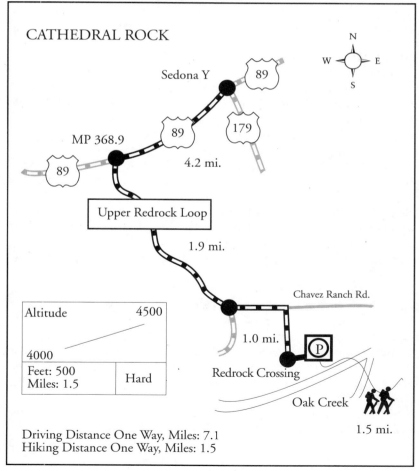

CATHEDRAL ROCK

Sedona Y

89

89

179

MP 368.9

89

4.2 mi.

Upper Redrock Loop

1.9 mi.

Chavez Ranch Rd.

Altitude   4500

4000

Feet: 500
Miles: 1.5   Hard

1.0 mi.

Redrock Crossing

Oak Creek

1.5 mi.

Driving Distance One Way, Miles: 7.1
Hiking Distance One Way, Miles: 1.5

CATHEDRAL ROCK, BACK O' BEYOND

General Information
Location Map F4
Sedona USGS Map
Coconino Forest Service Map

Driving Distance One Way: 4.1 miles *6.6 km* (Time 15 minutes)
Access Road: All cars, Last 0.7 miles *1.2 km* good dirt road
Hiking Distance One Way: 1.0 miles *1.6 km* (Time 30 minutes)
How Strenuous: Easy
Features: Views, Vortex spot

NUTSHELL: Cathedral Rock, a prominent Sedona landmark, is accessible from several points. This is the easiest and one of the most satisfying routes, featuring a marvelous natural walkway partly around the butte.

DIRECTIONS:
From the Sedona Y Go
　　　　South on Highway 179 a distance of 3.4 miles *5.5 km* (MP 310.2) to a point where you see a dirt road to the right into an area signed Back O' Beyond. Turn right onto the dirt road and follow it to the 4.1 mile *6.6 km* point, where you will see a marked and fenced parking area to your left.

TRAILHEAD: This is not a marked trail. It starts at the fence at the parking lot.

DESCRIPTION: At the parking area you are quite close to Cathedral Rock, and it dominates the skyline to your right. Enjoy the views of it before starting on the hike. You will see one of its outstanding features on the left end, a spire called The Mace, which is a large column that is larger at the top than the bottom.
　　　　The butte consists of two major parts, the upper sheer-walled cliffs and a lower platform with sloping sides. These slopes make it possible to climb to the top of the platform with relative ease.
　　　　Go through the gap in the fence and you will see several trails. Cattle used to graze this area and there are numberless false trails caused by them. Pass by the first trail that forks right and take the second right fork, about 40 paces from the fence. It goes downhill into a wash and up the other side.
　　　　Once across you will find another network of trails. Stay on the main one, which heads uphill toward the butte. At 0.2 miles *3.2 km* you will come to the top of a red slickrock ledge. Keep going up toward the central

mass and in a short distance you will find a wide lip that makes a natural walkway to your left. From here you simply hike the lip around to the south, hugging the butte all the way. This natural path is an unusual and delightful feature.

The views of the butte are eye-pleasing at every turn and you will also have some great views in the distance. This is a very restful and quieting kind of hike. Stop at the 1.0 mile *1.6 km* point, where the trail turns away from the butte and goes downhill into the junipers, a place where you encounter the remains of an old barbed wire fence. The trail goes on but is not very interesting beyond the fence.

We have not found a particular point that seems to be *the* Vortex spot on Cathedral Rock: no medicine wheels or other markers; but the place does have a nice restorative feeling of silent energy to both of us.

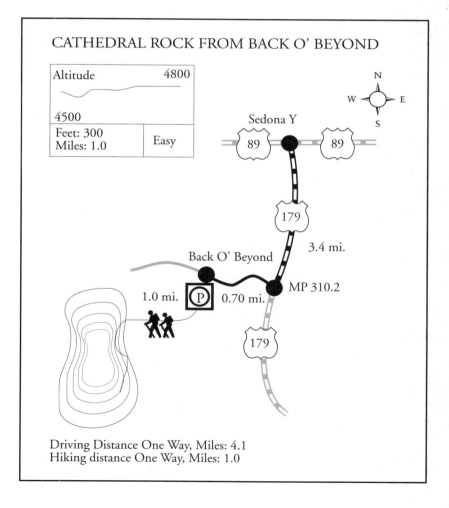

CATHEDRAL ROCK FROM BACK O' BEYOND

Altitude	4800
4500	
Feet: 300 Miles: 1.0	Easy

Sedona Y

89   89

179

3.4 mi.

Back O' Beyond

1.0 mi.   ⓟ   0.70 mi.   MP 310.2

179

Driving Distance One Way, Miles: 4.1
Hiking distance One Way, Miles: 1.0

CHICKEN POINT

General Information
Location Map E5
Sedona and Munds Mt. USGS Maps
Coconino Forest Service Map

Driving Distance One Way: 2.0 miles *3.2 km* (Time 10 minutes)
Access Road: All cars, All paved
Hiking Distance One Way: 1.2 miles *2.0 km* (Time 40 minutes)
How Strenuous: Moderate
Features: Rock formations, Views

NUTSHELL: Only a couple of miles southeast of Uptown Sedona, Chicken Point is a scenic gap that gives great views of Marg's Draw to the north and the Bell Rock country to the south. Short and easy, with good side tours, it is a great introductory hike to the area.

DIRECTIONS:
From the Sedona Y Go:
         South on Highway 179 (toward Phoenix) for 1.4 miles *2.3 km* (MP 312.1) to Morgan Road in the Broken Arrow Subdivision. Turn left (east) on Morgan Road and follow it to its end, at 2.0 miles *3.2 km*, where you park just beyond the cattle guard.

TRAILHEAD: Walk along the jeep road, FR 179F.

DESCRIPTION: Walk down the jeep road. You will see a sign at the cattle guard reading "Trail Walk-Through." We suggest that you disregard the walkthrough and just stay on the road. The road is widely used by the jeep tours that have proliferated in Sedona, so the road is well maintained, although sharing it with motor vehicles does detract from the natural qualities of the scene.
         As you walk the road, you will reach a spot at 0.34 miles *0.6 km* where a sunken road goes off to the right (south). This is the trail to the **Devil's Dining Room**, a large sinkhole. It is a short jaunt and worth seeing.
         At 0.42 miles *0.7 km*, the road splits but it doesn't matter which fork you take, as the roads converge on the other side of a hill. The high road gives better views. At 0.67 miles *1.1 km* you reach a T fork. Go straight. The right fork goes up to a nice viewpoint, again worth a short detour. The jeep tour drivers go up to the point for the view and to thrill the tourists, as they climb up a steep ledge. At 0.71 miles *1.2 km* you come to a Y fork. The left branch goes down into a gully and up to **Submarine Rock**, a worthwhile

side tour and a short easy one. Take the right fork to go to Chicken Point. You will hit another T intersection at 0.94 miles *1.5 km*. Go left.

At this part of the trail you are climbing and will get good views of the area to the north and east, a beautiful place known as Marg's Draw. It seems rather wild and remote and yet it is just a stone's throw from heavily populated areas of Sedona.

Chicken Point is a gap between Twin Buttes and the West Ridge of Lee Mountain. It is a great place for views both north and south and you stand right on beautiful red slickrock formations and are surrounded by interesting cliffs. Look for a famous formation called the Madonna and Nuns in the flutes of the rock face to your right. Depending on the light, it may be very obvious or you may have to use your imagination. It always seems to be windy at Chicken Point. Unfortunately this is not a place of solitude as it is very popular and when the jeep tours are running, load after load of them come to this justifiably popular spot.

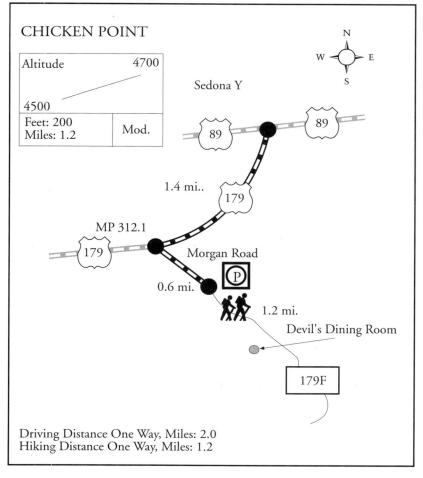

CHICKEN POINT

Altitude	4700
4500	
Feet: 200 Miles: 1.2	Mod.

N
W — E
S

Sedona Y

89   89

1.4 mi..   179

MP 312.1

179   Morgan Road

0.6 mi.   P

1.2 mi.

Devil's Dining Room

179F

Driving Distance One Way, Miles: 2.0
Hiking Distance One Way, Miles: 1.2

CHIMNEY ROCK

General Information
Location Map D4
Sedona USGS Map
Coconino Forest Service Map

Driving Distance One Way: 3.6 miles *5.8 km* (Time 10 minutes)
Access Road: All cars, All paved
Hiking Distance One Way: 0.65 miles *1.0 km* (Time 30 minutes)
How Strenuous: Moderate
Features: Rock formations, Views

NUTSHELL: This landmark located 3.6 miles *5.8 km* southwest of uptown Sedona can be climbed with moderate effort for great views.

DIRECTIONS:
From the Sedona Y Go:
       Southwest on Highway 89A (toward Cottonwood) for a distance of 2.5 miles *4.0 km* (MP 371.7), to Andante Drive. Turn right onto Andante Drive. Follow it to the 3.6 mile point *5.8 km* where it intersects Skyview. Drive just across Skyview onto a parking area on the dirt near the water tank.

TRAILHEAD: No signs posted. Follow the fence surrounding the water tank to the end of the fence. You will pick up the trail there.

DESCRIPTION:
       As you begin the hike, there are not many clues to the presence of the trail. You will see signs that people have parked just outside the fence surrounding the water tank. Walk along the fence to your left from where you parked and you will spot the trail heading down into a gully. Chimney Rock is in plain sight here, so you know which way you must walk.
       After going down into the wash, go upstream about 12 paces and you will find the trail going up the other side. In a couple of hundred feet, the path will intersect a major trail. Take the fork to the right, going uphill.
       At 0.5 miles *0.8 km* you will reach the top of a saddle between Chimney Rock and a ridge running over toward Capitol Butte. Take some time to explore around this ridgetop if you like. It is a good place. There are some great views.
       After you have explored the ridge, get back on the trail, following it for a short distance, looking for a faint trail to your left, which heads toward Chimney Rock.
       The trail up to the Chimney is not well developed, but this doesn't

matter much, as your objective is in sight always so that all you need to do is to keep working toward it. It is a bit of a scramble. From a distance Chimney Rock looks like a monolith, but when you get up close to it you can see that the formation is composed of three pillars. These probably were a single column thousands of years ago, but weathering has done its work. You can walk right up to the base of these pillars. They are fun to look at and you will have a great platform from which to view the surrounding countryside. You can see in all directions except to the north where Capitol Butte blocks your view.

It is possible to walk all the way around the Chimney. The ground is not level but making the loop is well worth the toil. We found it helpful to build a cairn to mark our starting point when we began the loop so that we would know where to descend. From the main trail up to the Chimney, around the Chimney and back down to the main trail is only 0.3 miles *0.5 km* .

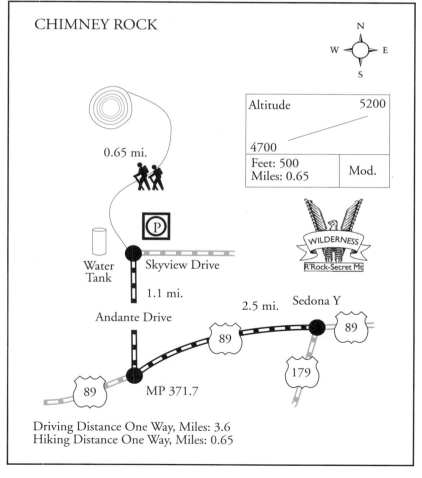

CHINUP

General Information
Location Map D4
Wilson Mt. USGS Map
Coconino Forest Service Map

Driving Distance One Way: 5.2 miles *8.4 km* (Time 15 minutes)
Access Road: All cars, All paved
Hiking Distance One Way: 0.5 miles *0.8 km* (Time 30 minutes)
How Strenuous: Moderate
Features: Views

NUTSHELL: This hike takes you to the top of a ridge projecting from the west face of Capitol Butte for fine views out over scenic country.

DIRECTIONS:
From the Sedona Y Go:
      Southwest on Highway 89A (toward Cottonwood) for a distance of 3.2 miles *5.2 km* (MP 371) to the Dry Creek Road, FR 152C. Turn right onto Dry Creek Road and follow it to the 5.2 mile *8.4 km* point, where FR 152 branches off to the right. The road is paved to this point. Pull onto FR 152 just far enough to find a parking place and park.

TRAILHEAD: This trail is not marked, but the trailhead is easily found. You will see a large metal sign frame, about 8 feet high, just up the road from where you park. Walk up the road about 75 paces from the sign frame and look to your right, where you will see a ditch and a blocked dirt road. This is the trailhead.

DESCRIPTION: Walk up the blocked road a few yards, where you will meet another trail. Go to your right. At 0.15 miles, the trail forks. Go to your left. At 0.08 miles you will reach another fork. The left fork (north), going uphill, is an old jeep road, and takes you on the Chinup hike. The right fork takes you on the **Capitol Butte** hike.
      Walk up the old jeep road. At 0.13 miles *0.2 km* it makes a hairpin turn to your left (northwest). Keep following the road. It will wind completely around the face of the ridge, climbing gradually as it does so. This gives the hiker the chance to see a panoramic view.
      At 0.24 miles *0.4 km* you will be around the side of the ridge at a point where there is a fork, with one branch going downhill. You want to turn right here and go uphill. In a few yards from this point you will come out onto a high shoulder of the ridge.

The road becomes less distinct on top and there are confusing cattle trails all over the ground. Look to your left (east), where you will see a knob about one hundred feet high. The top of this knob is your objective.

Keep picking your way through the scrub until you have climbed to the top of this knob. At the high point you will have great views. To the north you will see into the Dry Creek back country, to the west and south are equally fine views though not as wild, as you see many habitations. To the north look for an urn-shaped balanced rock on one of the cliffs of Capitol Butte. In the other direction, you will have a fine view of Lizard Head, a rock formation on the skyline.

You can then bushwhack to the head of the ridge, where it joins Capitol Butte and enjoy looking at the cliffs. This could even be the jumping off point for more exploration for those who have the time and energy.

CIBOLA MITTENS

General Information
Location Map D4
Munds Park and Wilson Mt. USGS Maps
Coconino Forest Service Map

Driving Distance One Way: 1.5 miles *2.4 km* (Time 10 minutes)
Access Road: All cars, Last 0.4 miles *0.65 km* good gravel road
Hiking Distance One Way: 1.5 miles *2.4 km* (Time 1 hour)
How Strenuous: Moderate
Features: Rock formations, Views

NUTSHELL: This unmaintained trail takes you to a landmark butte in the Soldier Pass area just 1.5 miles *2.4 km* north of the Sedona Y.

DIRECTIONS:
From the Sedona Y Go:
North on Highway on 89A (toward Flagstaff) for 0.30 miles *0.5 km* to Jordan Road, which is in the middle of uptown Sedona. Turn left (north) and take Jordan Road to its end, where the paving stops. Keep going on the unpaved road. Your goal is the former Shooting Range. At 1.1 miles *1.8 km*, you will intersect a private road. Turn left here. You will reach the Shooting Range gate at 1.5 miles *2.4 km*. Park outside.

TRAILHEAD: Use the **Brins Mesa East** Trail. Its trailhead is just beyond the gate.

DESCRIPTION: Hike the Brins Mesa East trail for about 0.7 miles *1.2 km*, to a point where you find an unmarked but distinct trail to the left marked by cairns.
Follow this left trail. At 0.75 miles *1.3 km* take the fork to the right.
You will climb up a butte and come out on top of the north end of **Shooting Range Ridge**. Take a minute while you are there to enjoy the view. You might even want to explore it a bit. Look for cairns leading right (north). The trail you want first goes down into a gully and then it goes up onto a redrock ledge.
Ahead of you, fully in view, is your objective, the gap between Cibola Mittens and Brins Ridge. The trail is fairly steep but it is short. Cairns mark the way.
At the top you will stand on a saddle from which you have out-standing views. To your right is the Mormon Canyon country, bounded to the north by Brins Mesa. To the east is Wilson Mountain. Behind you are

good views of uptown Sedona and the country beyond. To your left, west, is the Soldier Pass area. The saddle you are standing on divides Mormon Canyon and Soldier Pass.

You are at the base of one thumb of the mitten at this place. Keep going toward the hand of the mitten. You will find trails there. They seem to be deer trails but they work fine for humans.

There is a truly scenic gap between the first thumb and the hand. Just above head level at this gap you will find a rusted piton that was driven into the rock by a climber years ago. You can keep working your way around the hand of the mitten on a narrow but safe ledge to the other thumb, where the trail ends.

A subdivision under construction as we wrote this in Spring 1994 may change the appearance of the end of Jordan Road.

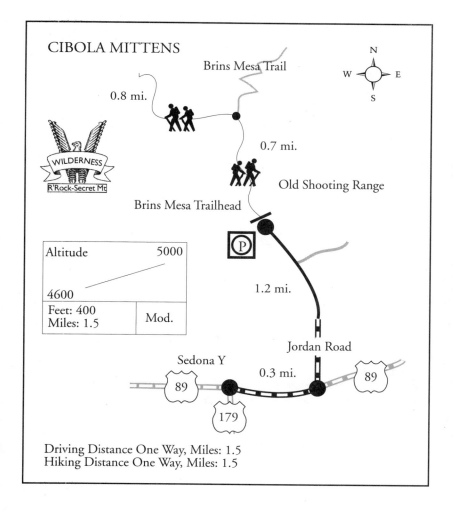

CIBOLA MITTENS

Brins Mesa Trail

0.8 mi.

0.7 mi.

Old Shooting Range

Brins Mesa Trailhead

WILDERNESS
R'Rock-Secret Mt

Altitude	5000
4600	
Feet: 400 Miles: 1.5	Mod.

1.2 mi.

Jordan Road

Sedona Y

0.3 mi.

89

179

89

Driving Distance One Way, Miles: 1.5
Hiking Distance One Way, Miles: 1.5

COCKSCOMB, THE

General Information
Location Map D3
Wilson Mountain USGS Map
Coconino Forest Service Map

Driving Distance One Way: 6.7 miles *11 km* (Time 20 minutes)
Access Road: All cars, All paved
Hiking Distance One Way: 2.5 miles *4.0 km* (Time 1.5 hours)
How Strenuous: Moderate
Features: Views

NUTSHELL: The trailhead is easy to reach, 6.7 miles *11 km* on paved roads. You hike 2.5 miles *4.0 km* along pleasant abandoned roads, then climb 400 feet to the top of a landmark butte southwest of Sedona.

DIRECTIONS:
From the Sedona Y Go:
Southwest on Highway 89A a distance of 3.2 miles *5.2 km* (MP 371) to Dry Creek Road (FR 152C) where you take a right turn onto Dry Creek Road. Follow it to the 6.1 mile *9.8 km* point, where it joins Long Canyon Road. Turn left here, staying on FR 152C. At the 6.7 mile *11 km* point, you will see a dirt road, FR 9586B, to your left (south). Park on it.

TRAILHEAD: Walk the closed road you park on.

DESCRIPTION: FR 9586B is a jeep road that goes to the south over gently rolling hills. Four-wheelers have driven all over the first part of this road, creating a confusing welter of tracks. The best clues to stay on the right path are: it is the main road everywhere; you always head southwesterly on it, never veering sharply east or west; look for bicycle tracks, as they mark the right route. You will hike the road a distance of 0.8 miles *1.3 km*, to a point where you will meet a power line. Make a short jog to your left (southeast) here and then continue taking the road southwesterly.

You are not in remote country as you move along this old road, but the juniper forest screens you so that you feel as if you are really out in the boondocks. From the power line onward you will be close to **Doe Mountain** and will move along beside it. At the 1.66 mile *2.7 km* point you will see an unexpected sight, a line of green-leafed deciduous trees and even bamboo at a boggy place where the road crosses a drainage. The fence you will see here surrounds The Tree Farm. You will pass through a gate and begin to climb uphill, moving away from the fence.

Ahead of you now, looming large, is the Cockscomb. At the 2.0 miles *3.2 km* point you will come to another corner of The Tree Farm fence at a point where the trail makes a hairpin turn to the east at the base of the Cockscomb. Look for a footpath to your right (south) here, going uphill. It is marked by cairns. The trail moves diagonally from the bottom right of The Cockscomb to its top left. About half way up you will meet the main trail, which is easy to follow. Stay on it, as it is the only route.

At the base of the ledge keep moving to your left (east). You will go just around the corner of the north face and climb three notches in the ledge. These are slightly risky but even with our aversion to risk we did not hesitate to make the climb. It's that safe. You will come out on top of the Cockscomb. The top is small and quite barren so you have good views all around. Walk about and enjoy looking. The cliffs of the Cockscomb itself are attractive. On the southern face you will look down on the spires that give the formation its name.

COFFEE POT TRAIL

General Information
Location Map D4
Sedona and Wilson Mt. USGS Maps
Coconino Forest Service Map

Driving Distance One Way: 2.6 miles *4.2 km* (Time 10 minutes)
Access Road: All cars, All paved
Hiking Distance One Way: 1.0 miles *1.6 km* (Time 45 minutes)
How Strenuous: Easy
Features: Rock formations, Views

NUTSHELL: Coffee Pot Rock is one of the most familiar Sedona land-marks. This trail allows you easy access to its base. You walk to a point under the "spout" where you enjoy great views.

DIRECTIONS:
From the Sedona Y Go:
      Southwest on Highway 89A (toward Cottonwood) for a distance of 1.7 miles *2.8 km* (MP 372.5) to Mt. Shadows Street. Turn right onto Mt. Shadows Street. Follow it to the 2.6 mile *4.2 km* point, where it meets Fabulous Texan Way. (The streets in this area are named after movies filmed in Sedona). There you will find a large water storage tank and a microwave tower inside a chain link fence. Drive across the road up onto the dirt apron around the fenced area, where there is parking space for a couple of cars.

TRAILHEAD: At the parking area. No signs posted. Follow the instructions below.

DESCRIPTION: To begin the hike, go through a crawl-through in the fence, a sort of window frame. On the other side you will find several trails, which can be confusing. We found no cairns or other markers. You can see Coffee Pot Rock ahead of you. Your first objective is to circle to the back of **Sugarloaf**, the hill at the parking place. At every trail fork take the branch that leads toward the back of the Sugarloaf, usually the left fork. The correct path circles the base of Sugarloaf and takes you around to the north side.

      You will pass under a power line. Beyond the line there is a wide cleared place. This is about 0.33 miles *0.5 km* from the beginning. In the clearing you will see a road going up Sugarloaf. The entrance to the road has been blocked by a row of flat red stones. Instead of going up Sugarloaf, look for a jeep road to your right. It heads up a low ridge that connects to the base of the cliffs where Coffee Pot Rock is located.

Once you get safely on this old road, the rest of the hike is easy. Whenever you come to a side path (and there are several of them), just remember where Coffee Pot Rock is and keep moving toward it.

The trail will take you to the base of the cliffs and then move along a ledge toward Coffee Pot. You will enjoy looking at the cliffs here, as they are very colorful and highly sculptured. As the trail nears Coffee Pot it becomes rougher and you have to watch carefully to see where it goes. Eventually the ledge you walk on will reduce down to the point where you can't walk it any further. Here you can look up and see the spout of Coffee Pot towering hundreds of feet above your head. It will seem that you are right under it, though you will be a little west of it.

At this farthest point, about 1.0 mile *1.6 km* from the parking spot, you will have some great views. The views to the north are marred by the substantial home building that has occurred there, but otherwise the views are fine.

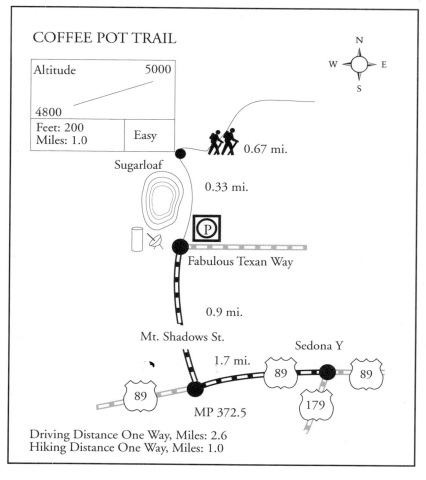

COOKSTOVE TRAIL #143

General Information
Location Map B5
Mountainaire USGS Map
Coconino Forest Service Map

Driving Distance One Way: 12.7 miles *20.4 km* (Time 20 minutes)
Access Road: All cars, All paved
Hiking Distance One Way: 0.75 miles *1.2 km* (Time 45 minutes)
How Strenuous: Hard
Features: Views

NUTSHELL: This is a marked and posted trail located just across Highway 89A from the Pine Flat Campground 12.7 miles *20.4 km* north of Sedona. It climbs the east wall of Oak Creek Canyon.

DIRECTIONS:
From the Sedona Y Go:
        North on Highway 89A (toward Flagstaff) for a distance of 12.7 miles *20.4 km* (MP 386.9) to the Pine Flat Campground. On your left at the upper end of the campground on the shoulder of the highway, you will see a structure about 5 feet high and 4 feet square made of round stones that houses a spring. You will see water flowing out of a pipe that sticks out the back of the structure. Park anywhere near here. There are wide aprons on both shoulders in this area.

TRAILHEAD: On the east side of the road just across Highway 89A from the spring. It is marked by a rusty sign reading, "Cookstove Trail #143."

DESCRIPTION: The water in the spring at Pine Flat is pure, and you will see people filling bottles and jugs these. We do this ourselves. There is a caution about this water, however: even though it is pure, it contains microbes that *your* system may not handle well, whereas local residents can drink it with no trouble.
        The Cookstove Trail is typical of all trails in upper Oak Creek Canyon that climb the east wall of the canyon: namely, it goes virtually straight up with little finesse. Similar trails are **Harding Spring, Purtymun, Thomas Point** and Thompson's Ladder**.** They are all strenuous hikes.
        The trail starts right by the highway and immediately begins to climb. At first the trail parallels Cookstove Draw. At 0.1 miles *0.16 km* you get a great view down into the draw, where there is a small waterfall during snow melt and after hard rains. Then the trail veers away from Cookstove

Draw as it rises.

The forest through which this trail passes is typical for upper Oak Creek Canyon, with pine at the beginning, changing into mixed pines and firs as you climb and the altitude increases.

The trail does a little zigging and zagging. When you top out, you are in a spot where you get good views of the west wall of Oak Creek Canyon, but the views are not as good as the views you get at the top of the Harding Spring trail.

The altitude at the rim is about 6600 feet, almost as high as Flagstaff, and the climate is similar to Flagstaff's climate. These hikes can often be pleasant in summer when hiking in Sedona would be too hot.

On the rim the country is flat and not scenic. The old-timers who built these trails would travel to Flagstaff once they got to the top. They did not build trails for the scenery. We like to walk along the rim looking for viewpoints, which are plentiful.

COOKSTOVE TRAIL #143

Altitude	6600
5600	
Feet: 1000 Miles: 0.75	Hard

N
W — E
S

89

ⓟ MP 386.9

Pine Flat
▲ C.G.

0.75 mi.

12.7 mi.

89

89   Sedona Y

179

Driving Distance One Way, Miles: 12.7
Hiking Distance One Way, Miles: 0.75

COURTHOUSE BUTTE BRIDLE TRAIL

General Information
Location Map F5
Mountainaire and Munds Mt. USGS Maps
Coconino Forest Service Map

Driving Distance One Way: 5.9 miles *9.5 km* (Time 20 minutes)
Access Road: All cars, All paved
Hiking Distance, Complete Loop: 6.0 miles *9.6 km* (Time 3.0 hours)
How Strenuous: Easy
Features: Views

NUTSHELL: This easy trail features Courthouse Butte, a landmark located 5.9 miles *9.5 km* south of Sedona.

DIRECTIONS:
From the Sedona Y Go:
    South on Highway 179 (toward Phoenix) for a distance of 5.9 miles *9.5 km* (MP 307.5) to a place where you will see crawlthrough frames in the barbed wire fence on the left side of the roadway. Pull over and park on the left shoulder near a crawlthrough.

TRAILHEAD: You will not find any signs marking this trail. Crawl through a frame in the fence and follow the unmistakable trail to the left, going toward Courthouse Rock.

DESCRIPTION: This trail looks like a jeep road at the start, then turns into a horse trail. It is often used by horse riders, so it is easy to follow.
    You will soon come to Bell Spring, which is located just below the famous **Bell Rock**. The spring can be located by the presence of the water-loving tall cottonwoods that grow around it. After that, you will come to a slickrock drainage coming from the spring and then the trail will take you along the south face of Courthouse Butte.
    Unlike many of the rock formations in Sedona that are attached to ridges, mountains or the rim, Courthouse Butte is freestanding and isolated.
    Courthouse Butte is very attractive and seems to be "built" on a more human scale than some of the gigantic formations around Sedona. It has undergone weathering that has created some very interesting erosion carvings and features. It feels friendly.
    The trail will take you beyond Courthouse Butte to a ridge behind a small subdivision. At 3.0 miles *4.8 km* the trail forks at a fence corner and turns left toward Lee Mountain. The trail takes you close to Lee Mountain

and climbs higher, up a talus slope, as it approaches the mountain. At the trail's highest point you have fine views to the south into the Jack's Canyon and Village of Oak Creek areas. The trail does not go very high against the side of Lee Mountain, just climbing the talus slope and then descending. From this point you follow a wash back to the beginning.

What is now called Courthouse Butte was originally called Cathedral Rock and *vice versa*. One of the early government map makers confused the two names and switched them. It doesn't seem to matter much, as either name seems appropriate, but some old-timers were pretty irate about the change.

The country through which this trail passes is cut by several arroyos that carry water that comes off Lee Mountain. These arroyos are fun to explore and can make hikes or hikelets in their own right.

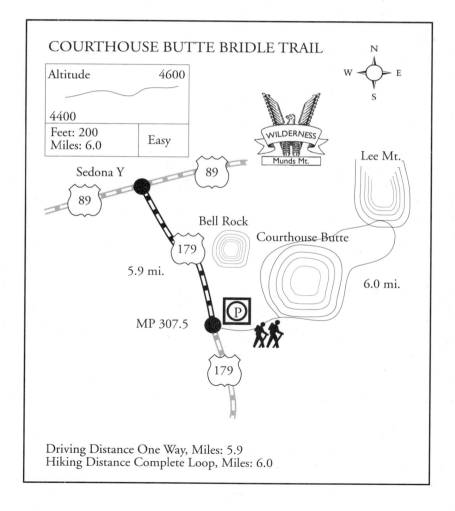

COURTHOUSE BUTTE BRIDLE TRAIL

Altitude   4600

4400

Feet: 200
Miles: 6.0

Easy

N
W   E
S

WILDERNESS
Munds Mt.

Sedona Y

89

89

Lee Mt.

Bell Rock

Courthouse Butte

179

5.9 mi.

6.0 mi.

MP 307.5

P

179

Driving Distance One Way, Miles: 5.9
Hiking Distance Complete Loop, Miles: 6.0

COW PIES

General Information
Location Map E5
Munds Mt. and Munds Park USGS Maps
Coconino Forest Service Map

Driving Distance One Way: 3.8 miles *6.1 km* (Time 20 minutes)
Access Road: All cars, Last 3.0 miles *4.8 km* good gravel road
Hiking Distance One Way: 1.5 miles *2.4 km* (Time 40 minutes)
How Strenuous: Easy
Features: Views, Fascinating rock formations and sculptures, Vortex

NUTSHELL: An ugly name for a beautiful area. The Cow Pies are redrock formations just off the Schnebly Hill Road, 3.8 miles *6.1 km* east of uptown Sedona. If you like redrocks, you will love the Cow Pies. **A personal favorite**.

DIRECTIONS:
From the Sedona Y Go:
        South on Highway 179 (toward Phoenix) for a distance of 0.3 miles *0.48 km* (MP 313.1) to the Schnebly Hill Road. It is just across the bridge past Tlaquepaque. Turn left onto the Schnebly Hill Road. It is paved for the first half mile and then turns into a gravel road that is all right for any car unless the road is muddy. At the 3.8 mile *6.1 km* point, pull over and park. There is an area off the road to your right for parking and there are more spaces on the shoulder.

TRAILHEAD: There are no signs. You will see a trail going over the left side of the road (to the west). Follow it.

DESCRIPTION: What's in a name? Many Sedona landmarks have grand names, such as the Crimson Cliffs. This hike takes place on a formation known by the ugly name, Cow Pies. The name does describe the appearance of the rock forms, but utterly fails to convey a sense of how beautiful and interesting they are. The "pies" look like hardened blobs of soft warm red mud, dropped into Bear Wallow Canyon the way you'd drop cookie dough onto a baking sheet. They are a unique Sedona experience, easy to reach and hike on. We prefer to call these formations "muffins."
        At 0.2 miles *0.32 km* you will come to the first muffin, a redrock shelf that had a very thin crust of volcanic basalt on top. This crust has broken up into small black stones which New Agers have arranged into a giant medicine wheel. This place is one of the fabled Sedona Vortex spots.

At 0.43 miles *0.7 km* you reach the next muffin. The trail you have been following continues in a straight line (for a hike called **Mitten Ridge**). You want to quit the trail here and turn to the left. Now you will get a better idea of the muffins. They are mounds of slickrock with many ridges and levels. Walk west, to your left, on the level area to the end of this muffin, where at 0.52 miles *0.84 km* you will find a land bridge linking it to the largest muffins, which sit by themselves in the bottom of the gorge.

You will top out on the Master Muffin at about 0.59 miles *1.0 km*. There is usually a cairn marking this spot. Take note of it, since it will help you find your way down on the return trip. From this point there is no trail. You just walk around and explore. In fact, it is so easy to walk around on these formations that you won't realize how substantial they are until you get to their edges and look down

The farthest extension of these rocks takes you out about 1.5 miles *2.4 km* from the parking place.

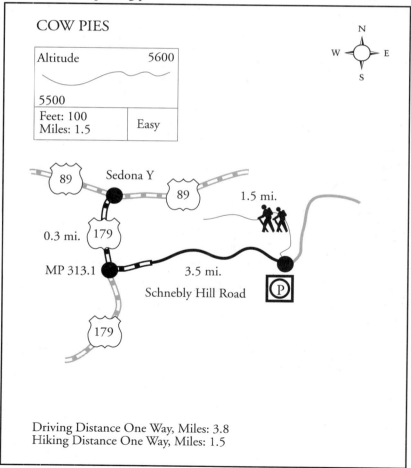

DAMFINO CANYON

General Information
Location Map E5
Munds Mt. and Munds Park USGS Maps
Coconino Forest Service Map

Driving Distance One Way: 1.85 miles *3.0 km* (Time 20 minutes)
Access Road: All cars, Last 1.05 miles *2.0 km* good gravel road
Hiking Distance One Way: 1.0 miles *1.6 km* (Time 45 minutes)
How Strenuous: Moderate
Features: Views, Arches

NUTSHELL: Located off the Schnebly Hill Road, just 1.85 miles *3.0 km* from uptown Sedona, this hike takes you straight up a side canyon in wild and unspoiled country.

DIRECTIONS:
From the Sedona Y Go:
South on Highway 179 (toward Phoenix) for a distance of 0.30 miles *0.48 km* (MP 313.1) to the Schnebly Hill Road, which is just across the bridge, past Tlaquepaque. Turn left onto the Schnebly Hill Road (the first half mile is paved) and follow it to the 1.85 mile *3.0 km* point.

TRAILHEAD: There are no signs marking this hike. There really is no trail. You work your way up the canyon floor.

DESCRIPTION: The Schnebly Hill Road is very popular and gets a lot of use. Sometimes it is in poor condition, but usually an ordinary passenger car can make it all right. If it is muddy you may need four-wheel drive.
At 1.85 miles *3.0 km*, at a hairpin turn, you will see Damfino Canyon to your right. There is a clearing at its entrance that is wide enough for four cars. This is the place to park.
There is an apparent trail on the left bank of the canyon, but do not take it. It vanishes soon, going nowhere. Instead, walk straight up the bottom of the canyon. As you climb, some side canyons will appear. Don't go into these. Stay in the main canyon. At 0.40 miles *0.65 km* you will reach a major fork. Go left there.
At 0.60 miles *1.0 km* you will see an arch in a redrock cliff ahead of you to your left. At 0.75 miles 1.2 *km* you will see an even bigger arch also on the left. At 1.0 miles *1.6 km* the going gets very rough and steep. This is a good place to stop although if you are hardy and in good shape you might try to struggle farther up the canyon. This is a good hike if you like

rock hopping. You get right in amongst the beautiful cliffs which form the walls of this canyon. It has a great remote wilderness feeling.

The original Schnebly Hill Road was built by a coalition of Sedona residents and Coconino County in 1902. Before that time, the only wagon road from Sedona to Flagstaff was along the difficult **Beaverhead** road, which is 11.2 miles south of Sedona. Damfino Canyon got its name during the 1930s when government officials were surveying the Schnebly Hill Road in order to realign and improve it. The survey party included a pioneer who had participated in the original road construction. When they came to this canyon, the head surveyor asked the old-timer for the name of the canyon. Although the veteran guide had provided the names of many a landmark for the engineer before that, this particular canyon stumped the old-timer and he replied, "Damn if I know," which came out sounding like "Damfino." The engineer thought he was reciting a name and wrote Damfino Canyon on the official map.

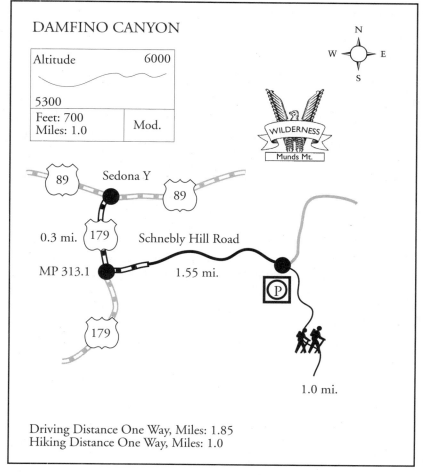

DAMFINO CANYON

Altitude	6000
5300	
Feet: 700 Miles: 1.0	Mod.

N
W — E
S

WILDERNESS
Munds Mt.

89   Sedona Y   89

0.3 mi. 179   Schnebly Hill Road

MP 313.1   1.55 mi.

179

1.0 mi.

Driving Distance One Way, Miles: 1.85
Hiking Distance One Way, Miles: 1.0

DEVIL'S BRIDGE #120

General Information
Location Map D4
Loy Butte and Wilson Mt. USGS Maps
Coconino Forest Service Map

Driving Distance One Way: 6.5 miles *10.5 km* (Time 30 minutes)
Access Road: All cars, Last 1.3 miles *2.1 km* medium dirt road
Hiking Distance One Way: 1.0 miles *1.6 km* (Time 30 minutes)
How Strenuous: Moderate
Features: Views, Arch

NUTSHELL: Located 6.5 miles *10.5 km* northwest of Sedona, this is a short hike to a fascinating arch.

DIRECTIONS:
From the Sedona Y Go:
　　　　Southwest on Highway 89A (toward Cottonwood) for a distance of 3.2 miles *5.2 km* (MP 371) to the Dry Creek Road, FR 152C. Turn right onto Dry Creek Road and follow it to the 5.2 mile *8.4 km* point, where FR 152 branches off to the right. The road is paved to this point. FR 152 is a dirt road that has been improved since the first edition of this book. Ordinary passenger cars can make it, though it can be rough. At 6.5 miles *10.5 km* you will reach a point where a dirt road takes off to the right. Turn onto it and park in the parking lot.

TRAILHEAD: This is a marked and maintained trail. There is a rusty sign where you park reading "Devil's Bridge #120."

DESCRIPTION: You will walk up an old road for about 0.4 miles *0.7 km*, to a point where a footpath forks off to your right. Follow this path. You will see that it leads up toward a red ledge on the east face of Capitol Butte. The path is steep but fairly short, being about 0.4 miles *0.7 km* from the fork.
　　　　Halfway up the trail from the fork you will begin to see the arch off to your left in the red ledge. It is hidden from your sight until you get to this point.
　　　　The path itself is very interesting as it begins to climb up the cliff. The Forest Service has used some natural stairsteps made by erosion and has added to these by cementing in some sandstone slabs to form stair steps.
　　　　At the top you have great views into colorful backcountry. You come out behind the arch. You can follow the trail to the end of the arch and loop around to stand on the arch if you are daring. The trail places you in a

spot where you are above the arch looking down on it.

To get under the arch, go back down to the bottom of the trail and look for cairns about 100 yards from the bottom, marking a small trail going off to your right. The trail goes down into a wash. You walk up the wash and find yourself under the arch.

This is a fine hike but attracts so many visitors that they may lessen your experience if you like solitude. Devil's Bridge is generally regarded as the largest of the natural arches around Sedona. It is an impressive sight.

If you face across the canyon you will be looking at the last leg of the **Lost Canyon Trail,** which is a personal favorite of ours.

DEVIL'S BRIDGE #120

Altitude   5200

5000

Feet: 200
Miles: 1.0   Mod.

152

1.3 mi.

152

WILDERNESS
R'Rock-Secret Mt

152C

2.0 mi.

1.0 mi.

152C

Dry Creek Road   Sedona Y

3.2 mi.

89   89

MP 371

179

Driving Distance One Way, Miles: 6.5
Hiking Distance One Way, Miles: 1.0

DEVIL'S DINING ROOM

General Information
Location Map E5
Sedona USGS Map
Coconino Forest Service Map

Driving Distance One Way: 2.0 miles *3.2 km* (Time 10 minutes)
Access Road: All cars, All paved
Hiking Distance One Way: 0.42 miles *0.7 km*
How Strenuous: Easy
Features: Sinkhole

NUTSHELL: The Devil's Dining Room is a sinkhole at the south end of Marg's Draw, only a few minutes from uptown Sedona. A short easy walk through scenic country brings you to this site, which is also the jumping off point for other good hikes.

DIRECTIONS:
From the Sedona Y Go:

South on Highway 179 (toward Phoenix) for 1.4 miles *2.3 km* (MP 312.1) to Morgan Road in the Broken Arrow Subdivision. Turn left (east) on Morgan Road and follow it to its end, at 2.0 miles *3.2 km*, where you park just beyond the cattle guard.

TRAILHEAD: You will see no trail signs. Walk the road, which is FR 179F.

DESCRIPTION: At the cattle guard you will see a sign indicating a "Trail Walk-through." We have tried this and see no reason to use it. It is better to walk right down the middle of the road.

This road is used by the jeep tours that abound in Sedona and you are likely to meet some of them on this hike in good weather. They act as if they own the road, and in a certain sense they do, as they have a maintenance agreement for it with the Forest Service.

At 0.26 miles *0.42 km* turn right, going up on a red sandstone ledge. The jeeps go up there to thrill the dudes, so the trail is easy to follow. You stay on the lower part of the ledge and walk across it, where the dirt road resumes.

At 0.34 miles *0.6 km* go to the right on a sunken road. This will lead you to the Devil's Dining Room at 0.42 miles *0.7 km*. At the site, you will come out into a small clearing where you will see a line of boulders and a barbed wire fence. These surround the sinkhole.

This sinkhole isn't nearly as big as **Devil's Kitchen** but it is impressive. Sinkholes develop when underground cavities undermine a ledge of rock to the point where it collapses into the void. Some geologists speculate that this sinkhole and Devil's Kitchen were both caused by the same underground river that removed the supporting subsoil from both places. After being "dormant" for decades, Devil's Kitchen became active again in November 1988, when a large chunk of ledge fell into the hole. We were at the site a month later and saw warning signs all around the rim. One of the jeep tour guides was there looking into the pit in awe and told us that he had gone to the bottom not long before the rockfall, being unaware of the danger. Since then there have been more cave-ins there. Devil's Dining Room appears to be stable, but so did Devil's Kitchen before November 1988. The natural undermining continues. Something for you to contemplate as you stand on the rim.

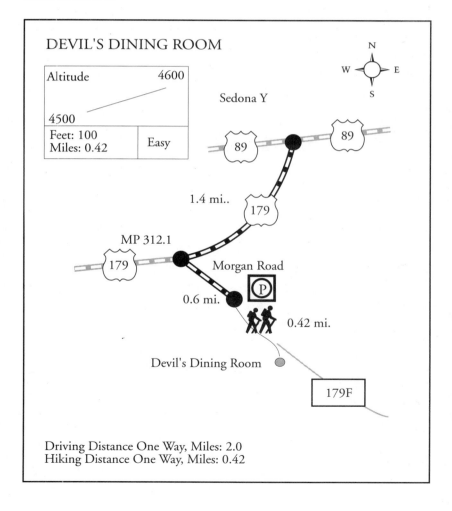

Driving Distance One Way, Miles: 2.0
Hiking Distance One Way, Miles: 0.42

DEVIL'S KITCHEN

General Information
Location Map D4
Sedona and Wilson Mt. USGS Maps
Coconino Forest Service Map

Driving Distance One Way: 3.0 miles *5.0 km* (Time 10 minutes)
Access Road: All cars, All paved
Hiking Distance One Way: 0.35 miles *0.56 km* (Time 15 minutes)
How Strenuous: Easy
Features: Sinkhole

NUTSHELL: The Devil's Kitchen is a sinkhole in the Soldier Pass area, only a few minutes from uptown Sedona. The hike is short, easy and scenic.

DIRECTIONS:
From the Sedona Y Go:
      Southwest on Highway 89A (toward Cottonwood) for a distance of 1.25 miles *2.4 km* (MP 372.8) to Soldier Pass Road. Turn right onto Soldier Pass Road and follow it to the 2.75 mile *4.4 km* point, where it intersects Rim Shadows Drive, where you turn right. Follow Rim Shadows a short distance, to a three-way intersection. Go straight onto Canyon Shadows and follow it to the 3.0 miles *5.0 km* point. There you will see a sign saying "National Forest Access." Take the road to your left there and park in the parking area. This is well defined and spacious.

TRAILHEAD: You will see a rusty sign at the parking area reading "Soldier Pass Trail #66."

DESCRIPTION: The trail is an old jeep road and it is still in use by jeep tours. Walk down this road for 0.10 miles *0.16 km* where you will see a road branching off to your right, marked FR 904B. Take this road. You will climb it uphill for a short distance and will reach Devil's Kitchen at 0.35 miles *0.56 km.*
      Devil's Kitchen is the biggest sinkhole in the Sedona area. The original cave-in occurred in the late 1800s, causing an implosion that was heard for miles. It raised a dust cloud that darkened the sky over a wide area.
      Cave-ins here have not ceased. This is an active sinkhole. The hole was dormant for many years but then became active again in 1988 when a large chunk of the rim fell into the cavity. Since then there have been other collapses. There are warning signs around the perimeter of the crater warning you not to get close to the edge. They aren't kidding. Another collapse

could happen at any time. This is an active sinkhole, rather like an active volcano. You can see a thin white layer of mineral exposed on most of the sheared stone faces. This layer looks like a film of calcium sandwiched between the layers of stone along fault lines, making a weak bond and creating natural weak points along which the collapsing occurs.

The hole is about one hundred feet deep. It was caused by an underground stream cutting away the strata underneath a redrock ledge. This created an underground cave. Deprived of its support, the cap eventually gave way along fault lines. Scientists believe that the same underground stream created the **Devil's Dining Room** several miles south of Devil's Kitchen.

There is a large tree, perhaps ninety feet tall, in the bottom of the crater. Since it is older than the crater it is assumed that it was growing on the top, fell in during the collapse and continued to grow. Plucky tree.

DOE MOUNTAIN #60

General Information
Location Map D3
Wilson Mt. USGS Map
Coconino Forest Service Map

Driving Distance One Way: 8.9 miles *14.3 km* (Time 20 minutes)
Access Road: All cars, Last 1.2 miles *1.9 km* good dirt road
Hiking Distance One Way: 1.8 miles *2.9 km* (Time 1 hour)
How Strenuous: Moderate
Features: Views

NUTSHELL: This small mesa, 8.9 miles *14.3 km* west of uptown Sedona, is fairly easy to climb. Its weathered cliffs are a delight to explore and it provides great views. **A personal favorite**

DIRECTIONS:
From the Sedona Y Go:
Southwest on Highway 89A (toward Cottonwood) for 3.2 miles *5.2 km* (MP 371) to Dry Creek Road. Go right on Dry Creek Road to the 6.1 mile *9.8 km* point, where Dry Creek Road joins the Long Canyon Road, both paved. Turn left here, on FR 152C, and go to the 7.7 mile *12.4 km point*, where it joins the Boynton Canyon Road. Turn left here on the Boynton Pass Road, FR 152C. The paving soon ends, to be replaced by a good dirt road. Stop at the 8.9 mile *14.3 km* point, just before a cattle guard. The parking area is on the right. This is also the parking place for the **Bear Mountain** hike.

TRAILHEAD: You will see a rusty sign across the road reading "Doe Mountain #60."

DESCRIPTION: Doe Mountain is a small mesa standing by itself. It is one of the most southerly redrock formations in the west-of-Sedona area. Only the **Cockscomb** is farther south. The trail zigzags to the top of the mesa, climbing steadily. It is a good trail, but a fairly steep pull. Though it seems improbable, there are often cattle on top.
The top of Doe Mountain is not bare rock as you might think when you see it from a distance. Soil has formed through weathering and low junipers and shrubs grow there, plus forage for the cattle. The best part of this hike is working your way around the rim. The edge of the rim is mostly bare redrock. This means that there are no trees to obstruct your views, so Doe Mountain is a terrific viewpoint and it is situated so that there are inter-

esting things to look at. Views of Sedona are particularly good from here.

In addition to the views of far off objects, you will see some wonderful things nearby, where erosion has worked the cliff faces into some really fantastic rock sculptures. The Sedona Westerners report that there are Indian ruins on the top of the mesa but in three trips we have never seen any. The south side of Doe looks down on a tree farm, which is an unexpected and interesting sight. The farm lies between Doe Mountain and the Cockscomb.

On trips we took in 1988, 1989 and 1990 we saw three feral goats perched on a narrow ledge halfway up a cliff face. The first time we saw this we could not believe our eyes. Then we saw a ribbon around the neck of one goat and came to believe that these were pets who heard the call of the wild.

The peacefulness and wildness of this hike were spoiled for us twice when helicopter tours touched down here to show tourists the views. If this is progress, spare us.

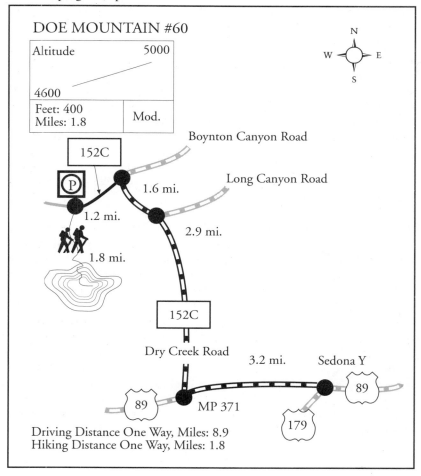

DOE MOUNTAIN #60

Altitude	5000
4600	
Feet: 400 Miles: 1.8	Mod.

N
W — E
S

Boynton Canyon Road

152C

Ⓟ

1.6 mi.

Long Canyon Road

1.2 mi.

2.9 mi.

1.8 mi.

152C

Dry Creek Road

3.2 mi.

Sedona Y

89

89

MP 371

179

Driving Distance One Way, Miles: 8.9
Hiking Distance One Way, Miles: 1.8

DOGIE TRAIL #116

General Information
Location Map C1
Loy Butte and Clarkdale USGS Maps
Coconino Forest Service Map

Driving Distance One Way: 20.7 miles *33 km* (Time 45 minutes)
Access Road: All cars, Last 11.1 miles *17.6 km* good dirt road
Hiking Distance One Way: 4.0 miles *6.4 km* (Time 2.5 hours)
How Strenuous: Moderate
Features: Sycamore Canyon access, Views

NUTSHELL: This hike provides access into Sycamore Canyon at Sycamore Pass, located 20.7 miles *33 km* northwest of Sedona.

DIRECTIONS:
From The Y in Sedona Go:
Southwest on Highway 89A (toward Cottonwood) a distance of 9.6 miles *15.4 km* (MP 364.5) to the Red Canyon Road. Turn right on Red Canyon Road, also known as FR 525, and follow it to the 12.4 mile *19.8 km* point where FR 525C branches to the left. Turn left on FR 525C and stay on it to the 15.6 mile *25 km* point where it meets FR 761, the Bill Gray Road. Your destination is Sycamore Pass. Go right here, staying on FR 525C to the 19.7 mile *31.6 km* point, where it meets FR 9529. Turn left here and go to the 20.7 mile *33 km* point, where the road meets FR 9528. Park near this intersection. Don't try to drive on FR 9528.

TRAILHEAD: At the intersection beyond your parking spot you will see a road sign reading, *"Sycamore Pass, Dogie Trail"* with an arrow pointing to the right. Follow the arrow and walk down the road. You will reach a fork in the road, where you should take the right hand path. From there you will walk down a jeep road to the trailhead. Distance from the parking area to the trailhead is 0.5 miles *0.8 km.*

At the trailhead you will see a sign: *"Sycamore Canyon 5 miles, Sycamore Basin Trail 5.5 miles, Road 525C 0.5 miles, Dogie Trail #116."*

DESCRIPTION: From the beginning, this trail slopes gradually toward Sycamore Canyon. You will walk down an old stock trail that is very rocky, but the grade is gentle. After hiking a few hundred yards, the landscape will open up to some great views ahead of you, where you will see redrock spires and buttes that are just as impressive as those nearer Sedona.

There are two cattle tanks on this trail. To get to the first one, you must detour to your left. The path goes right around the rim of the second one.

We recommend that you stop at about the 3.0 *4.8 km* or 4.0 mile *6.4 km* point rather than going all the way into Sycamore Canyon, for it is a very strenuous hike to go to the bottom. By staying on top you will have a fine hike and enjoy tremendous views. Remember that the return leg of this hike is all uphill.

Sycamore Canyon is a huge wild place. Even experienced hikers should not attempt a multi-day trip through it unless they are thoroughly prepared and know what they are doing. The brief sight of the canyon you get on a day hike like this is misleading and understates the rigors of the place. It is very beautiful and deserves to be better known and visited, as we hope to encourage in this book, but please do not overextend yourself.

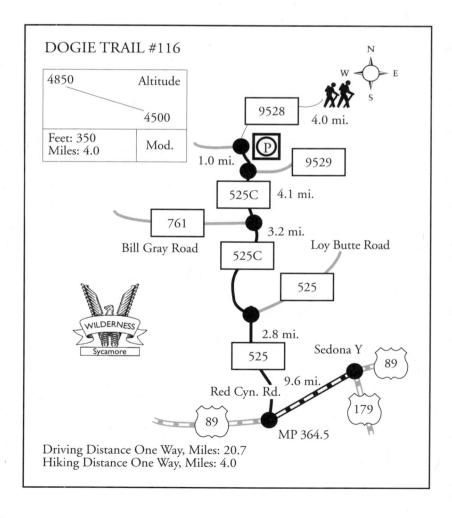

DOGIE TRAIL #116

| 4850 | Altitude |
| | 4500 |

| Feet: 350 Miles: 4.0 | Mod. |

9528 — 4.0 mi.

1.0 mi.

9529

525C — 4.1 mi.

3.2 mi.

761 — Bill Gray Road

525C

Loy Butte Road

525

2.8 mi.

525 — Sedona Y

89

9.6 mi.

Red Cyn. Rd.

179

89

MP 364.5

WILDERNESS Sycamore

Driving Distance One Way, Miles: 20.7
Hiking Distance One Way, Miles: 4.0

DRY CREEK TRAIL #52

General Information
Location Map C4
Loy Butte and Wilson Mt. USGS Maps
Coconino Forest Service Map

Driving Distance One Way: 9.6 miles *15.4 km* (Time 45 minutes)
Access Road: Most cars, Last 4.4 miles *7.0 km* Medium unpaved
Hiking Distance One Way: 2.0 miles *3.2 km* (Time 1 hour)
How Strenuous: Moderate
Features: Scenic canyon

NUTSHELL: Located 9.6 miles *15.4 km* north of Sedona, this is a wilderness hike that follows the course of Dry Creek to its head at the base of the Mogollon Rim.

DIRECTIONS:
From The Y in Sedona Go:
Southwest on Highway 89A (toward Cottonwood) for 3.2 miles *5.2 km* (MP 371) to Dry Creek Road. Turn right on Dry Creek Road (FR 152C) and proceed to the 5.2 mile *8.4 km* point. Turn right on FR 152, the Vultee Arch Road, and follow it to the 9.6 mile *15.4 km* point. Here there is a parking loop, with the **Vultee Arch** Trailhead at the tip. Curve around and head back, and you will see the parking for the **Bear Sign** and Dry Creek trails to your right, just a few yards beyond the Vultee Arch parking spot.

TRAILHEAD: The parking area is in a grove of trees. Walk west across a little gully. There you will see a rusty sign marked "Dry Creek #52."

DESCRIPTION: Since the first edition of this book came out, FR 152 has been improved and can now be driven by any car with reasonable clearance if you keep a lookout for rocks and ruts.

From the parking place walk across a little arroyo and around the toe of a hill for about 0.10 miles *0.16 km* where you will encounter Dry Creek. Where you enter it, the canyon cut by Dry Creek is rather shallow and wide. The trail follows up the creek that usually is *dry*, living up to its name, in a northerly direction.

If there is any appreciable amount of water in the creek, you might want to postpone this hike for another day when the creek is dry because the trail crosses the creekbed at least a dozen times.

As you walk the trail gains altitude but this is a gradual climb and you are barely conscious of it. The walking is pretty easy and the trail is a good one.

At 0.63 miles *1.0 km* you reach a point where the creek forks at a reef. The left hand channel is the **Bear Sign Trail** and the right fork is the Dry Creek Trail. There is a rusty sign in the left channel marked "Bear Sign #59." From this point the canyon deepens and you are treated to the sight of giant redrock buttes on both sides of the creek. As you proceed you will notice a change in the vegetation as the increase in altitude causes changes in the life zones.

The trail ends where it intersects a channel running east and west. We are informed that this channel can be hiked but it would be very steep and rugged, for advanced hikers only. To the east, it appears to go all the way to the top of the rim to East Pocket, where the East Pocket fire lookout tower is located.

EAGLES' NEST TRAIL

General Information
Location Map F3
Sedona USGS Map
Coconino Forest Service Map

Driving Distance One Way: 8.8 miles *14.1 km* (Time 15 minutes)
Access Road: All vehicles, All paved
Hiking Distance Complete Loop: 3.23 miles *5.2 km* (Time 1.5 hours)
How Strenuous: Moderate
Features: Oak Creek, Red Rock State Park, Views

NUTSHELL: This moderate trail is located in Red Rock State Park 8.8 miles *14.1 km* southwest of Sedona. It takes you along the banks of a creek, then to the top of a redrock butte for exceptional views.

DIRECTIONS:
From the Sedona Y Go:
　　　　Southwest on Highway 89A (toward Cottonwood) for a distance of 5.5 miles *8.8 km* (MP 368.6) to the Lower Red Rock Loop Road. Turn left on the Lower Red Rock Loop Road and follow it to the 8.5 miles *13.6 km* point, where you will see the entry to Red Rock State Park. Turn right into the park. You will come to a toll booth where an admission is charged. From that point, drive to the Visitor Center and park there, at 8.8 miles *14.1 km.*

TRAILHEAD: This is a marked and maintained trail, part of the network of trails in the park. Go through the Visitor Center. Though the center is not marked as the trailhead for this hike, it is the starting point for it.

DESCRIPTION: Enjoy the Visitor Center and then walk through it, turning right on the paved trail. At 0.08 miles *0.13 km* you will come to the first trail junction. Here the **Smoke Trail** forks to the right, where Sentinel Crossing is located. Keep moving straight ahead and go across the creek on Kingfisher Bridge. Just beyond the bridge, at the 0.34 mile *0.55 km* point turn right and follow the **Kisva Trail** to its end (about 1.0 miles *1.6 km* from the Visitors Center). This portion of Kisva is lovely. The trail is bounded by the creek on your right and pretty redrock cliffs on your left. Large sycamores and other deciduous trees line the creek bank. The Armijo Ditch, an historic irrigation canal, runs along the cliff base and its banks are covered with blackberries.
　　　　Where the Kisva Trail ends, the Eagles' Nest Trail goes off to your left, uphill. It takes you by twists and turns to the top of the red cliffs at the

base of which you have been walking. At the top (1.4 miles *2.3 km* from the Visitor Center) there is a viewpoint with a couple of benches. The views from this place are great. You see red buttes all around you forming a basin through which Oak Creek cuts a curving path.

The trail from the top drops down the other side of the butte, meets the **Coyote Ridge Trail** and then drops down from the butte, reaching ground level where it joins the Kisva Trail at a point where there is a trail toilet. You would then return to the Visitor Center the way you started. An alternative is to cross the creek at the Sentinel Crossing, 0.1 miles *0.16 km* to your right.

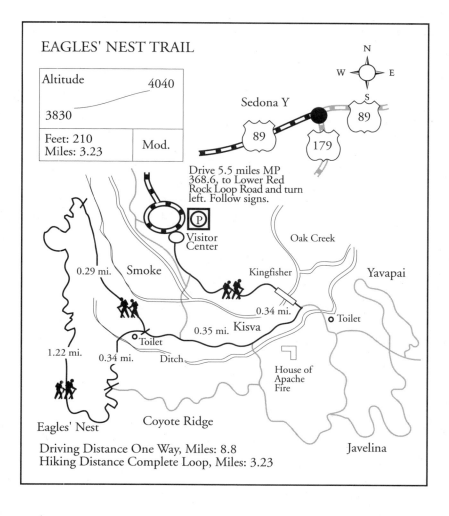

EAGLES' NEST TRAIL

Altitude 4040
3830
Feet: 210
Miles: 3.23   Mod.

Sedona Y

89   89   179

Drive 5.5 miles MP 368.6, to Lower Red Rock Loop Road and turn left. Follow signs.

Visitor Center

Oak Creek

0.29 mi.   Smoke   Kingfisher   Yavapai

0.34 mi.   Toilet

0.35 mi.   Kisva

1.22 mi.   Toilet

0.34 mi.   Ditch   House of Apache Fire

Eagles' Nest   Coyote Ridge   Javelina

Driving Distance One Way, Miles: 8.8
Hiking Distance Complete Loop, Miles: 3.23

FAY CANYON #53

General Information
Location Map C3
Wilson Mt. USGS Map
Coconino Forest Service Map

Driving Distance One Way: 8.2 miles *13.2 km* (Time 20 minutes)
Access Road: All cars, Last half mile good dirt road
Hiking Distance One Way: 1.2 miles *2.0 km* (Time 30 minutes)
How Strenuous: Moderate
Features: Views, Arch, Indian ruins

NUTSHELL: This is an easy hike 8.2 miles *13.2 km* northwest of uptown Sedona, featuring a lovely canyon on the side of Bear Mountain with a natural arch and Indian ruins. **A personal favorite.**

DIRECTIONS:
From the Sedona Y Go:
Southwest on Highway 89A (toward Cottonwood) for a distance of 3.2 miles *5.2 km* (MP 371) to Dry Creek Road. Turn right onto Dry Creek Road (also known as FR 152C) and follow it to the 6.1 mile *9.8 km* point, where it intersects the Long Canyon Road, where you turn left. Stay on FR 152C to the 7.7 mile *12.4 km* point, where it intersects the Boynton Canyon Road. Here you will turn left onto the Boynton Pass Road. It is paved for a short distance and then becomes unpaved. At the 8.2 mile *13.2 km* point you will reach the driveway to the parking area, which is off to your right. Pull in and park there.

TRAILHEAD: You will see a rusty sign at the gate: "Fay Canyon #53."

DESCRIPTION: The trail is gentle and wide. You will find a forest of oaks, many of them quite sizable. Though the canyon is short, about one mile long, it is broad and very scenic. There are impressive red cliffs on both sides with buff colored cliffs rimming the back of the canyon.
At just over 0.50 miles *0.8 km*, a side trail branches off to the right (east) and makes a sharp climb up the east side of the canyon to Fay Arch. This trail is usually marked with cairns. The path to the arch is nothing like the main trail. It seems to have just been scratched out of the side of the canyon willy nilly. It is steep and there are places where the footing is tricky. Aunt Maude would have no trouble with the main trail along the canyon floor but the climb to the arch would be too much for her.
There is a small Indian ruin just before you reach the arch. This

isn't much of a ruin, just knee high walls outlining one room in a low, shallow cave. There are a few rock art figures on the cliff face above the ruin but we suspect that they are modern. Canyon wrens, tiny birds with a glorious call, live in this cliff face. If you are lucky you will hear one.

There is a narrow slot between the arch and the wall it has broken away from. You can stand underneath it and look up through it for an interesting view. The clamber up the side of the canyon would be worthwhile for the views even if there were no arch. Spectacular.

After visiting the arch, return to the main trail and continue up the canyon. Near its end it forks around a redrock fin that sticks out like the prow of a ship. You can quit right where you are for a 1.2 mile *2.0 km* hike or you can climb up on the fin. You can go in either direction around the fin, but we recommend the left hand fork. It will take you up and out on a slickrock shelf where you will find a few caves that contain fragmentary Indian ruins.

FAY CANYON #53

0.7 mi.

Boynton Cyn.

Long Cyn.

0.5 mi.

1.6 mi.

0.5 mi.

2.9 mi.

152C

Dry Creek Road

3.2 mi.

Sedona Y

89

89

89

MP 371

179

WILDERNESS
R'Rock-Secret Mt

Altitude		4800
4500		
Feet: 300 Miles: 1.2		Mod.

Driving Distance One Way, Miles: 8.2
Hiking Distance One Way, Miles: 1.2

FLUME ROAD TRAIL #154

General Information
Location Map G6
Strawberry USGS Map
Coconino Forest Service Map

Driving Distance One Way: 52.2 miles *83.5 km* (Time 1.5 hours)
Access Road: All cars, Last 16.8 miles *26.7 km* good dirt road
Hiking Distance One Way: 4.0 miles *6.4 km* (Time 2.0 hours)
How Strenuous: Moderate, but you have to wade across Fossil Creek
Features: Historic flume, Gorgeous riparian creek, Wide easy trail, Views

NUTSHELL: This adventure is worth making for the sake of the drive alone, but includes wild country, an historic electrical power plant and flume, a spring-fed creek and great natural beauty. NOTE: You must be equipped with wading shoes and shorts to wade across the creek at the beginning.

DIRECTIONS:
From the Sedona Y Go:
          South on Highway 179 (toward Phoenix) for 14.7 miles *23.6 km*, to the I-17 Interchange. Turn south on I-17 and go to the 23.6 miles *37.8 km* point, where you take Exit 289 for Camp Verde. Go into Camp Verde, where you will come to a stop sign at 27.3 miles *43.6 km*. Turn left here and go east on Highway 260 to the 35.4 mile *56.6 km* point (MP 228.5), where you turn right (south) on unpaved FR 708. It is signed. Follow this narrow winding mountain road to the 49.5 mile *79.2 km* point, where it meets FR 502. Turn left (east), staying on FR 708 and go just past the Irving power plant. At the 52.2 mile point *83.5 km*, turn left into the trailhead parking. It is signed.

TRAILHEAD: At the parking lot.

DESCRIPTION: The flume you will follow on this hike carries water through two hydroelectric turbines, one at Irving, and the other at Childs. This hike follows the road used when the flume was built in 1916. The road is still used for maintenance.
          Crossing the creek means wading across a swift mountain stream. You will want wading shoes for this and perhaps a stick for balancing. The water will be knee to hip high, so be prepared. Once across, you must turn to your left (west) and hike about twenty yards to pick up the trail. (There is also a path to the right [east], along the creekbank, but it is not the hiking trail). From the creek level, the trail goes up steeply for 0.5 miles *0.8 km* to

meet the road.

Once on the road, you walk east up the canyon for 3.5 miles *5.6 km*, with the flume as your constant companion. The flume construction was quite a project for 1916.

You climb, but the grade is gradual, and this is not a killer hike. Along the way, you will enjoy the scenery, from the rich geological diversity to the sweeping views. The canyon is impressive, and so are the surrounding cliffs, whose rocks are multi-hued.

In the last quarter mile, the road dips down to lush riparian creek level, ending at a dam. From the dam, the flume begins its seven mile journey down to the Verde River. The steep fall of the canyon and the copious springs mean that the water develops plenty of power, enough to keep those turbines humming.

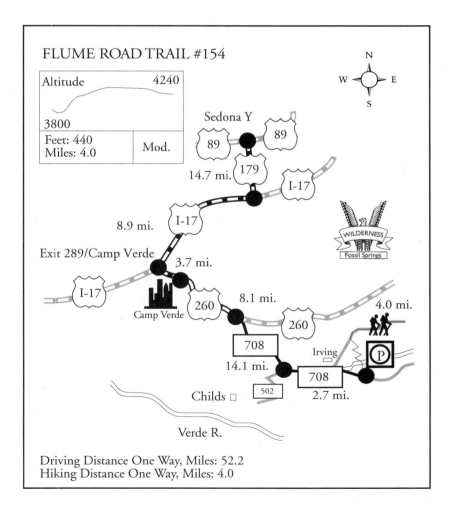

FLUME ROAD TRAIL #154

Altitude	4240
3800	
Feet: 440 Miles: 4.0	Mod.

Sedona Y
89
89
179
14.7 mi.
I-17
8.9 mi.
I-17
Exit 289/Camp Verde
3.7 mi.
I-17
Camp Verde
260
8.1 mi.
260
4.0 mi.
708
Irving
14.1 mi.
708
Childs □
502
2.7 mi.
Verde R.
WILDERNESS
Fossil Springs

Driving Distance One Way, Miles: 52.2
Hiking Distance One Way, Miles: 4.0

HARDING MOUNTAIN

General Information
Location Map B5
Mountainaire and Munds Park USGS Maps
Coconino Forest Service Map

Driving Distance One Way: 11.8 miles *18.9 km* (Time 20 minutes)
Access Road: All cars, All paved
Hiking Distance One Way: 0.66 miles *1.1 km* (Time 1.0 hour)
How Strenuous: Hard
Features: Views

NUTSHELL: This hike in the cool upper Oak Creek Canyon takes you across the creek to scale a small mountain hidden away by cliffs and forest. It's a hard climb up animal trails to the top but the view is splendid.

DIRECTIONS:
From the Sedona Y Go:
North on Highway 89A (toward Flagstaff) for a distance of 11.8 miles *18.9 km* (MP 386) not far above the entrance to the Cave Spring Campground. There is a wide parking apron on the west wide of the road at the 386 milepost.

TRAILHEAD: This is not a marked trail, but once across the creek, you will easily find it. The trail requires hard scrambling and climbing. For experienced hikers.

DESCRIPTION: From the place where you park, look to your left. Just below you is a flat grassy plain bordering Oak Creek. Find a place to hike down to the grass. Your task from there is to find a place to cross the creek. You will see several footpaths worn into the grass, leading down to the stream. Depending on how high the water is, you either boulder hop or wade across.

Once across, you will see your target, a small mountain with a pinpoint top hidden in the trees. Bushwhack your way over to it. As you near its base, you will see a distinct sandy track that loops around the mountain on its south face. You can also see the remains of the old Oak Creek road higher up on the flank of the mountain. This was a difficult way that crossed the creek a dozen times getting down to the Thomas Place (West Fork).

The trail will take you around behind (the west side of) the mountain and then head north. Soon it will follow along under a power line, and this part of the trail seems to be the service road that was used for the construction of the line.

At about the half mile point, the trail goes uphill steeply to the top of a ridge. At this point you leave it and go to your right (east). There are several game trails going up the west side of Harding Mountain here. We just followed the most likely looking one. The game trails start out very steep and get much steeper toward the top. We wondered about deer even making the effort, but hoof prints showed us that they do, indeed, go to the summit.

Muttering and stumbling, we clawed our way to the top and were glad that we made the effort. There are several bare ledges there, allowing the hiker to have superb views of the area.

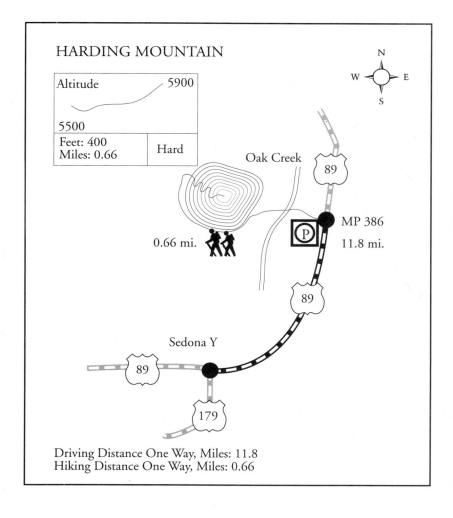

HARDING MOUNTAIN

Altitude	5900
5500	
Feet: 400 Miles: 0.66	Hard

Oak Creek

89

MP 386

0.66 mi.

11.8 mi.

89

Sedona Y

89

179

Driving Distance One Way, Miles: 11.8
Hiking Distance One Way, Miles: 0.66

HARDING SPRING TRAIL #51

General Information
Location Map B5
Mountainaire and Munds Park USGS Maps
Coconino Forest Service Map

Driving Distance One Way: 11.4 miles *18.3 km* (Time 20 minutes)
Access Road: All cars, All paved
Hiking Distance One Way: 0.80 miles *1.3 km* (Time 45 minutes)
How Strenuous: Hard
Features: Views

NUTSHELL: This is a marked and posted trail located just across Highway 89A from the Cave Spring Campground 11.4 miles *18.3 km* north of Sedona. It climbs the east wall of Oak Creek Canyon.

DIRECTIONS:
From the Sedona Y Go:
        North on Highway 89A (toward Flagstaff) for a distance of 11.4 miles *18.3 km* (MP 385.6) to the entrance to the Cave Spring Campground, which is on your left (west). Park anywhere around here on the shoulder of the road.

TRAILHEAD: On the east side of Highway 89A just across from the Cave Spring Campground entrance. It is marked by a rusty sign reading, "Harding Spring Trail #51."

DESCRIPTION: There is no official parking area for this hike. Cars park all along the shoulders of the road wherever there is a wide spot. If you are lucky you might find a parking spot in the Cave Spring Campground but don't count on it. Camping in the campground requires the payment of a fee.
        Since you will be so near the Cave Spring Campground after you park, you might as well walk into the campground and take a look at Cave Spring. It is an interesting place.
        Like the other trails going up the east wall of upper Oak Creek Canyon the Harding Spring trail goes virtually straight up with little finesse. You start in a pine and spruce forest and then reach a more open area as you climb above tree line. Then you get into a region of pine forest again at the top.
        The trail zigzags in such a way that it isn't a killer, like the **Purtymun Trail** or Thompson's Ladder. It is more like the **Cookstove Trail** or the **Thomas Point Trail.**

The trail was built in the 1880s to provide access to the canyon rim so that families living down in the canyon could get to the top and go to Flagstaff. They could lead a horse up such a trail or hike it, but it was not a wagon road, as you will see when you hike it. They would leave a wagon chained to a tree at the top and hitch the horse to it for the trip to town. When they brought their goods back, they would park the wagon and pack the goods down by horseback. Such a trip often took several days and was considered to be a major undertaking. Most of the east rim hikes are old family trails.

These east rim trails all predate the present Highway 89A, which is much newer than you might think. It was completed in the 1930s. Before that the only road good enough for a wagon was the Schnebly Hill Road and using it meant a long trip from the upper canyon south to Sedona, then doubling back to the north to go to Flagstaff.

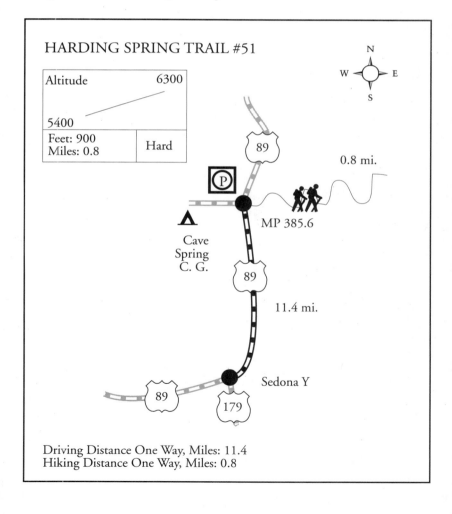

HARDING SPRING TRAIL #51

Altitude	6300
5400	

Feet: 900 Miles: 0.8	Hard

N
W ☆ E
S

89

0.8 mi.

P

▲
Cave
Spring
C. G.

MP 385.6

89

11.4 mi.

Sedona Y

89

179

Driving Distance One Way, Miles: 11.4
Hiking Distance One Way, Miles: 0.8

HERMIT RIDGE

General Information
Location Map D5
Munds Mt. and Munds Park USGS Map
Coconino Forest Service Map

Driving Distance One Way: 2.6 miles *4.2 km* (Time 10 minutes)
Access Road: All cars, All paved
Hiking Distance One Way: 1.4 miles *2.3 km* (Time 1.5 hours)
How Strenuous: Moderate
Features: Views

NUTSHELL: This hike is located 2.6 miles *4.2 km* north of Sedona. There is no marked trail, but for those who enjoy bushwhacking and steep climbs, it is very rewarding.

DIRECTIONS:
From the Sedona Y Go:
 North on Highway 89A (toward Flagstaff) a distance of 2.6 miles *4.2 km* (MP 376.8) where you park at the mouth of a closed road.

TRAILHEAD: Walk down the closed road a few feet beyond a pole gate to a place where you will see a sign, "Casner Canyon #11."

DESCRIPTION: Follow the **Casner Canyon Trail** down to Oak Creek. When you get to the floor of the gorge, you will find it strewn with boulders. You will see a canyon on the other side. Head for it. When you get to the creek, you will have to wade it or rock hop over it, depending on the depth of the water.
 Once across, hike into Casner Canyon, its entrance marked by a high jutting ledge. Keep jumping boulders to get to the right hand (south) side, where you will soon pick up the Casner Canyon Trail. At 0.33 miles *0.53 km*, the trail goes up a knob and then starts down at the base of an undercut cliff. At the top of this knob you will see a faint trail going steeply uphill by a barbed wire fence. Take it.
 You will come out onto a shoulder of Hermit Ridge near a power line. The highest point of the ridge is just above your head here. You can make reaching the top easier by walking southwest along the shoulder for about 0.1 mile *0.16 km*, then going up. There are no marked paths, but there are game trails. Look for a likely spot to make the short, steep climb to the top.
 Hermit Ridge is quite narrow, covered with manzanita and other

scrub through which there are many open lanes made by cattle. Your destination is to the south, toward Sedona, where you will see the towering cliffs of Mitten Ridge. Bushwhack, following open alleys through the growth.

We picked up a deer trail that follows along the west side of the ridge, overlooking the creek and the highway. Great views from here. On the east side of the ridge you have equally fine views. Near the 1.0 mile *1.6 km* point you will be directly opposite the popular Grasshopper Point Picnic Ground. The creek makes a pretty picture here.

As you get closer to the buttes you will climb again, then reach an area where wide eroded ledges on the face of the ridge are almost like roadways. As you approach the cliffs, these paths turn into bare redrock ledges. At this point you can move upward or hike the ledges on the lower levels. We recommend the low ones. Finally the ledges pinch out in a scenic bowl, where it is dangerous to try to go any farther.

HERMIT RIDGE

Altitude	5300

5000

Feet: 300 Miles: 1.4	Mod.

89

Oak Creek

Casner Cyn.

MP 376.8

0.33 mi.

2.6 mi.

89

1.07 mi.

89

Sedona Y

179

Driving Distance One Way, Miles: 2.6
Hiking Distance One Way, Miles: 1.4

HOT LOOP TRAIL #94

General Information
Location Map G5
Munds Mt. USGS Map
Coconino Forest Service Map

Driving Distance One Way: 8.7 Miles *14 km* (Time 15 Minutes)
Access Road: All cars, Paved except last 0.10 miles *0.16 km*
Hiking Distance One Way: 4.0 Miles *6.4 km* (Time 75 Minutes)
How Strenuous: Hard
Features: Views

NUTSHELL: Located south of the Sedona Y 8.7 miles *14 km*, this trail follows the Woods Canyon Trail and then branches off to the top of Wild Horse Mesa where you will have exciting views.

DIRECTIONS:
From the Y in Sedona, Go:
South on Highway 179 (toward Phoenix) for 8.6 miles *13.8 km* (MP 304.8) to an unmarked dirt road to your left. Turn left on the road, follow it for 0.10 miles *0.16 km* and then park.

TRAILHEAD: Right at the highway you will see a gate and a rusty sign reading, "Woods Canyon #93."

DESCRIPTION: The gate is unlocked. Go through it. We recommend that you park just beyond the gate. You can drive farther but the road conditions are dicey, especially if the road is wet. We have driven in as far as a mile but do not recommend this unless you are sure your vehicle can handle it. If you park near the highway as we recommend this is a four mile hike each way.
To follow the trail just walk along the main jeep road. At 2.0 miles *3.2 km* from the highway you will come to a fence. Just beyond the fence you will find a rusty sign marked, "#93 Hot Loop." This is the place where the Hot Loop Trail branches off to the left, going uphill. It looks like a road. The **Woods Canyon Trail** path forks to the right here and turns into a footpath descending to the bottom of the canyon.
From this place the Hot Loop Trail is a hard steep climb up the road. When you reach a point 3.0 miles *4.8 km* from the highway the jeep road disappears and the road turns into a footpath over loose lava stones. It is hard to see the trail in these stones. Be sure to look for the cairns that mark the trail.
When you finally struggle to the top of Wild Horse Mesa at 3.7

miles *6.0 km* from the highway, the trail gets better again with more soil and fewer rocks. At a point 4.0 miles *6.4 km* from the highway it will be obvious to you where the rim of the mesa is to your left. Walk over to it and see the view. It is a great vantage point from which to see Pine Valley, Jacks Canyon and Lee Mountain.

There is very little shade on this hike and the trail is rocky almost everywhere. It is not very scenic until you reach the top. This trail was built as a livestock trail, not a scenic one.

When the first homesteaders came into the Sedona area in 1876 (after the Apaches had been subdued by the federal troops located at Camp Verde) they found many wild horses in the grasslands. Some of the men made a pretty good living trapping these horses and selling them. Wild Horse Mesa was the location for a sizable horse herd and that is how it got its name. It is also called Horse Mesa.

HOT LOOP TRAIL #94

Altitude	5200
4000	

Feet: 1200 Miles: 4.0	Hard

WILDERNESS
Munds Mt.

Sedona Y

89   89

179

8.6 mi.

Wild Horse Mesa

MP 304.8

P

4.0 mi.

179

Driving Distance One Way, Miles: 8.7
Hiking Distance One Way, Miles: 4.0

HOUSE MOUNTAIN

General Information
Location Map G3
Sedona and Lake Montezuma USGS Maps
Coconino Forest Service Map

Driving Distance One Way: 14.5 miles *23.2 km* (Time 40 minutes)
Access Road: High clearance vehicles, last 3.9 miles *6.24 km* dirt
Hiking Distance One Way: 2.25 miles *3.6 km* (Time 70 minutes)
How Strenuous: Easy
Features: Views

NUTSHELL: This sprawling mountain located 14.5 miles *29.2 km* south of Sedona is rather drab but is a platform for great views.

DIRECTIONS:
From the Sedona Y Go:
    South on Highway 179 (toward Phoenix) for a distance of 10.6 miles *17 km* (MP 303) to unpaved road FR 120. Turn right on FR 120 and follow it to the 12.4 miles *20 km* point, where FR 9120A intersects it. Turn right onto FR 9120A. The road up to this point has been good, but from here to the end it is rough, with deep ruts, rocks and other hazards. At the 14.5 mile *23.2 km* point you will be on top of House Mountain. The road here becomes too rough to drive farther. Pull off the road and park in this area.

TRAILHEAD: No trail markings. Walk the road, FR 9120A.

DESCRIPTION: House Mountain is a shield volcano so it is more rounded than conical on top. A shield volcano doesn't erupt with a big upthrusting bang. It sort of rises like a pimple and then oozes lava. As a result it can create a sprawling low mountain, which is exactly what House Mountain is.
    The driving instructions take you to the top of House Mountain and along the top to a point where the road gets extremely rough. Using a truck with high clearance, or a bike, you could go two miles more on the road, almost to the north face of the mountain, the face that looks at Sedona.
    The top of the mountain is uninteresting. There has been some livestock activity here and some woodcutting. It was for these purposes that the road was built. As you walk along the road you are not close enough to the rim of the mountain to get any views. You must walk across the top to the north edge to get to a viewpoint.
    Once you are at the north edge, the location of the rim will be obvious to you. Just leave the road and bushwhack your way along to the rim.

Once there you will have tremendous views. You will find some places where lava has formed bare columns where no trees grow. These spots are excellent viewpoints.

There is another hike in the book that goes to the top of House Mountain. This is The **Turkey Creek Trail** that climbs the northwest face, with access from the Verde Valley School Road. Though the Turkey Creek Trail is a steep climb, it is much more scenic and enjoyable than the hike described in this article.

The top of House Mountain shows signs of considerable ranching activity. When we first began to hike around Sedona, we were surprised to find signs of cattle grazing (and sometimes the cattle themselves) on mountain tops, including some that must be hard for cattle to climb, such as **Doe Mountain**. House Mountain would be fairly easy to climb from the south approach used on this hike. So, if you hear a large animal crashing through the brush, it is much more likely to be a Guernsey than a Grizzly.

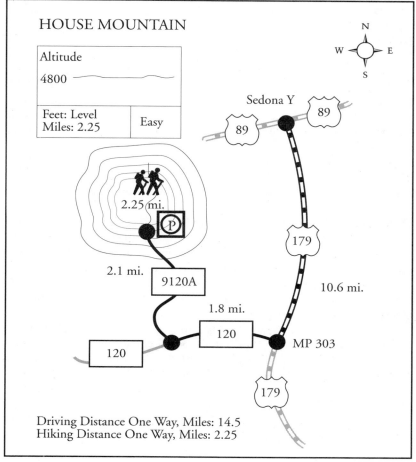

HOUSE MOUNTAIN

Altitude

4800

| Feet: Level Miles: 2.25 | Easy |

N
W — E
S

Sedona Y

89

89

2.25 mi.

P

2.1 mi.

9120A

179

10.6 mi.

1.8 mi.

120

120

MP 303

179

Driving Distance One Way, Miles: 14.5
Hiking Distance One Way, Miles: 2.25

HS CANYON #50

General Information
Location Map C4
Loy Butte and Wilson Mt. USGS Maps
Coconino Forest Service Map

Driving Distance One Way: 8.6 miles *13.8 km* (Time 30 minutes)
Access Road: Last 3.4 miles *5.5 km* rough dirt
Hiking Distance One Way: 2.0 miles *3.2 km* (Time 70 minutes)
How Strenuous: Moderate
Features: Views, Remote side canyon

NUTSHELL: This beautiful canyon, 8.6 miles *13.8 km* northwest of uptown Sedona, provides a delightful hike but the access road is rough.

DIRECTIONS:
From the Sedona Y Go:

Southwest on Highway 89A (toward Cottonwood) for 3.2 miles *5.2 km* (MP 371) to Dry Creek Road. Turn right on Dry Creek Road (FR 152C) and proceed to the 5.2 mile *8.4 km* point. Turn right on FR 152, the Vultee Arch Road, and follow it to the 8.6 mile *13.8 km* point. You will see a road sign pointing to the trail turnoff. Make a sharp turn to your left into the parking area.

TRAILHEAD: Hike the Secret Canyon Trail, which starts at the parking area, for 0.6 miles *1.0 km* to reach the HS Canyon trailhead.

DESCRIPTION: The access road, FR 152, road is often rough. but it has been improved since we came out with the first edition of this book. Unless there has been a recent washout, we think most ordinary passenger cars, unless they are very low slung, can make it.

Once you get to the trailhead, you hike the **Secret Canyon Trail**. It goes immediately over to Dry Creek and then proceeds along the Dry Creek drainage. If water is running in Dry Creek you may not be able to make this hike because the trail winds across the creekbed several times.

At 0.6 miles *1.0 km* you will see a trail going off to the left marked with a rusty sign reading, "H S Canyon #50." Take this trail. H S Canyon is narrow. It goes mostly to the west toward the north face of Maroon Mountain, and you can see a huge fin of Maroon Mountain in the distance. H S Canyon is a pretty little canyon and not very well known. We have never encountered any other hikers on this trail, but usually find them on the better known Secret Canyon Trail.

An easy walk, the trail is mostly shaded by a pleasant forest. It climbs but the climb is so gradual that it is not exhausting. There are great views. The canyon walls here are lower than those flanking some of the other hikes in this book. As a result they seem to be on a more human scale, and consequently the canyon has a nice friendly feeling.

The trail takes you to the base of Maroon Mountain where it ends in a box canyon surrounded by thousand foot high white cliffs—truly an impressive place. The end of the trail gives a false appearance of climbing out of the canyon but that is an illusion, for it plays out against the mountain.

The old cowboys who named many of the Sedona landmarks were an earthy bunch. They called this place Horse Shit Canyon, but that was too salty for the map makers, who have sanitized it to HS Canyon.

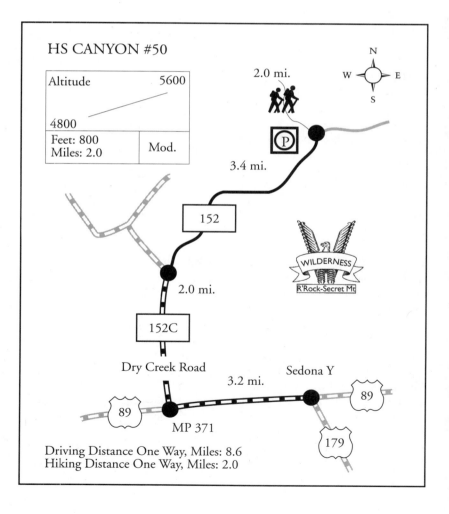

HS CANYON #50

Altitude	5600
4800	

| Feet: 800 Miles: 2.0 | Mod. |

2.0 mi.

3.4 mi.

152

WILDERNESS
R'Rock-Secret Mt

2.0 mi.

152C

Dry Creek Road

3.2 mi.

Sedona Y

89

89

MP 371

179

Driving Distance One Way, Miles: 8.6
Hiking Distance One Way, Miles: 2.0

JACK'S CANYON TRAIL #55

General Information
Location Map F5
Munds Mountain and Sedona USGS Maps
Coconino Forest Service Map

Driving Distance One Way: 9.8 miles *15.7 km* (Time 15 minutes)
Access Road: All cars, All paved
Hiking Distance One Way: 4.5 miles *7.2 km* (Time 2.5 hours)
How Strenuous: Moderate
Features: Old cattle trail, Views

NUTSHELL: Located 9.8 miles *15.7 km* south of the Sedona Y, this old cattle trail starts in an inhabited area. It then proceeds into some remote back country.

DIRECTIONS:
From the Sedona Y Go:
    South on Highway 179 (toward Phoenix) for a distance of 7.2 miles *11.5 km* (MP 306.2) to Jack's Canyon Road. There is a stoplight. Turn left (east) onto Jack's Canyon Road and follow it. It is paved all the way to the 9.8 miles *15.7 km* point, at the entrance to the Pine Valley subdivision, where the paving ends. There is a sign for the trailhead there. Pull in to the right and park.

TRAILHEAD: You will see a pole gate and rusty sign reading, "Jack's Canyon #55."

DESCRIPTION: You start this hike by following a road. The first mile of the hike is not very attractive because you are always in sight of the houses in a subdivision. For a time you will feel as if you are walking through people's backyards.
    Jack's Canyon runs between the substantial Lee Mountain on your left (west) and the lower Wild Horse Mesa (also known as Horse Mesa) on your right and curves around Lee Mountain going to the north. Eventually it climbs up to the top of the Mogollon Rim at Jack's Point, where it meets the **Munds Mt. Trail**. The rim in that location is quite flat and open and makes a good grazing area for cattle. The purpose of this trail was to provide a means of taking cattle herds up to the top of the rim in the summer and bringing the critters back to the low country in the winter.
    The trail follows an eastward course for about 2.0 miles *3.2 km* to Jack's Tank. Just beyond the tank the jeep road ends and your route turns

into a foot path that branches off to the right, down into the canyon floor. The canyon curves at the tank and begins a northerly course from there. (The jeep road continues about 0.50 miles *0.8 km* from Jack's Tank parallel to the canyon but up on the shoulder of the hill. It terminates at a pasture and is not worth hiking).

The hiking trail is more interesting from Jack's Tank onward, especially if there is some water running in the canyon. You don't want a lot of water, just a bit, since you will be walking across the canyon bottom.

Over many centuries the intermittent flow of water has worn the soil in the channel down to redrock and in many places the water has carved interesting sculptures in the soft stone. The canyon is narrow and scenic.

We recommend stopping at the 4.5 mile *7.2 km* point, which is where the trail leaves the canyon bottom and begins its steep ascent to the rim, which requires you to climb over 1200 feet in 2.0 miles *3.2 km*. The trail tops out on Munds Ridge, near the **Munds Mt.** Trailhead.

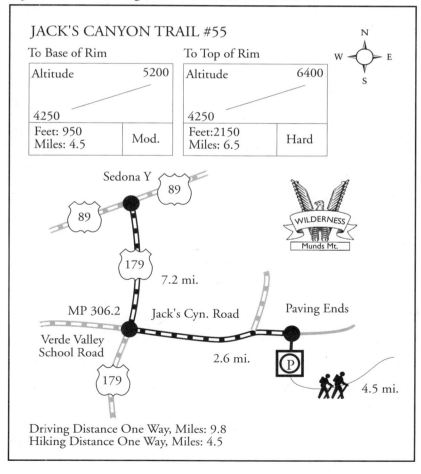

JACK'S CANYON TRAIL #55

To Base of Rim		To Top of Rim	
Altitude 5200		Altitude 6400	
4250		4250	
Feet: 950 Miles: 4.5	Mod.	Feet:2150 Miles: 6.5	Hard

N
W — E
S

Sedona Y

89

89

179

7.2 mi.

MP 306.2

Jack's Cyn. Road

Paving Ends

WILDERNESS
Munds Mt.

Verde Valley School Road

2.6 mi.

179

P

4.5 mi.

Driving Distance One Way, Miles: 9.8
Hiking Distance One Way, Miles: 4.5

JAVELINA TRAIL

General Information
Location Map F3
Sedona USGS Map
Coconino Forest Service Map

Drive Distance One Way: 8.8 miles *14.1 km* (Time 15 minutes)
Access Road: All vehicles, All paved
Hiking Distance, Complete Loop: 1.98 miles *3.2 km* (Time 1.0 hours)
How Strenuous: Moderate
Features: Oak Creek, Red Rock State Park, Views

NUTSHELL: This moderate trail is located in Red Rock State Park 8.8 miles *14.1 km* southwest of Sedona. It takes you through some scenic back country for interesting views.

DIRECTIONS:
From the Sedona Y Go:
Southwest on Highway 89A (toward Cottonwood) for a distance of 5.5 miles *8.8 km* (MP 368.6) to the Lower Red Rock Loop Road. Turn left on the Lower Red Rock Loop Road and follow it to the 8.5 miles *13.6 km* point, where you will see the entry to Red Rock State Park. Turn right into the park. You will come to a toll booth where an admission is charged. From that point, drive to the Visitor Center and park there, at 8.8 miles *14.1 km*.

TRAILHEAD: This is a marked and maintained trail, part of the network of trails in the park. Go through the Visitor Center. Though the center is not marked as the trailhead for this hike, it is the starting point.

DESCRIPTION: Enjoy the Visitor Center and then walk through it, turning right on the paved trail. At 0.08 miles *0.13 km* you will come to the first trail junction. Here the **Smoke Trail** forks to the right, where Sentinel Crossing is located. Go straight here. The sign at this junction shows your destination as *"Kingfisher Crossing, House of Apache Fire."*
Soon after this you will reach another junction. Turn right here, to Kingfisher Crossing, which is a major bridge across the creek. You will see the House of Apache Fire on a hilltop, a pueblo style house of native rock.
When you cross the bridge you will reach another trail junction at 0.34 miles *0.54 km*, where the **Kisva** and **Eagles' Nest** trails go right. You will go left there and at 0.44 miles *0.7 km* thereafter will be at the base of the knoll on which the house is located. You will see a driveway going uphill to your right to get to the house. To your left is a short flight of redrock steps

and a sign for the **Apache Fire Trail.** Begin the first leg of this hike on the Apache Fire Trail.

Walk up the steps and you will find yourself on a nice gentle trail heading south, away from the park and into undeveloped country. This part of the trail is a welcome getaway from the developed area. The trail makes a big loop. Toward the far end of the loop the **Javelina Trail** takes off, making a sharp turn to your left. From here you begin to climb.

The trail winds around the contours of a canyon, with a couple of interesting sidepaths to viewpoints, then turns north to intersect the East Gate Road. Directly across the road is the beginning of the **Yavapai Ridge Trail**.

Here you turn left and follow the road down to the main path just across the Kingfisher Bridge, from where you cross the bridge and return to the Visitor Center.

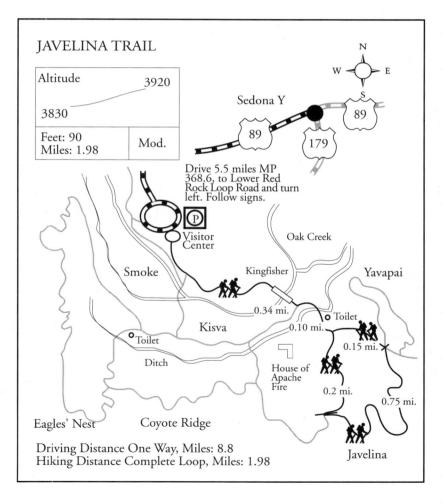

KISVA TRAIL

General Information
Location Map F3
Sedona USGS Map
Coconino Forest Service Map

Driving Distance One Way: 8.8 miles *14.1 km* (Time 15 minutes)
Access Road: All vehicles, All paved
Hiking Distance One Way: 0.98 miles *1.6 km* (Time 30 minutes)
How Strenuous: Easy
Features: Oak Creek, Red Rock State Park, Views

NUTSHELL: This easy trail is located in Red Rock State Park 8.8 miles *14.1 km* southwest of Sedona. It takes you along the banks of Oak Creek on a level path.

DIRECTIONS:
From the Sedona Y Go:
Southwest on Highway 89A (toward Cottonwood) for a distance of 5.5 miles *8.8 km* (MP 368.6) to the Lower Red Rock Loop Road. Turn left on the Lower Red Rock Loop Road and follow it to the 8.5 miles *13.6 km* point, where you will see the entry to Red Rock State Park. Turn right into the park. You will come to a toll booth where an admission is charged. From that point, drive to the Visitor Center and park there, at 8.8 miles *14.1 km*.

TRAILHEAD: This is a marked and maintained trail, part of the network of trails in the park. Go through the Visitor Center. Though the center is not marked as the trailhead for this hike, it is the starting point for it.

DESCRIPTION: Enjoy the Visitor Center and then walk through it, turning right on the paved trail. At 0.08 miles *0.13 km* you will come to the first trail junction. Here the **Smoke Trail** forks to the right, where Sentinel Crossing is located. Keep going on the paved path to the Kingfisher Crossing bridge. Go across the creek on the bridge, where you will emerge onto a sandy trail Go straight for about ten yards, where you will find the trail junction for the **Apache Fire Trail** and the **Eagles' Nest Trail**.
Turn right. Soon you will see a sign marking the Kisva (pronounced **Keese**-va) Trail. The trail follows an old ranch road that is still in use by officials of the Red Rock State Park, so it is wide and easy to walk. Kisva, the sign tells you, means "Shady Water" in Hopi. It is an appropriate name, as many trees grow along the creekbank and provide shade for the trail. The shade and the cool creek water make this a good hot weather trail.

Near the end of the trail you come to a place where the trail goes along the base of a redrock ridge. There is an irrigation ditch to your left, at the cliff base, with the creek running along to your right. This abundance of water supports the growth of large sycamores, stunning with their beautiful white bark. They overarch the trail. There are many blackberries along the ditch bank. It is a gorgeous spot.

The trail ends at a point that is 0.98 miles *1.6 km* from the Visitors Center. The road continues, but it is for use by park officials only. The Eagles' Nest Trail starts here, going uphill to your left.

This is a very pleasant and easy ramble that would be appreciated by people who are not strong enough to take a more strenuous hike yet want to experience a walk that will display the main attractions of Sedona: redrocks and Oak Creek. Return to the Visitors Center by Sentinel Crossing.

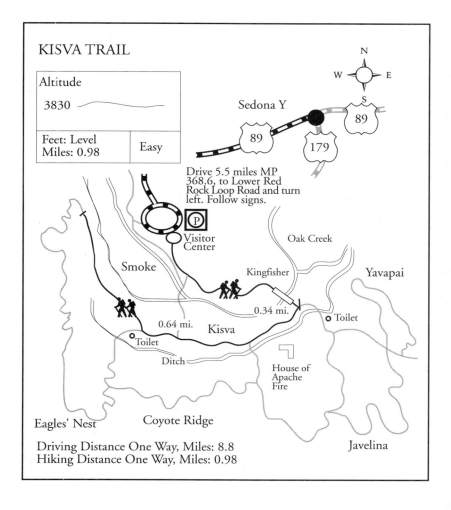

KISVA TRAIL

Altitude	
3830	
Feet: Level Miles: 0.98	Easy

Sedona Y

89

89

179

Drive 5.5 miles MP 368.6, to Lower Red Rock Loop Road and turn left. Follow signs.

Visitor Center

Oak Creek

Smoke

Kingfisher

Yavapai

0.34 mi.

Toilet

0.64 mi.   Kisva

Toilet

Ditch

House of Apache Fire

Eagles' Nest   Coyote Ridge

Javelina

Driving Distance One Way, Miles: 8.8
Hiking Distance One Way, Miles: 0.98

KUSHMAN'S CONE

General Information
Location Map E2
Page Springs, Sedona USGS Maps
Coconino Forest Service Map

Driving Distance One Way: 10.4 miles *16.7 km* (Time 35 minutes)
Access Road: High clearance vehicle for last 0.5 miles *0.8 km*
Hiking Distance One Way: 0.55 miles *0.9 km* (Time 40 minutes)
How Strenuous: Moderate
Features: Views

NUTSHELL: This volcanic cone located 10.4 miles *16.7 km* southwest of Sedona is a fairly hard climb but rewards the hiker with marvelous views.

DIRECTIONS:
From the Sedona Y Go:
      Southwest on Highway 89A (toward Cottonwood) for a distance of 8.2 miles *13.2 km* (MP 365.9) to a place where you will see a dirt road, FR 9573C, going off to your right through a gate in a barbed wire fence. Go through the gate and follow FR 9573C. At 8.3 miles *13.3 km*, an unmarked road forks right. Ignore it. At 8.7 miles *14 km* FR 9573 branches to the left. Ignore it. At 8.9 miles *14.3 km* there is a fork. Take the right turn and begin to circle around the mountain headed north. At 9.3 miles *15 km* you will be on the north side and you will see a big power line. FR 9573P branches to the left here. Go right, staying on FR 9573C. At 9.8 miles *15.7 km you* reach a junction where FR 9573A goes to the left. Take FR 9573A. You will be at the power line. At 10.0 miles *16 km* you will see FR 9544 going right. Take it. It follows the power line. Go down to the bottom of a long hill and park at 10.4 miles *16.7 km*, where the road meets a wash. Don't try to cross the wash, as the road beyond is very bad and you will only gain 0.1 miles, as the road totally ends at 10.5 miles *16.9 km*.

TRAILHEAD: There are no signs. You will see a faint jeep trail going into the wash and up the other side. This must have been a service road for the construction of the power line.

DESCRIPTION: Walk across the wash, and take the jeep road going up to the power line, then follow it to the Northeast. Soon after, the road disappears, but you can see a path along the power line. By now you are on the shoulder of the mountain. Kushman's Cone is a small extinct volcano, and broken lava is everywhere. The footing is very rocky and the going is quite slow. You will reach a point where it seems that there really is no trail, but you can see paths through the shrubbery all over the place. Don't worry, just keep picking your way along, following the power line until it starts to dip down, at which point you want to begin working uphill as you curve around to the east. At about 0.33 miles *0.53 km* you will come to a worn path marked by cairns and you want to take this path to the top.

Many mountain tops are elusive. You think you have come to the mountain's crest only to find that it is merely a bench. That is not the case on Kushman's Cone, where you will find a definite pinpoint top. From the top you can enjoy thrilling views to the west. To the Northeast you can see parts of Sedona. Immediately below you to the east is a subdivision—not so thrilling—but the views beyond it are great.

On your way back down, don't follow the marked trail all the way, as it veers off to a subdivision. You will need to leave the trail and get back to the power line, using the line as your marker for the return to your car.

LITTLE HORSE TRAIL #61

General Information
Location Map E5
Munds Mt. and Sedona USGS Maps
Coconino Forest Service Map

Driving Distance One Way: 3.75 miles *6.0 km* (Time 10 minutes)
Access Road: All cars, All paved
Hiking Distance One Way: 3.0 miles *4.8 km* (Time 1.5 hours)
How Strenuous: Moderate
Features: Views, Redrocks, Secluded canyon

NUTSHELL: Located near downtown Sedona, this hike takes you across relatively flat land to the beautiful redrocks below Chicken Point, then on to Briant Canyon, a hidden gem.

DIRECTIONS:
From the Sedona Y Go:
South on Highway 179 (toward Phoenix) for a distance of 3.75 miles *6.0 km* (MP 309.7). Your target is an unmarked dirt road to your left (east). As you near the road, look sharp, for there are no clues that the road is there, and the entrance is narrow. Drive onto the road about 100 yards and park near the trailhead sign.

TRAILHEAD: There is a rusty sign, "Little Horse #61" where you park.

DESCRIPTION: The trailhead sign is a bit misleading, as it seems to point you to a washed out and unusable road. Hike down the main road. In a few paces there is a fork, where you go right (south). Soon you will reach another fork, where you go left (east).
At 0.25 miles *0.4 km* you will come to a streambed at the base of a small red cliff, where you go left (north) and walk along the bed for a few yards. At 0.4 miles *0.65 km* you will come to a power line. From here you can see the top of the Chapel of the Holy Cross in the distance. It helps to know what your destination is from here, since there are many paths in the area, which can cause confusion. You want to go to the Madonna and Nuns redrock formation, two pyramidal spires at the east end of Twin Buttes— that is to say, the far end of the buttes against which the Chapel is built. The correct trail will always head in this direction, which is northeast.
The trail will bring you to the base of the redrocks of Twin Buttes. At 1.35 miles *2.2 km*, you will come to a gate. Go through the gate. Just beyond the gate you will be at the foot of **Chicken Point**, which is at the top

of the redrocks to your left, a slickrock saddle between red buttes. The jeep tours drive there frequently so don't be surprised if you hear people on top, towering above you. From here the trail heads on easterly through a lovely cypress forest and at about the 2.0 miles point *3.2 km* it reaches Briant Canyon, a hidden fold on the side of Lee Mountain.

The trail turns southeast, dips to the canyon bottom, then climbs out of the bottom and goes up on a ledge, where you hike to the end of the trail at 3.0 miles. Briant Canyon has a nice secluded feeling, away from all signs of man, and yet it is quite close to town.

Trail's end seems rather mysterious, as the trail just stops without reaching any apparent destination.

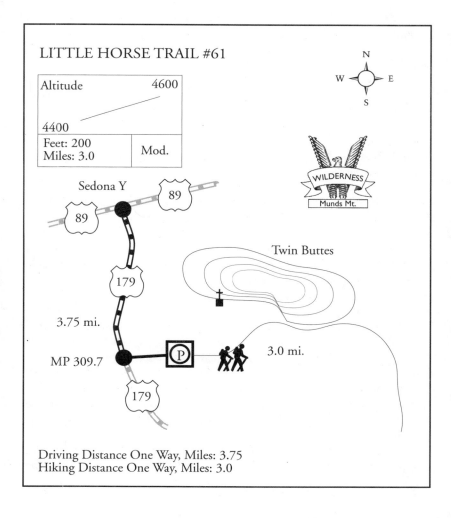

LITTLE PARK HEIGHTS

General Information
Location Map F4
Sedona USGS Map
Coconino Forest Service Map

Driving Distance One Way: 5.1 miles *8.2 km* (Time 15 minutes)
Access Road: All cars, All paved
Hiking Distance One Way: 1.0 miles *1.6 km* (Time 40 minutes)
How Strenuous: Hard
Features: Views

NUTSHELL: Located across the highway from Bell Rock, just south of Sedona, this tall butte rewards your steep climb with great views.

DIRECTIONS:
From the Sedona Y Go:
South on Highway 179 (toward Phoenix) for a distance of 5.1 miles *8.2 km* (MP 308.5) to Bell Rock Vista. There is a parking place for several cars at the vista. Pull in and park.

TRAILHEAD: There are no signs. A trail marked with cairns starts just south of the outhouse at Bell Rock Vista.

DESCRIPTION: On the south end of the parking area at Bell Rock Vista there is a public toilet. This is set back from the highway. Just south of this you will find two trails leading away from the highway. Take the trail that is farther south. It dips down at its start. Look carefully for cairns as you start this hike. Many false trails meander through this area as a result of cattle grazing so it is important to use the cairns for guides.
You will climb constantly on this hike. The climb is gradual for the first quarter of a mile and then steep.
Your destination will be obvious from the beginning. It is the saddle in the high butte located west of Bell Rock Vista. **Bell Rock** merits its fame, as it is an interesting place. It is listed in this book and makes for a fine hike. Its neighbor across the highway, the subject of this hike, is not well known but deserves to be. When you begin the hike it will seem as if it is an impossible task, that, "You can't get there from here." Then you will see how the trail makes use of the terrain and will realize that it is not only possible but that you are going to do it.
As you climb up to the saddle you will reach two major benches before you come to the top. Each of these benches becomes a natural resting

place and a good observation point. From the benches you can see Bell Rock, Courthouse Butte and the colorful country between them and the Chapel of the Holy Cross.

Above the second bench you will have a hard steep haul and then you will reach the saddle. The saddle is at 1.0 miles *1.6 km*. From there you can go to knobs on either the north or south ends of the butte. There is also an extension to the west where the main trail leads you onto a bare finger of rock from which you get excellent views. Depending on how much you roam around on the top, you can easily add another mile to this hike.

Once you are on top you can see to the west. There you will have views down on the Verde Valley School and the Red Rock Loop Road areas.

Some hikers report finding fossils on top of this butte. We were there on a windswept January day when it was so cold that we did not take time to look for fossils but the rock certainly did appear to be a fossil bearing stratum.

LITTLE PARK HEIGHTS

Altitude	5200
4300	
Feet: 900 Miles: 1.0	Hard

Sedona Y

89   89

179

5.1 mi.

Bell Rock Vista

P   MP 308.5

1.0 mi.

179

Bell Rock

Driving Distance One Way, Miles: 5.1
Hiking Distance One Way, Miles: 1.0

LONG CANYON #122

General Information
Location Map C3
Wilson Mt. USGS Map
Coconino Forest Service Map

Driving Distance One Way: 6.7 miles *11 km* (Time 15 minutes)
Access Road: All cars, All paved
Hiking Distance One Way: 3.0 miles *4.8 km* (Time 2 hours)
How Strenuous: Moderate
Features: Views, Great cliffs

NUTSHELL: Located 6.7 miles *11 km* northwest of uptown Sedona, this trail takes you right up against the base of gorgeous red cliffs. This is one of the best trails for viewing rock formations. **A personal favorite.**

DIRECTIONS:
From the Sedona Y Go:
Southwest on Highway 89A (toward Cottonwood) for a distance of 3.2 miles *5.2 km* (MP 371) to the Dry Creek Road, FR 152C. Turn right onto Dry Creek Road and follow it to the 6.1 mile *10 km* point, where there is a stop sign. The paved road to your right is the Long Canyon Road. Take it to the 6.7 miles *11 km* point, where you will see an unpaved road to your left. The entrance to the road is blocked with boulders. There is a parking area in front of the boulders. Park there.

TRAILHEAD: This is a marked and maintained trail. There is a rusty sign where you park reading, "Long Canyon #122."

DESCRIPTION: The trail begins as a wide jeep road. In fact, the Forest Service has moved several boulders across the road at its entrance to keep vehicles from using it.
At 0.30 miles *0.48 km* you will come to a 3-pronged fork. Take the left fork. At 0.60 miles *1.0 km* you will come to a big gate. This marks the entrance to the Redrock-Secret Mt. Wilderness Area. Go through the gate. The trail is a footpath from this point. At 1.0 miles *1.6 km* you will reach another fork. Here one trail goes left parallel to a power line and the other trail goes right. Take the right fork. The left fork goes to Boynton Canyon.
For the first 1.5 miles *2.4 km* on this trail you will be walking in open country with almost no shade. This part of the trail isn't much fun in hot weather. After that you will enter a cypress forest where there is shade. By then you will have moved fairly close to Maroon Mountain which is to

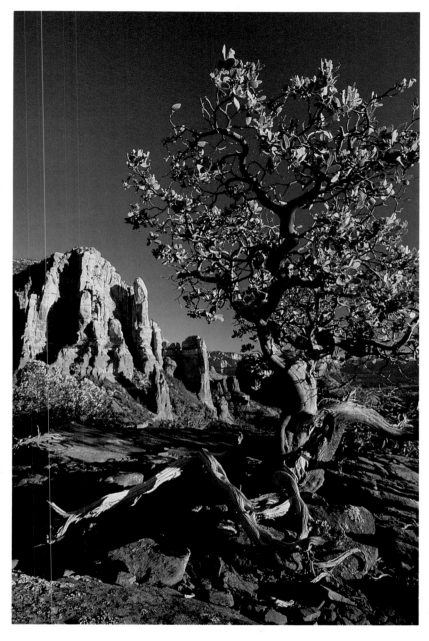

Earth Angel Spire from Brins Mesa

Front Cover: *View from The Shooting Range West Trail*

Reflection of Mitten Ridge

Soldier Pass Arches

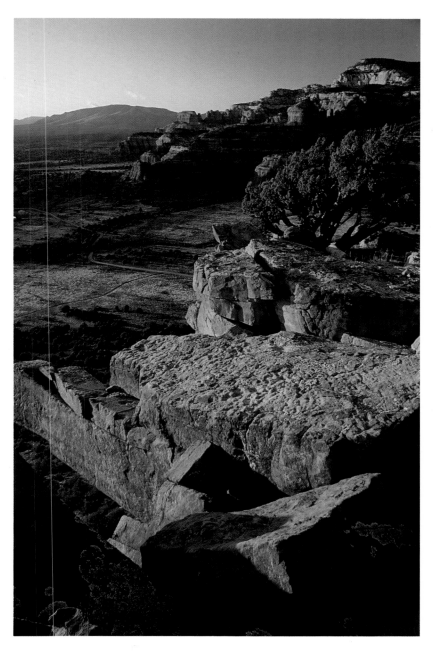

Bear Mountain from Doe Mountain

Bear Mountain

Steamboat Rock and Spires

Sinagua Cliff Dwelling

Red Canyon

Silhouette of Kushman's Cone

Sinagua Petroglyphs

Sunset on Schnebly Hill

your right (north). You will catch glimpses through the trees of the magnificent red and white sculptured cliffs of Maroon Mountain as you hike.

Beyond the 2.5 mile *4.0 km* point the vegetation becomes more
alpine and less desert-like. Here you will encounter many oaks and huge alli-
gator bark junipers. Some of the junipers are many centuries old.

At 3.0 miles *4.8 km* the trail, which has been generally following a
northwest course parallel to the base of the mountain, turns and goes straight
north, climbing steeply. This is the stopping point for this hike. Here you
will find genuine alpine conditions with pines and firs and a carpet of green
on the forest floor. The canyon walls are nearer to you now and you get
tremendous views.

The trail continues but becomes difficult. It plays out completely at
4.0 miles *6.4 km* in a side canyon, in a place that is one of the wildest in the
Sedona area. It really feels remote. The path narrows there to a barely dis-
cernible game trail where you are totally out of sight of the works of man.

LONG CANYON TRAIL #122

3.0 mi.

0.6 mi.

Long Cyn. Rd.

0.9 mi.

152

Altitude   5300

4550

2.0 mi.

Feet: 750
Miles: 3.0   Mod.

152C

Dry Creek Road   Sedona Y

3.2 mi.

89   89

MP 371

179

Driving Distance One Way, Miles: 6.7
Hiking Distance One Way, Miles: 3.0

WILDERNESS
R'Rock-Secret Mt

LONG CANYON TRAIL #63

General Information
Location Map G6
Casner Butte, Buckhorn Mtn. USGS Maps
Coconino Forest Service Map

Driving Distance One Way: 18.0 miles *29 km* (Time 30 minutes)
Access Road: All cars, Last 0.80 miles *1.28 km* good dirt road
Hiking Distance One Way: 2.5 miles *4.0 km* (Time 2 hours 30 minutes)
How Strenuous: Hard due to steep climb on first leg
Features: Views

NUTSHELL: Starting on the east bank of Wet Beaver Creek, this hike takes you along an old cattle trail, as you climb over one thousand feet.

DIRECTIONS:
From the Sedona Y Go:
          South on Highway 179 (toward Phoenix) for 14.7 miles *23.52 km*, to the I-17 Interchange. Instead of going onto I-17, go underneath it and get onto the paved country road FR 618. You will pass the Beaver Creek Ranger Station and the bridge over Beaver Creek, where the paving ends. Just after the paving ends, you will reach a three-way fork at 17.4 miles *28.0 km*. Turn left here. You will see a sign for Southwest Academy. At 18.0 miles *29.0 km,* look to your right. You will see the trail sign just beyond a fence. There is almost no parking. We found a pullout big enough for one car behind us.

TRAILHEAD: The trailhead is uphill to your right, where you will see a couple of vertical railroad ties used as fence supports. There is a wire gate with a hiker symbol on a fence post. On the other side is a sign that says, "Long Canyon Trail #63. Bell Trail #13—10 miles. Trail difficult to find after 2 miles." [We had no trouble finding the trail].

DESCRIPTION: This is an old cattle trail, like several others in the area, such as the **Bell Trail**. The Long Canyon Trail climbs steeply, rising 700 feet in the first 0.4 miles *0.64 km.*
          As you rise, you begin to enjoy views. At first these views are of the nearby creek. You can see a ranch to the south and some of the buildings of the academy to the north of your starting point. Climbing even higher, you begin to see over the banks of Beaver Creek. The climb is steep, but the trail zigzags and is well maintained.
          You climb to a ridge that is more level, and walk east along it. You can walk over to the rim of the ridge anywhere and have views of the Verde

Valley. You can also see some of the colored cliffs of the Sedona country. At the 1.0 miles *1.6 km* point you make another climb, but this one is not as steep or as long as the first climb.

When you finish the second climb, you emerge onto the top of a mesa, where it is fairly flat and the walking is easy—except for the fact that the ground is strewn with rocks everywhere, making for hard footing.

You will find the trail marked by wire-cage cairns. In spite of the warning sign at the trailhead, we had no trouble seeing the trail.

On top, we found the hike disappointing, as it passes through flat and uninteresting county. The trail moves east, parallel to the south side of Long Canyon. Maps indicate that the trail nears the edge of the canyon at about the 4.0 mile *6.4 km* point, and meets the Bell Crossing Trail, which skirts along the north side of Long Canyon, at the canyon's mouth. We stopped at the 2.5 mile point.

LOST CANYON

General Information
Location Map C4
Wilson Mt. USGS Map
Coconino Forest Service Map

Driving Distance One Way: 7.7 miles *12.4 km* (Time 25 minutes)
Access Road: Most cars, Last 2.5 miles *4.0 km*, medium dirt road
Hiking Distance One Way: 2.2 miles 3.6 km (Time 80 minutes)
How Strenuous: Moderate, one short stretch is strenuous
Features: Scenic canyon, Indian ruins, Cave

NUTSHELL: This little known destination is reached by a trail that branches off the **Brins Mesa West Trail** on the road to Vultee Arch a few miles northwest of Sedona. **A personal favorite.**

DIRECTIONS:
From The Y in Sedona Go:
Southwest on Highway 89A (toward Cottonwood) for 3.2 miles *5.2 km* (MP 371) to Dry Creek Road. Turn right on Dry Creek Road (FR 152C) and proceed to the 5.2 mile *8.4 km* point. Turn right on FR 152, the Vultee Arch Road, and follow it to the 7.7 mile *12.4 km* point. Pull off to the right into the big parking area and park.

TRAILHEAD: Use "Brins Mesa #119."

DESCRIPTION: Start this hike by taking the **Brins Mesa West** trail. From the rusty sign walk up the trail 210 feet. At this point you will see a minor trail going off to the right marked by a cairn. Take it.
You must watch for cairns to guide you. You will cross one wash and go across country to an arroyo that cuts across a redrock ledge. Here you turn left and hike up the arroyo for a short distance to a point where the trail branches off to the right. The trail is very steep here.
At 0.40 miles *0.65 km* you will come to the top of a ledge where you will have spectacular views. Beyond that you have another short climb to the top of a higher ledge. The trail follows the rim of this higher ledge. Before you is a giant red reef marking the toe of Lost Canyon. The trail takes you around the toe and into the canyon.
When you get into Lost Canyon you will find that the canyon walls are tall and sheer. At times the trail comes very close to the edge of the rim. It you aren't bothered by heights this is one of the finest canyon hikes. The ledge you walk on is made of harder stone than the layers of rock above it.

The upper layers have weathered and receded leaving the ledge rather like a balcony all around the canyon. Above you are beautiful red cliffs topped with cream stone. Below are sheer drops.

At 0.75 miles *1.2 km* you will see above you to your left a long narrow cave half way up the cliff. There is a ruin in the cave. Cairns mark the place where you turn to go up to the ruin. It is a scramble.

From the ruin come back down to the ledge and continue to the head of the canyon. Look down into the bottom and you will see another ruin. You can reach it by taking the **Lost Canyon Ruin** hike.

If you want a one mile hike, the head of the canyon is a good place to stop. However, the trail goes on. It follows back out to the canyon mouth and then curves around another toe and goes into the canyon where the natural arch called **Devil's Bridge** is located. You can keep going to the 2.2 mile *3.6 km* point, where the trail vanishes.

LOST CANYON

Altitude	5100

4600

Feet: 500
Miles: 2.2

Mod.

N
W — E
S

WILDERNESS
R'Rock-Secret Mt

2.5 mi.

Ⓟ

Brins Mesa Trail

152

2.0 mi.

2.2 mi.

152C

Dry Creek Road

Sedona Y

3.2 mi.

89

89

MP 371

179

Driving Distance One Way, Miles: 7.7
Hiking Distance One Way, Miles: 2.2

LOST CANYON RUINS

General Information
Location Map C4
Wilson Mt. USGS Map
Coconino Forest Service Map

Driving Distance One Way: 7.1 miles *11.4 km* (Time 25 minutes)
Access Road: Most cars, Last 1.9 miles *3.0 km* medium dirt road
Hiking Distance One Way: 0.60 miles *0.96 km* (Time 30 minutes)
How Strenuous: Easy
Features: Indian ruins

NUTSHELL: On this easy hike you bushwhack up a canyon bottom to a hidden Indian ruin.

DIRECTIONS:
From The Y in Sedona Go:
Southwest on Highway 89A (toward Cottonwood) a distance of 3.2 miles *5.12 km* (MP 371) to the Dry Creek Road. Turn right on Dry Creek Road, also known as FR 152C, and follow it to the 5.2 mile point *8.32 km* where unpaved FR 152 branches to the right. Take FR 152. Follow the road to the 7.1 miles point *11.4 km*, where you will see a canyon that comes from your right and cuts under the road. Find a parking place nearby.

TRAILHEAD: There is no marked trail. You walk the canyon bottom to the head of the canyon.

DESCRIPTION: The Sedona area has so many remarkable land features, monuments, spires, buttes, etc., that naming them all was a real chore. We have never been able to find a name for this charming little canyon with its gem of an Indian ruin, so we decided to bestow a name upon it and have called it Lost Canyon.

We have taken many hikes in the Sedona area that require hiking a streambed in the bottom of a canyon. Some of these are quite difficult because of brush and obstacles in the watercourse. This hike is one of the nicest, easiest streambed hikes, because the actual floor of the canyon is redrock, with most of the soil washed off, so nothing grows in its middle, leaving it clear for walking. There are a couple of places where the channel is blocked, one by a boulder and the other by fallen trees. Both are easy to detour.

The canyon is forested with Arizona cypresses, one of the prettiest stands in the region. They are of all ages and sizes, making for an interesting mixture. We love cypress forests, they're so quiet and pleasant. The trees often take fantastic shapes. Some are twisted while neighbor trees of the same age are straight as an arrow.

The canyon climbs gently. At the start, as you begin the hike, look high up to your left and you will see a cave. This contains the Indian ruin you visit on the **Lost Canyon** hike. Some of the smaller caves "upstairs" show signs of rock work too and are probably Indian ruins.

As you go farther up the canyon, the middle cliffs fill the horizon so you can't see the tallest cliffs. At the end of the canyon you enter a box. The ruin is under an overhang to your right, and you have an easy climb of about 20 feet to get to it. It has been pothunted but is fairly intact. Enjoy it and then walk up to the very end of the canyon and look up. The water has undercut the cliff so that it projects over you. This would be a terrific sight when a gentle waterfall was running.

LOST CANYON RUINS

Altitude	4900
4700	
Feet: 200 Miles: 0.6	Easy

1.9 mi.

0.6 mi.

152

2.0 mi.

152C

WILDERNESS

R'Rock-Secret Mt

Dry Creek Road

Sedona Y

3.2 mi.

89

89

MP 371

179

Driving Distance One Way, Miles: 7.1
Hiking Distance One Way, Miles: 0.6

LOST WILSON MOUNTAIN

General Information
Location Map C4
Wilson Mt. USGS Map
Coconino Forest Service Map

Driving Distance One Way: 7.7 miles *12.5 km* (Time 30 minutes)
Access Road: Most cars, Last 2.5 miles *4.2 km* medium dirt road
Hiking Distance One Way: 1.3 miles *2.1 km* (Time 45 minutes)
How Strenuous: Easy
Features: Scenic stroll through Arizona cypress forest

NUTSHELL: Located 7.8 miles *12.5 km* north of Sedona, this hike follows a closed road to a point near the southwest face of Wilson Mountain.

DIRECTIONS:
From the Sedona Y Go:
Southwest on Highway 89A (toward Cottonwood) a distance of 3.2 miles *5.2 km* (MP 371) to the Dry Creek Road. Turn right on Dry Creek Road, also known as FR 152C, and follow it to the 5.2 mile *8.4 km* point where FR 152 branches to the right. Take FR 152. Follow the road to the 7.8 miles *12.5 km* point where you will see a dirt road blocked with red boulders branching off to the right. The best parking is at the **Brins Mesa West** trailhead 0.1 mile *0.17 km* behind you.

TRAILHEAD: This trail is neither marked nor maintained. Walk the blocked road.

DESCRIPTION: FR 152 has been improved since the first edition of our book. It is still rough, but anything but a low rider can negotiate it. Another change is that the mouth of the road that you will hike has been blocked by boulders so that a car cannot enter it—a good thing for hikers.

The road goes through a beautiful forest of Arizona cypress, juniper, manzanita, agave and cactus. The route ambles along, curving here and there to follow the terrain and you do not have a very good sense of its purpose. It primarily goes north, parallel to the base of Brins Mesa and then turns east toward Mt. Wilson. Just about the time you think that it is going to take you right to the mountain, it stops, where the road is deeply eroded at a steep bank. The stopping point does not make any sense. You will not feel that you have reached a destination. The road just ends. We explored all the likely routes from the end point but could find none.

In spite of this strange end, the road provides a very easy pleasant walk, far from the crowds. We have hiked it several times and found it a calming, easy stroll.

At the 0.90 mile *1.5 km* point, where the road makes a hairpin turn, there is a small clearing to the right. We walked over there and found a cairn that seemed to mark a trail down into a streambed. We tried to follow it but found no other cairns, and the streambed became choked with manzanita to the point that it was too difficult to hike through it.

How do you *lose* a mountain? Usually the term refers to a seldom seen aspect. In this case the name *Lost* Wilson refers to a nub projecting from the northwest face of the main mass of Wilson Mountain.

LOY BUTTE (HONANKI RUINS)

General Information
Location Map C1
Loy Butte and Page Springs USGS Maps
Coconino Forest Service Map

Driving Distance One Way: 19.9 miles *32 km* (Time 45 minutes)
Access Road: All cars, Last 10.3 miles *16.5 km* good dirt road
Hiking Distance One Way: 0.25 miles *0.4 km* (Time 10 minutes)
How Strenuous: Easy
Features: Best Indian ruins in the Sedona area

NUTSHELL: Located 19.9 miles *32 km* northwest of Sedona, this is a short hike to excellent Indian ruins.

DIRECTIONS:
From The Y in Sedona Go:
        Southwest on Highway 89A (toward Cottonwood) a distance of 9.6 miles *15.4 km* (MP 364.5) to the Red Canyon Road. Turn right on Red Canyon Road, also known as FR 525, and follow it to the 12.4 mile *20 km* point where FR 525C branches to the left. Stay on FR 525, the road to the right. Follow FR 525 to the 15.4 mile *25 km* point, where it intersects the Boynton Pass Road, FR 152C. Stay on FR 525, the road to the left. At 15.6 miles *25.5 km* you will reach an intersection with FR 795. Turn left here on FR 525. At 16.8 miles *27 km* you will come to an intersection with FR 525D. Turn right, still on FR 525. At 19.5 miles *31.2 km* you will reach the Hancock Ranch. Here the road goes through the ranch, which is private property. Take the left fork here, still on FR 525. At 19.9 miles *32 km* you will come to the parking area for the ruins. Pull off to the right and park.

TRAILHEAD: This trail is not marked with a sign but you will see a distinct path heading toward the nearby cliff.

DESCRIPTION: Don't be alarmed by the Hancock Ranch signs as you drive into the region of the ruins. An easement for the road runs through the ranch and you are welcome so long as you stay on the road and abide by the rules: no shooting, no hunting, no wandering around on the private property, etc.
        The ruins are located in a large cave in the cliff face. The official name for these ruins is the Honanki Ruins. In recent years the Forest Service has done some work to stabilize the ruins. There is no caretaker for them and over the years careless and malicious visitors have caused some damage.

Even so, the ruins are well preserved and definitely worth a visit. You will see some names carved and painted on the walls. Some of them are fairly old. The Smithsonian Institute did a survey of Indian ruins in northern Arizona in the 1920s, headed by archaeologist Jesse Fewkes. He spent some time at this ruin and thought that it was a major find. In spite of his glowing reports, the government did little about the ruins except to preserve public access to them. They were little known and not very frequently visited until lately. Now they seem to be on the menus for all the jeep tours.

It is fun to explore the ruins and walk along the cliff face on both sides of the ruins. Try to imagine yourself as an occupant of the place centuries ago when the tribe of Indians lived there and picture the life you would have led. There is a small streambed running along the cliff bottom but it seldom carries water. Maybe in the days when these ruins were inhabited water ran in the stream year around.

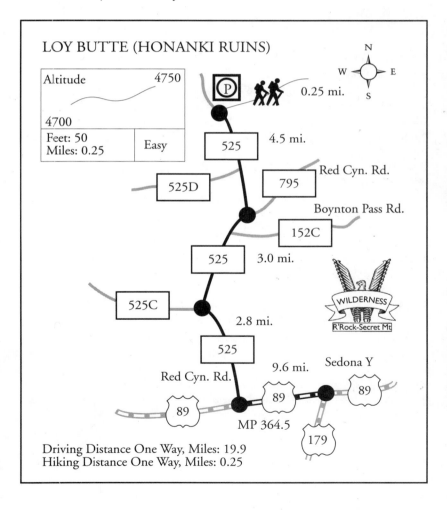

LOY CANYON #5

General Information
Location Map C1
Loy Butte and Page Springs USGS Maps
Coconino Forest Service Map

Driving Distance One Way: 19.2 miles *31 km* (Time 40 minutes)
Access Road: All cars, Last 9.6 miles *15.4 km* good dirt road
Hiking Distance One Way: 4.0 miles *6.4 km* (Time 2.5 hours)
How Strenuous: Moderate
Features: Indian ruins, Scenic canyon, Views

NUTSHELL: Located 19.2 miles *31 km* northwest of Sedona, this trail takes you through a pleasant canyon to the base of the Mogollon Rim.

DIRECTIONS:
From The Y in Sedona Go:
      Southwest on Highway 89A (toward Cottonwood) a distance of 9.6 miles *15.4 km* (MP 364.5) to the Red Canyon Road. Turn right on Red Canyon Road, also known as FR 525, and follow it to the 12.4 mile *20 km* point where FR 525C branches to the left. Stay on FR 525, the road to the right. Follow FR 525 to the 15.4 mile *25 km* point, where it intersects the Boynton Pass Road, FR 152C. Stay on FR 525, the road to the left. At 15.6 miles *15.5 km* you will reach an intersection with FR 795. Turn left here on FR 525. At 16.8 miles *27 km* you will come to an intersection with FR 525D. Turn right, still on FR 525. At 19.2 miles *31 km* you will reach a fence. Park on either side of the road at the fence.

TRAILHEAD: You will see a rusty sign marked, "Loy Canyon #5" on the right side of the road in front of the fence.

DESCRIPTION: Since you are so close, drive on down the road another 0.7 miles *1.2 km* and visit the Honanki Indian ruins located at **Loy Butte** if you haven't seen them. They are the Sedona area's finest Indian ruins.
      The Loy Canyon trail was built as a cattle trail in the late 1890s. Like many other cattle trails now used for hiking, the purpose of this trail was to drive cattle to the top of the Mogollon Rim. The cattle would be kept in the warm low country during the winter and then walked to the cool high country for the summer. The rim is over 1000 feet high in most places, so it was hard to find spots where a trail could be built.
      You start this hike by skirting the fence around a ranch for about half a mile, then begin to walk up the canyon bottom.

Look for a small Indian ruin set in a cave at 0.75 miles *1.3 km*. It is in a cliff face to your left.

The trail rises gradually through a forest for 4.0 *6.4 km* miles. It meanders across the creekbed a few times, so you don't want to make the hike when water is running high. Because the trail gains in altitude the vegetation along the trail also changes. It is very desert-like at the beginning, with cactus and low shrubs. As you progress, you enter a pine forest.

At the end of 4.0 miles *6.4 km* you are at the base of the cliffs forming the rim, where we stop for an easy day hike. To go to the top requires some serious work. The trail becomes much steeper and you climb about one thousand feet in a mile.

MARG'S DRAW

Driving Distance One Way: 0.9 miles *1.4 km* (Time 5 minutes)
Access Road: All cars, All paved
Hiking Distance One Way: 1.0 miles *1.6 km* (Time 40 minutes)
How Strenuous: Easy
Features: Views

NUTSHELL: Marg's Draw is a beautiful area in Sedona's backyard, a bowl surrounded by the Crimson Cliffs, Munds Mountain, Lee Mountain and Twin Buttes. This short hike takes you into the center of the area.

DIRECTIONS:
From the Sedona Y Go:
South on Highway 179 (toward Phoenix) for a distance of 0.7 miles *1.2 km* (MP 312.8) to Sombart Lane, which is just beyond a Circle K store. Turn left onto Sombart Lane and follow it to the 0.9 mile *1.4 km* point, where there is an unpaved parking area to your right. Park there.

TRAILHEAD: You will see no trail signs. You will see a footpath going uphill through a wooden gate framed by high steel pipe fence posts.

DESCRIPTION: You will climb uphill a bit to get through the wooden gate and then you will reach a flat. There are several paths and trails through the area. Follow directions carefully so that you don't take the wrong trail. At 0.27 miles *0.44 km* you will reach a fork. Take the left fork. In a few feet, the trail splits three ways. Take the middle trail. At 0.4 miles *0.64 km* the Marg's Draw Trail goes to the right along a redrock shelf. You will know you are on the right trail if it swings away from the red cliff and heads south. Another trail described in this book, **The Schnebly-Marg's Connection**, takes you around the base of the cliffs and to the north. **The Snoopy Rock Trail** heads straight for the cliff.

This is an easy walk, being quite level. You will feel at times that you are in a remote area and then a view will open up allowing you to look at Sedona, reminding you that you are just a stone's throw from it. How nice to have such an area so close to town.

The story goes that the Thompsons, a family of early settlers in the area, had a mule named Marg. They used her to perform hard hauling tasks.

One of the toughest jobs was pulling a wagon up the steep road to Flagstaff.

Mules are pretty intelligent animals and Marg learned how to tell when the family was about to go somewhere when she saw them get out the wagon, harness and tack. When she saw such activity she would gallop away into a draw to hide. But Marg wasn't smart enough, because the natural bowl shape of the draw made it easy to box her in and catch her. The family referred to the area as Marg's Draw and the name stuck.

The draw is accessible from the north end by the route covered in this article. The south end can be reached easily by taking Morgan Road. There is no connection in the middle. We have tried to bushwhack through the middle a couple of times. We would find what seemed to be a trail and follow it only to have it play out.

Your trail ends at one mile, on a large redrock shelf, with strange quartz bubbles imbedded in its surface. There are great views from here.

MARG'S DRAW

Altitude   4600

4500

Feet: 100
Miles: 1.0   Easy

N
W   E
S

WILDERNESS
Munds Mt.

Sedona Y

89

89   Schnebly Hill Road

179

0.7 mi.
MP 312.8   Sombart Lane

179   0.2 mi.   1.0 mi.

P

Driving Distance One Way, Miles: 0.9
Hiking Distance One Way, Miles: 1.0

General Information
Location Map E5
Munds Mt. and Munds Park USGS Maps
Coconino Forest Service Map

Driving Distance One Way: 5.0 miles *8.0 km* (Time 30 minutes)
Access Road: All cars, Last 4.2 miles *6.7 km* good dirt road
Hiking Distance, Complete Loop: 1.0 miles *1.6 km* (Time 45 minutes)
How Strenuous: Moderate
Features: Historic road, Redrocks, Views

NUTSHELL: This hike takes you to a prominent landmark on the Schnebly Hill Road just east of Sedona, where you climb a rock formation and then hike part of an historic road.

DIRECTIONS:
From the Sedona Y Go:
South on Highway 179 (toward Phoenix) for a distance of 0.3 miles *0.48 km* (MP 313.1) to the Schnebly Hill Road. It is just across the bridge past Tlaquepaque. Turn left onto the Schnebly Hill Road. It is paved for the first half mile and then turns into a dirt road that is all right for any car unless the road is muddy. At 5.0 miles *8.0 km* you will see a gate made of very thick steel pipes. This is used to close the road in winter. You will see a parking area on the left side of the road just before the gate. Park here.

TRAILHEAD: The trail starts at the parking place. It is unmarked and unsigned.

DESCRIPTION: At the parking place you will see a line of three boulders blocking what looks like a road going uphill to a couple of redrock spires just above your head. This hike has two levels. First take the uphill portion of the path, making a mental note of the fork downhill to the left (south).

The uphill path takes you on a steep but short climb to the base of the two spires. It is fun to explore these. If you are adventuresome, you can climb them. This whole area on top is a good viewpoint from which to enjoy the eye-filling delights of the area. We sat here one memorable evening and watched a thrilling sunset.

After you have finished enjoying the top, go back downhill and take the lower path. Although unmarked, it is well worn and you will have no trouble following it. In about 0.10 miles *0.16 km* you will intersect the old Schnebly Hill Road. Take the left fork first and follow the old road about

0.05 miles *0.08 km*, around the bend of a small arroyo that cuts it. When you look to your right here you will see the red butte whose top you just climbed. Circling the butte is a layer of rusty mauve stone about 12 feet thick. This is the Ft. Apache formation, a harder stone than the redrock above and below it. There are a couple of small windows in this layer. The old road followed this circular ledge around the butte and was referred to as the Merry-Go-Round.

Now go back to the trail fork and take the Merry-Go-Round. Step away from the road and go to the lip of the ledge all along the way to enjoy the many fine views into some of the most scenic areas around Sedona.

You will soon have girdled the butte. Keep following the old road uphill. You will see how the Merry-Go-Round was an ideal natural road, being flat and sandy, while the road above and below it was steep and rocky. You will intersect the present Schnebly Hill Road in about 0.25 miles *0.4 km* from the butte. From there walk back down the present road to your car.

MERRY-GO-ROUND

N

W ← → E

S

Altitude	5400
5300	

| Feet: 100 Miles: 1.0 | Mod. |

89 Sedona Y 89

1.0 mi.

0.3 mi. 179

4.7 mi. (P)

MP 313.1

Schnebly Hill Road

179

Driving Distance, One Way, Miles: 5.0
Hiking Distance Complete Loop, Miles: 1.0

MESCAL MOUNTAIN

General Information
Location Map C3
Wilson Mt. USGS Map
Coconino Forest Service Map

Driving Distance One Way: 6.7 miles *11.0 km* (Time 15 minutes)
Access Road: All cars, All paved
Hiking Distance One Way: 2.5 miles *4.0 km* (Time 90 minutes)
How Strenuous: Moderate
Features: Views, Indian ruins

NUTSHELL: Mescal Mountain is a small mesa at the mouth of Boynton Canyon 6.7 miles *11.0 km* northwest of Sedona. It takes a bit of scrambling to get to its top but the effort is worthwhile.

DIRECTIONS:
From the Sedona Y Go:
        Southwest on Highway 89A (toward Cottonwood) for a distance of 3.2 miles *5.2 km* (MP 371) to the Dry Creek Road, FR 152C. Turn right onto Dry Creek Road and follow it to the 6.1 mile *10 km* point, where there is a stop sign. The paved road to your right is the Long Canyon Road. Take it to the 6.7 miles *11 km* point, where you will see an unpaved road to your left. The entrance to the road is blocked with boulders. There is a parking area in front of the boulders. Park there.

TRAILHEAD: You will begin this hike on a marked and maintained trail. There is a rusty sign where you park reading "Long Canyon #122."

DESCRIPTION: Start the hike by taking the **Long Canyon Trail**, which begins as a wide jeep road. In fact, the Forest Service has moved several boulders across the road at its entrance to keep vehicles from using it.
        At 0.30 *0.48 km* miles you will come to a 3-pronged fork. Take the leftmost fork. At 0.60 *1.0 km* miles you will come to a big gate. This marks the entrance to the Redrock-Secret Mt. Wilderness Area. Instead of going through the gate, stay outside it and walk north along the fence. At the 1.0 mile *1.6 km* point you will reach a butte. Here the trail begins to climb sharply.
        You will see a cave to your right that looks large enough to contain an Indian ruin. It is large enough but there is no ruin due to a large crack in the cave roof that allows water to pour into the cave when it rains. There is a side trail over to this cave and it is worth taking for the fun of exploring.

From the cave the trail zigzags to a saddle on Mescal Mountain. Just below the saddle you will see a shallow cave containing a rudimentary Indian ruin.

From this point the trail gets steeper. You will see a distinct footpath marked with cairns going up to the south. A few yards above the saddle there is the ruin of a pit house. Beyond it the trail winds right up to the face of the highest point on Mescal Mountain and then curves, hugging the cliff at its base. It is fairly easy hiking, though steep, until you get to a point just below the top. There you will have to do some climbing if you want to go to the top.

We don't do any rock climbing. We are risk-averse and true rock climbing scares us. The small climb involved here is no worse than climbing a high ladder, though. Once you are on top, walk around the perimeter to enjoy the view. The distance to the top is 1.5 miles *2.4 km.* Fully exploring the top can add another mile to the hike.

MITTEN RIDGE

VORTEX

General Information
Location Map E5
Munds Mt. and Munds Park USGS Maps
Coconino Forest Service Map

Driving Distance One Way: 3.8 miles *6.1 km* (Time 20 minutes)
Access Road: All cars, Last 3.0 miles *4.8 km* good gravel road
Hiking Distance One Way: 2.5 miles *4.0 km* (Time 2 hours)
How Strenuous: Moderate
Features: Views, Fascinating rock formations and sculptures, Vortex

NUTSHELL: Just 0.3 miles *0.48 km* from the Y, the Schnebly Hill Road is enjoyed by thousands of people. The hike takes you part way up the road, then across Bear Wallow Canyon to explore the redrock buttes on the west side of the canyon.

DIRECTIONS:
From the Sedona Y Go:
        South on Highway 179 (toward Phoenix) for a distance of 0.3 miles *0.48 km* (MP 313.1) to the Schnebly Hill Road. It is just across the bridge past Tlaquepaque. Turn left onto the Schnebly Hill Road. It is paved for the first half mile and then turns into a dirt road that is all right for any car unless the road is muddy. At the 3.8 mile *6.1 km* point, pull over and park. There is a bare redrock ledge off the road to your right for parking.

TRAILHEAD: There are no signs. There is a trail going downhill off of the left side of the road (to the west). Follow it.

DESCRIPTION:
        As you drive up Schnebly Hill Road you will become conscious of a deep streambed to your left. This is Bear Wallow Canyon. You will also be aware of a big butte between the road and Oak Creek Canyon. This is Mitten Ridge, one of the major Sedona landmarks, and it is your goal on this hike.
        At the parking place you can park on the shoulder or drive up onto a slickrock shelf. Then you walk across the road and look for the trail. It dips down and heads toward Mitten Ridge.
        In about 200 yards you will come to a redrock shelf that was capped with a very thin layer of gray lava. This cap has broken up into small stones. This place is one of the Sedona Vortex spots and believers often arrange some of these gray stones into a huge medicine wheel.

Thus far you are following the same trail that we have described for the **Cow Pies** hike. At 0.50 miles *0.8 km*, the paths split. You will go straight instead of turning left as you would for the Cow Pies hike. You will walk toward ledges at the base of Mitten Ridge. Cairns usually mark the trail. It goes across several lower ledges to get up near the base of the cliffs. Once there you work your way west, at times ascending to a higher ledge. At first you will be walking through brush but at 1.5 miles *2.4 km* you will break out onto clear slickrock.

Here you will find an upper and lower trail. Try the lower one. You will soon see a saddle above you to the right. The saddle is a great viewpoint. You probably will not find a regular trail going to the saddle but it is easy and fun to walk up the sloping redrock face of the ridge to the saddle. The trail pinches out at the 2.5 miles *4.0 km* point.

MITTEN RIDGE

Altitude	5400
5100	

Feet: 300 Miles: 2.5	Mod.

N
W ← → E
S

89 Sedona Y

89

2.5 mi.

0.3 mi. 179

3.5 mi.

MP 313.1

Schnebly Hill Road

P

179

Driving Distance, One Way, Miles: 3.8
Hiking Distance One Way, Miles: 2.5

MOONEY TRAIL #12

General Information
Location Map C1
Loy Butte USGS Map
Coconino Forest Service Map

Driving Distance One Way: 18.1 miles *29 km* (Time 30 minutes)
Access Road: All cars, Last 8.5 miles *13.6 km* good dirt road
Hiking Distance One Way: 3.75 miles *6.0 km* (Time 2.5 hours)
How Strenuous: Hard
Features: Views

NUTSHELL: This cattle trail starts at Black Tank 18.1 miles *29 km* southwest of Sedona and climbs to the base of the Mogollon Rim (or, alternatively, to the top)

DIRECTIONS:
From the Sedona Y Go:
Southwest on Highway 89A (toward Cottonwood) a distance of 9.6 miles *15.4 km* (MP 364.5) to the Red Canyon Road. Turn right on Red Canyon Road, also known as FR 525, and follow it to the 12.4 mile *20 km* point where FR 525C branches to the left. Sycamore Pass is your target. Turn left onto FR 525C. Follow it to the 18.1 mile *29 km* point, where FR 551 branches to the right. Pull in on FR 551 and park.

TRAILHEAD: This is a marked and maintained trail. You will see a rusty sign near the road reading, "Mooney Trail #12."

DESCRIPTION: You are near the trailhead when you see the red earth bank of a dam with fence posts on top on your right. This is Black Tank. Just as you curve around the tank there is a road to your right, FR 551. You will see the trail's rusty sign as you pull in.

Park near the tank. If you have a high clearance vehicle you can drive about 1.0 miles *1.6 km* on FR 551, parking just before the road crosses a gully. The gully is Spring Creek.

If you park at the tank, then walk through the fenced area toward the pumphouse, a small brick building. When you exit the gate at the other end of the tank area, turn right. You will see many trails because cattle are still run here and wherever they wander, they leave false trails. Follow the most heavily traveled jeep trail for 0.25 miles *0.4 km*, to a point where the road forks. Take the left fork marked FR 551A.

The trail goes along foothills, gradually climbing to a ridge top.

Then you walk along the top of the ridge. The ridge is javelina country and you will see plenty of sign. It is hard to see these critters, as they are shy. Sometimes you may get a whiff of them. The javelina odor smells just like a cow barn. From the ridge top you get good distant views, particularly to the north, of the Mogollon Rim, but there isn't much to see close at hand. In fact, this is a rather drab trail.

You will reach another cattle tank called Sebra Tank. Beyond Sebra Tank you will come to the base of the Mogollon Rim, where the trail begins a steep ascent. There is an arch located in the cliff face here.

The trail to the top is hard. It is a severe climb and most of it is in the open, exposed to full sunlight. You wouldn't want to do this on a hot sunny day. At the top you will come out on a ridge at a place where the Mooney Trail, Taylor Cabin Trail and **Casner Mountain** trails all converge. If you turn left here, you will go to Casner Mountain; if you turn right, you will go to the top of the rim.

MOONEY TRAIL #12

Altitude	5500
4500	
Feet: 1000 Miles: 3.75	Hard

Black Tank

3.75 mi.

5.7 mi.

761

Bill Gray Road

525C

Loy Butte Road

525

WILDERNESS
Munds Mt.

2.8 mi.

525

Sedona Y

89

9.6 mi.

Red Cyn. Rd.

89

179

MP 364.5

Driving Distance One Way, Miles: 18.1
Hiking Distance One Way, Miles: 3.75

MUNDS MOUNTAIN TRAIL #77

General Information
Location Map E5
Munds Mt. and Munds Park USGS Maps
Coconino Forest Service Map

Driving Distance One Way: 6.6 miles *10.6 km* (Time 30 minutes)
Access Road: All cars, Last 5.8 miles *9.3 km* good dirt road
Hiking Distance One Way: 2.9 miles *4.64 km* (Time 2.5 hours)
How Strenuous: Hard
Features: Views

NUTSHELL: This hike takes you to the top of the north end of Munds Mountain, from where you have glorious views.

DIRECTIONS:
From the Sedona Y Go:
South on Highway 179 (toward Phoenix) for a distance of 0.3 miles *0.5 km* (MP 313.1) to the Schnebly Hill Road. It is just across the bridge past Tlaquepaque. Turn left onto the Schnebly Hill Road. It is paved for the first half mile and then turns into a dirt road that is all right for any car unless the road is muddy. At 5.0 miles *8.0 km* you will see a gate made of very thick steel pipes. This gate is locked across the road in winter, usually about mid-November to mid-April. (Call the Sedona Forest Service Ranger Station to find out whether it is open.) Drive to the top, 6.6 miles *10.6 km* from the Y, where you will find the Schnebly Hill Vista with a big parking area to your left. Park there.

TRAILHEAD: Your approach to the trailhead is over old jeep roads. From the parking area walk up the main road about 100 paces, where you will see a dirt road to your right (south). Take it. The road is the Old Schnebly Hill Road, following the alignment it had from 1902 until the 1930s. If you have a high clearance vehicle, you can drive a portion of it, though it has not been maintained for years and is very rough. At 0.88 miles *1.45 km* on this road you come to a fork. Go left (south) here. You will soon see a small microwave tower. At 1.2 miles *2.0 km* you will come to a fork. Here the old road goes right, on to meet the **Schnebly Hill Trail.** Turn right and walk a short distance, to the point where the road makes a hairpin curve to your right. At this point you will see a footpath to the left (south) marked by a cairn. Take this path, which is the second leg of the Schnebly Hill Trail.

From here the trail follows the edge of the rim, with many excellent viewpoints along the way. You will pass through two gates, the second being located at Committee Tank. Soon after this the trail goes out on a thin ridge connected to Munds Mt. At 2.4 miles *3.9 km* you will find the trailhead sign, "Munds Mt. Trail 77," just beyond the point where the **Jacks Canyon Trail** meets the ridge.

DESCRIPTION: At the trailhead the trail splits. Take the right fork, a sandy groove. The footing on this trail is poor, as it is covered with small white slippery rocks. The cairns are hard to see. The trail goes to the top by switchbacks, improving about halfway up. Beyond the midpoint, you will get thrilling glimpses into the Mitten Ridge area. At the top you emerge onto a rather bare park. Move around its edge for unsurpassed views.

     In winter, when the Schnebly Hill is closed above the 5.0 mile *8.0 km* point, you can use the Schnebly Hill Trail as your approach and still make this hike. The top is above 6000 feet, so there may be snow or mud, so keep this in mind.

MUNDS MOUNTAIN TRAIL #77

Altitude 6700

6200

Feet: 500
Miles: 2.9   Hard

N
W E
S

WILDERNESS
Munds Mt.

Rim

89   Sedona Y   89

P

Schnebly Hill Trail   Vista

0.3 mi.   179   6.3 mi.

1.2 mi.

MP 313.1

Schnebly Hill Road

179

0.5 mi.   1.2 mi.

Driving Distance, One Way, Miles: 6.6
Hiking Distance One Way, Miles: 2.9

MUSHROOM ROCK

Driving Distance One Way: 8.0 miles *13 km* (Time 20 minutes)
Access Road: All cars, All paved
Hiking Distance One Way: 2.25 miles *3.6 km* (Time 90 minutes)
How Strenuous: Hard
Features: Gorgeous canyon, Indian Ruins, Vortex

NUTSHELL: A hike in **Boynton Canyon** 8.0 miles *13 km* northwest of Sedona. You branch off the main trail into a side canyon for a clifftop hike of eye-popping beauty.

DIRECTIONS:
From the Sedona Y Go:
    Southwest on Highway 89A (toward Cottonwood) a distance of 3.2 miles *5.0 km* (MP 371), to Dry Creek Road, where you take a right turn onto Dry Creek Road (FR 152C). Follow it to the 6.1 *10 km* mile point, where it joins Long Canyon Road. Take a left here, staying on FR 152C. At the 7.7 mile *12.4 km* point, you reach another junction. Go right. At 8.0 miles *13 km*, just before the gatehouse to the Enchantment Resort, you will see a parking area to the right. Park there. There is also a small parking area on the left side of the road.

TRAILHEAD: It is marked at the parking area by a sign reading, "Boynton Canyon #47."

DESCRIPTION: Hike the Boynton Canyon Trail for 1.3 miles *2.1 km*, where the trail is a corridor through a thicket of head-high mazanitas. Take an unmarked but distinct trail to the right (east) going downhill into a wash, on the other side of which is a canyon full of Arizona cypress trees.
    On the far side of the wash the trail turns left (north), leaves the forest and climbs to a saddle on a ridge. At the saddle you will find that the ridge forms the south wall of yet another canyon. Go east, toward the head of the canyon, where you will find a walkable ledge under a ten foot high groove in the redrock. This groove is a magic place. Plants in natural "baskets" hang on its wall and we saw one pictograph there. Some hikers will want to stop at the groove's end.
    For those unafraid of heights who don't mind some redrock scram-

bling, deeper magic lies ahead. Follow cairns up a steep path. About half way up you will see a side path to your left. Take it to a pristine cliff dwelling in a large cave, then return to the main trail for a stiff climb to the next top.

You will emerge onto a terrace. Below you are ridges. Above you are ledges crowned with sheer cliffs. There are more ruins in a grooved ledge high above. You see into two canyons. Standing in this glorious place, we were transfixed with beauty. Following cairns, hike west along the north wall, climbing up and down to use walkable ledges. Some are wide as a street and some are narrow and scary. You round the corner of a giant reef at 2.0 miles *3.2 km* and, bang!, there is Mushroom Rock at the head of a steep V-shaped gorge, perfectly framed by giant rippling walls. The trail goes on another 0.25 miles *0.4 km*, pinching down to an irreducible end where you stand on the tip of a finger ridge.

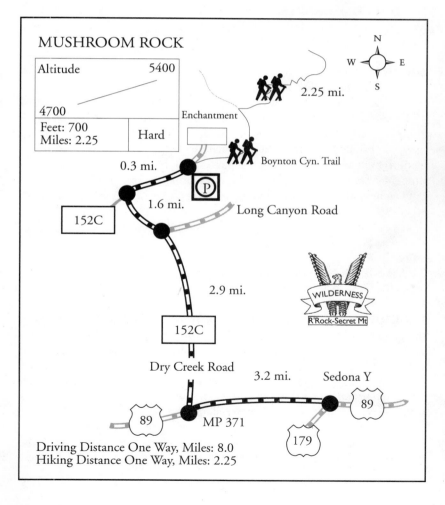

OAK CREEK & VERDE CONFLUENCE

General Information
Location Map G1
Cornville USGS Map
Coconino Forest Service Map

Driving Distance One Way: 22.2 miles *35.6 km* (Time 40 minutes)
Access Road: All cars, Last 4.0 miles *6.4 km* good dirt road
Hiking Distance One Way: 2.0 miles *3.2 km* (Time 1 hour)
How Strenuous: Easy
Features: Indian ruins, River confluence

NUTSHELL: Located 22.2 miles *35.6 km* southwest of Sedona, this hike has no trail but offers interesting exploration along a stream bank to see a river confluence and an Indian ruin.

DIRECTIONS:
From The Y in Sedona Go:
        Southwest on Highway 89A (toward Cottonwood) a distance of 17.2 miles *27.6 km* (MP 357), to a point where the Cornville Road intersects Highway 89A. A sign identifies this as Cornville and I-17 access. Turn left on the Cornville Road and follow it one mile, to the 18.2 mile *29.2 km point*. Turn right there onto FR 671, an unpaved road. Follow this road to the 21.5 mile *34.5 km* point, where there is a three-pronged fork. Take the left fork onto an unmarked dirt road. Follow this road to the 22.1 mile *35.4 km* point, where there is a two-pronged fork. Take the left fork here. At 22.2 miles *35.6 km* you will be near the Indian ruin at the rim of Oak Creek canyon. Park here.

TRAILHEAD: No trail. You will see Indian ruins to your left at the parking spot. View them and then hike to the confluence.

DESCRIPTION: The Indian ruin is a two-story structure located on a prominent knob of land near the riverbank. It is on private land and protected by a fence festooned with "No Trespassing" signs. You can get close enough for a good look without going onto the land. This is an unusual ruin for the area, as it is neither a pit house nor a cliff dwelling. Instead it is a freestanding "apartment building." It is built with distinctive round boulders from the river, which add to its unusual appearance.

        From the ruin you can walk along the riverbank back to the confluence or you can drive there. To drive to the confluence just go back to the last fork in the road and turn left, from where it is about 0.40 miles *0.64 km* to the spot where the rivers converge.

The two streams meet at a V-shaped point overlooked by a high white bluff. This bluff provides a natural perch, a place to sit and watch the meeting of the waters. As you sit on the point looking forward, downstream, Oak Creek is to your left and the Verde River is to your right. After a rain, Oak Creek runs red, while the Verde (true to its name, which means "green" in Spanish) runs green. It is fascinating to watch the waters mix. Oak Creek seems to run faster than the Verde.

This is not a wilderness experience. Right across the river is a big trailer and RV park and there are several ranches in the area. You could actually make this trip with no hiking at all. It is an excellent hike, though, if you explore along the river bank for a couple of miles as we did.

Look sharp as you are walking and you may find pottery shards and arrowheads along the river rim, as this area was inhabited by Indians for hundreds of years. Leave them in place. Never take artifacts.

OLD HIGHWAY 79

General Information
Location Map F2
Page Springs and Sedona USGS Maps
Coconino Forest Service Map

Driving Distance One Way: 8.5 miles *13.6 km* (Time 15 minutes)
Access Road: All cars, Last 0.3 miles good dirt road
Hiking Distance One Way: 2.5 miles *4.0 km* (Time 75 minutes)
How Strenuous: Moderate
Features: Views

NUTSHELL: This old dirt road has been replaced by the present Highway 89A. It provides a pleasant stroll from a point on Highway 89A to a point on the lower Red Rock Loop Road.

DIRECTIONS:
From the Sedona Y Go:
 Southwest on Highway 89A (toward Cottonwood) for a distance of 8.2 miles *13.2 km* (MP 366), to a point where you see a dirt road going through a gate on the left (east) side of the highway. Turn left and go through the gate, which is unlocked. Drive on the old road about 0.30 miles *0.5 km* and park.

TRAILHEAD: No signs posted. You walk the old road.

DESCRIPTION:
 From Highway 89A you can see the unlocked gate to your left. Go through it and drive down the dirt road for about 0.30 miles *0.5 km*. The road is good to this point and any car can make it that far. If you want to try to shorten the hike, you can drive farther if you have a high clearance vehicle. You will reach a bad place in the road at about 0.50 miles *0.8 km* where the road dips down into the Dry Creek streambed. The road is steep here and suffers lots of damage from washouts. Most vehicles, even with high clearance, should park here, at the hilltop. Don't go down to the river unless you are a hardy soul and are equipped with a high clearance four-wheel drive vehicle.
 In the old days this road was the main road south of Sedona. It was the only wagon road connecting Sedona to the Verde Valley, Cottonwood and Jerome. The right of way was a good one and might have been preserved except for the fact that it crosses Dry Creek at creek level. Dry Creek isn't always dry. It carries water every spring when the snow in the high country

is melting, and after hard rains, and at such times may be impassable Every now and then a real gully-washer comes along and rips things up, requiring a rebuilding. The present location of Highway 89A crosses Dry Creek on a good high bridge, thereby avoiding the flooding problem.

The scenery along the road is not very interesting, but the road provides a good stroll, as it is open, flat and wide. You get some good views.

The road ends on the Lower Red Rock Loop Road, which was paved in 1990. There are horse stables here and you will run into many horse trails near the end of the hike. The main old road is obvious because it is so much bigger than the horse trails, so if you stay on it, you will have no trouble finding your way.

The area where Old Highway 79 meets the Lower Red Rock Loop Road used to be called Elmerville, a name that has now faded into disuse. There was and is a collection of small homes at the site and it may even have had its own post office.

OLD HIGHWAY 79

Altitude

4000

Feet: Nearly flat
Miles: 2.5   Mod.

N
W ← → E
S

Sedona Y

89

8.2 mi.

179

89

Red Rock
LoopRoad

MP 366

89   0.3 mi.

2.5 mi.

Dry Creek

Driving Distance One Way, Miles: 8.5
Hiking Distance One Way, Miles: 2.5

OLD JIM THOMPSON ROAD

General Information
Location Map D5
Munds Park and Wilson Mt. USGS Maps
Coconino Forest Service Map

Driving Distance One Way: 1.1 miles *1.8 km* (Time 10 minutes)
Access Road: All cars, All paved
Hiking Distance One Way: 2.6 miles *4.2 km* (Time 2 hours)
How Strenuous: Moderate
Features: Rock formations, Views

NUTSHELL: Located in uptown Sedona's backyard, this old road starts at Midgley Bridge, skirts along the base of Steamboat Rock, and ends overlooking the upper Jordan Road area.

DIRECTIONS:
From the Sedona Y Go:
North on Highway 89A (toward Flagstaff) for a distance of 1.1 miles *1.8 km* (MP 375.9). Go just across Midgley Bridge and turn left into the parking area.

TRAILHEAD: You will see a rusty sign at the parking lot. It reads, "Wilson Canyon #49."

DESCRIPTION: Walk along the Wilson Canyon Trail for the first leg of this hike. The trail crosses a streambed and then you walk along the bank of the canyon. At 0.37 miles *0.6 km*, the trail crosses the creek where the canyon curves to the west. Walk up out of the canyon here to your left (west) on a wide but very rocky trail going uphill. This is the old wagon road built by pioneer Jim Thompson in the early 1900s.

In about 100 yards after starting to climb, you will meet another path. Turn left (south) here, and continue going uphill. At about 0.6 miles *1.0 km*, you will reach a ridge top, where there is another trail intersection. Again go to your left (south). At 1.1 miles *1.8 km* you will come to Steamboat Tank, marked by the deciduous trees growing there. Side trails go to the tank. The main trail follows along the edge of the ridge. The trails may seem confusing here, but you can't get lost, because your way is bounded by Steamboat Rock on one side and the edge of the ridge on the other.

The old road stays at about the same level as it curves around west and south, following the contour of Steamboat Rock. At the 2.1 mile *3.4 km* point, you will find a power line. There is a path going off to your left here, which is the only private trail we know about, going down to Red Rock Lodge in 1.0 miles *1.6 km.* Stay on top, on the old road. You are moving away from Steamboat Rock and following west along the base of Wilson Mountain. The road is easy to walk and is quite level.

At the 2.6 mile *4.2 km* point you will come to a gate. We believe that this is a good stopping point for the hike. From here the trail drops down to the northern extension of Jordan Road. In the Spring of 1994 as this was written, the land through which this last leg of the trail passes is being sub-divided. We have been told that the developers are obligated to provide an easement for the trail, but we do not know at this time where it will be.

OLD JIM THOMPSON ROAD

Altitude	5250
4600	
Feet: 650 Miles: 2.6	Mod.

N
W — E
S

2.6 mi.

89

⊕ (P)

MP 375.9

1.1 mi.

Midgley Bridge

89

Sedona Y

89

179

Driving Distance One Way, Miles: 1.1
Hiking Distance One Way, Miles: 2.6

PARSONS TRAIL #144

General Information
Location Map F1
Clarkdale and Sycamore Basin USGS Maps
Coconino Forest Service Map

Driving Distance One Way: 34.3 miles *55 km* (Time 1 hour)
Access Road: All cars, Last 10.5 miles *17 km* good dirt road
Hiking Distance One Way: 4.0 miles *6.4 km* (Time 2 hours)
How Strenuous: Moderate
Features: Tremendous canyon, Year around stream

NUTSHELL: This trail enters the south end of Sycamore Canyon, 34.3 miles *55 km* SW of Sedona. It is the easiest trail into the canyon.

DIRECTIONS:
From The Y in Sedona Go:
Southwest on Highway 89A a distance of 19.4 miles *32 km*, which will take you into the town of Cottonwood. Go straight through Cottonwood on Main Street and then on Broadway, headed toward Tuzigoot National Monument. At 23.4 miles *37.5 km* you will reach the road to Tuzigoot. Turn right onto it and follow it to the 23.8 mile *38.1 km* point, just over the bridge. You will see signs there for the Verde Valley Country Club and Sycamore Canyon Wilderness. Turn left on this dirt road, FR 131. Stay on FR 131 to the 34.3 mile *55 km* point, a parking area at the top of Sycamore Canyon.

TRAILHEAD: The trail is well marked at the parking area. A rusty sign reads, "Parsons Trail #144."

DESCRIPTION: You enter the south end of Sycamore Canyon, where the canyon walls are not as tall as they are upstream. The walls display interesting rock formations. The hue of the red stone is rosier than the rock in Sedona. It is mixed with white rock and is very rough, grainy and chunky. Basalt is blended in, rather than being a cap as it is in Sedona.

The trail follows along Sycamore Creek, usually on the right bank, though it does cross the creek twice. It is fairly level. In all but extremely dry years, water runs year around up to Parsons Spring at 4.0 miles *6.4 km*, so you have the pleasant experience of walking beside running water. The vegetation is lush. Cows often graze through the area.

The canyon for the first two miles seems wide and spacious. At 1.3 miles *2.1 km* you will reach Summers Spring. It usually seeps water across the trail. Although the water looks clear and pure, the Forest Service advises not to drink it unless you treat it. Also be careful about eating the water-cress growing there.

Upstream from Summers Spring the trail gets rough. A heavy flood in 1980 tore out a lot of the trail and the Forest Service lacks funds to rebuild. In spots you have to scramble over boulders. Stay near the streambed and you will pick up the surviving parts of the trail every time you pass one of the washouts. There are large pools that hold fish.

Sycamore Canyon is in a mineralized zone and before it became a Wilderness Area some mining occurred there. You will pass the entrance to an agate mine at 2.7 miles *4.4 km*. It has been plugged but bits of hardware are still around.

The canyon narrows and the walls get steeper as you work your way up the canyon. You will reach Parsons Spring at 4.0 miles *6.4 km*. Above this point the stream is only intermittent. This is the place to stop for a day hike. The trail continues but becomes very difficult.

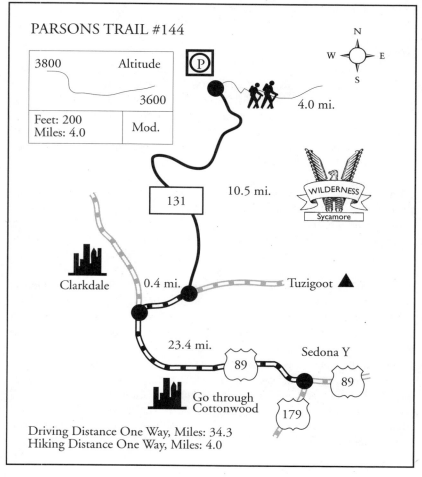

PARSONS TRAIL #144

3800	Altitude
	3600
Feet: 200 Miles: 4.0	Mod.

4.0 mi.

10.5 mi.

131

WILDERNESS
Sycamore

Clarkdale   0.4 mi.   Tuzigoot

23.4 mi.

Sedona Y

89   89

Go through
Cottonwood

179

Driving Distance One Way, Miles: 34.3
Hiking Distance One Way, Miles: 4.0

PINK SAND CANYON

General Information
Location Map B5
Mountainaire USGS Map
Coconino Forest Service Map

Driving Distance One Way: 12.7 miles *20.1 km* (Time 20 minutes)
Access Road: All cars, All paved
Hiking Distance One Way: 0.25 miles *0.4 km* (Time 30 minutes)
How Strenuous: Easy
Features: Scenic canyon

NUTSHELL: Starting at the Pine Flat Campground in upper Oak Creek Canyon, this hike takes you across the creek and up an unusual narrow canyon, the floor of which is covered with pink sand.

DIRECTIONS:
From the Sedona Y Go:
        North on Highway 89A (toward Flagstaff) for a distance of 12.7 miles *20.1 km* (MP 386.9) to the Pine Flat Campground. On your left at the upper end of the campground on the shoulder of the highway, you will see a standpipe, a structure about 5 feet high and 4 feet square made of round stones that houses a spring. Park anywhere near here. There are wide aprons on both shoulders in this area.

TRAILHEAD: Go into the campground at the north entrance just below the standpipe. A roadway branches to the right as you enter. Take it. It becomes unpaved and goes down to Oak Creek, where you will find the remains of a concrete driveway going across the creek. This is the trailhead. It is unmarked.

DESCRIPTION: The water in the spring at the Pine Flat campground is pure. Caution: with any spring water, even though it tests pure, there are natural microbes in the water. Local residents are used to these microbes and their immune systems can handle them. This may not be true of visitors; so be careful. Just because you see someone drinking from a spring doesn't mean that the water is good for *you.*
        The center of the concrete driveway was ripped out by heavy floods in 1993, but you can walk across on the debris. Follow the old sunken road you will find on the other side. After walking it a short distance you will come to a three-way fork. Take the center road here, which is still a sunken lane. In about 0.1 mile *0.16 km* this road will wind around to a point under

a power line, where it turns into a footpath heading west into a canyon.

Follow this trail into the canyon. Although the trail is not posted, it is distinct at the entrance to the canyon. It goes up on the top of the bank until it is about half way up the canyon. There it reaches a place where it is better to hike down into the canyon bottom and follow it the rest of the way.

You will find the bottom of this attractive canyon covered with an unusual pink sand, almost a coral color. The canyon is narrow, getting narrower as it goes. A thousand feet above your head are soaring white cliffs, though you will be walking in redrock.

At a point 0.25 miles *0.4 km* from the beginning, the canyon becomes a narrow slot choked with boulders. It would take a lot of effort to scramble over these boulders, so most hikers will want to quit in this spot, where you can see the canyon end a few hundred yards ahead of you in a beautiful box.

This hike is shaded all the way and would be cool even in summer.

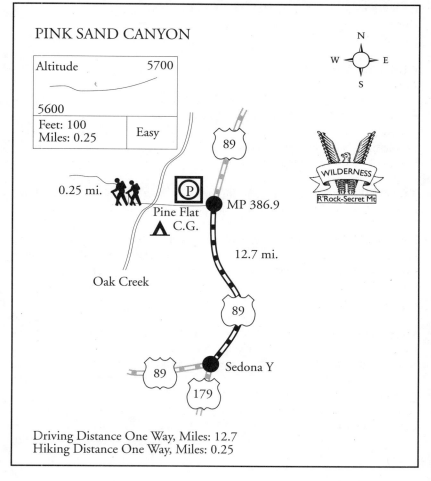

PINK SAND CANYON

Altitude	5700
5600	
Feet: 100 Miles: 0.25	Easy

0.25 mi.

89

Pine Flat ▲ C.G.

⊓P⊔ MP 386.9

12.7 mi.

Oak Creek

89

89 Sedona Y

179

WILDERNESS
R'Rock-Secret Mt

Driving Distance One Way, Miles: 12.7
Hiking Distance One Way, Miles: 0.25

PUMPHOUSE WASH

General Information
Location Map B5
Mountainaire USGS Map
Coconino Forest Service Map

Driving Distance One Way: 13.5 miles *22 km* (Time 20 minutes)
Access Road: All cars, All paved
Hiking Distance One Way: 1.5 miles *2.4 km* (Time 1.5 hours)
How Strenuous: Moderate
Features: Scenic canyon

NUTSHELL: Pumphouse Wash is a tributary canyon meeting Oak Creek at the bottom of the Highway 89A switchbacks. There is no trail. You rock hop along the canyon bottom, enjoying the sight of immense towering cliffs, redrock sculptures and a get-away-from-it-all feeling.

DIRECTIONS:
From the Sedona Y Go:
North on Highway 89A (toward Flagstaff) for a distance of 13.5 miles *22 km* (MP 387.7) to the bridge that spans Pumphouse Wash. It is posted. Below (south) of the bridge there is a wide apron that will hold a couple of cars on the right hand side of the road (east), or you can cross the bridge and park on a wide apron on the left side of the road (south).

TRAILHEAD: There is no marking or official trail. Look for a way down into the bottom of the wash. There are paths from both parking areas.

DESCRIPTION: Once you are in the canyon bottom, you walk along the streambed in an upstream direction, away from Oak Creek. The bottom is strewn with large boulders and you have to hop from rock to rock. As a result of this, the hike is harder than the mileage and altitude would seem to indicate.

Pumphouse Wash does not carry water year around. During the spring snowmelt it can run high, but after the first of June it is usually dry except for a few pools. The trick is to make the hike when there is enough water in the wash to add to the enjoyment of the hike but not so much as to make it impassable. Try mid-May. If you see water running under the bridge, there is too much water to make the hike.

Soon after you enter the canyon, your attention will turn from the boulders under your feet to the heights overhead. The walls of the canyon are extremely high and sheer, giving the hiker a real awestruck feeling of just how small humans are in the scale of things.

At about 0.3 miles *0.48 km* you will reach the first of a chain of half a dozen pools. These are situated so that you cannot bypass them, but must go through them. Depending on how much water is present, this can mean walking, wading or swimming. When the water is low, an old pair of tennies is good gear. You just wade through and keep on going, walking in wet shoes. If the water is deep enough, there are some good swimming holes.

You will be out of the pool zone in about 0.6 miles *1.0 km* and soon after will see a transition. The rock you hike on changes from white to red. We love this middle part of Pumphouse Wash. It seems virgin and primitive. Oak Creek Canyon itself must have looked like this before it was developed. The cutting action of the water has carved chutes and swirls and all kinds of fascinating sculptures in this red stone. You will see evidence of beaver activity.

We think that the 1.5 mile *2.4 km* point is a good place to stop.

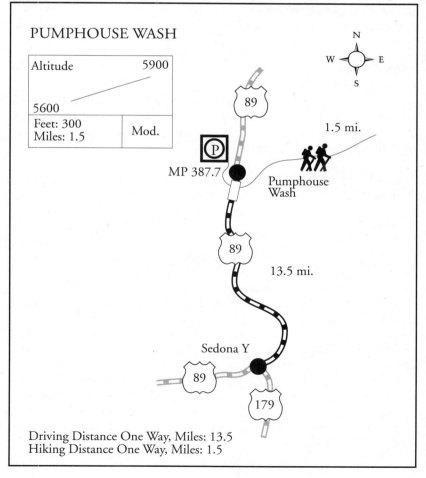

PUMPHOUSE WASH

N
W — E
S

Altitude	5900
5600	
Feet: 300 Miles: 1.5	Mod.

89

1.5 mi.

MP 387.7

Pumphouse Wash

89

13.5 mi.

Sedona Y

89

179

Driving Distance One Way, Miles: 13.5
Hiking Distance One Way, Miles: 1.5

PURTYMUN TRAIL

General Information
Location Map B5
Munds Park and Wilson Mt. USGS Maps
Coconino Forest Service Map

Driving Distance One Way: 8.4 miles *13.5 km* (Time 20 minutes)
Access Road: All cars, All paved
Hiking Distance One Way: 1.0 miles *1.6 km* (Time 1 hour)
How Strenuous: Hard
Features: Views

NUTSHELL: This hard hike climbs the east wall of Oak Creek Canyon from a point directly across Highway 89A from the Junipine Resort in the upper canyon, 8.4 miles *13.5 km* north of Sedona. The trail is in poor condition.

DIRECTIONS:
From the Sedona Y Go:
        North on Highway 89A (toward Flagstaff) for a distance of 8.4 miles *13.5 km* (MP 382.6) to the entrance to the Junipine Resort, which is on your left (west). There are some public parking spaces at the north end of the property, adjacent to the highway.

TRAILHEAD: There are no markings for this trail. Go across the highway to the Fire Station. The trail starts there.

DESCRIPTION: The people at Junipine have created a parking lot at the north end of their property that has space for several cars. If it is full then park along the road shoulder nearby. The trailhead is not conspicuous. You will see a Fire Station across the highway from the resort. The trail starts at the south side of the Fire Station where there is a yellow fire plug.
        This trail was built by the Purtymun family, which homesteaded the Junipine property in the late 1800s. Like other families in the canyon they needed a way to get to the rim so that they could go to Flagstaff, so they built this trail. They did not have sophisticated equipment, just picks, shovels, crowbars and maybe a little dynamite. Their practice was to leave a wagon at the top. When they wanted to go to town they would walk a horse to the top, hitch it to the wagon and then drive to Flagstaff. In town they would load the wagon with goods, perhaps bartering some of the vegetables and fruits they had grown for flour and coffee. They would then drive the wagon back to Oak Creek Canyon and chain it to a tree at the top of the trail.

After that they would carry the goods down in saddlebags. Such a trip could take three or four days.

In spite of the hardships of using the trail, the alternative was worse. There was no convenient wagon road from Sedona to Flagstaff until the Schnebly Hill Road was built in 1902. Before that the only wagon road was the old **Beaverhead** route several miles farther south. Highway 89A did not come onto the scene until much later. It was built in phases starting in the early 1920s, and it took a decade to complete.

This trail is so steep and so rough that we don't see how the Purtymuns could ever have gotten a horse up and down it. It is hard climbing for humans, who can grab onto trees for support. We rate this the worst kept and most difficult trail in the book. We do not recommend this hike but we include it as an historic trail.

If you want a good hike up the east rim of upper Oak Creek Canyon try **Cookstove**, **Harding Spring** or **Thomas Point**.

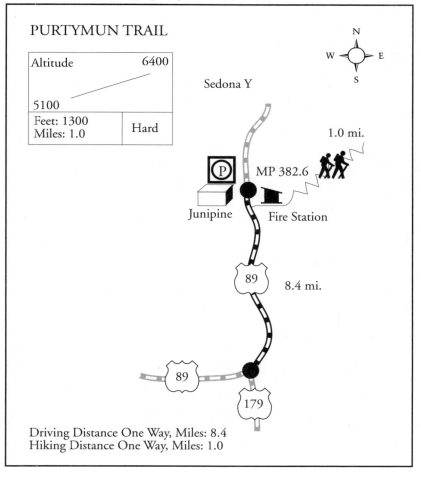

PURTYMUN TRAIL

Altitude 6400

5100

Feet: 1300
Miles: 1.0

Hard

Sedona Y

1.0 mi.

MP 382.6

Junipine

Fire Station

89

8.4 mi.

89

179

Driving Distance One Way, Miles: 8.4
Hiking Distance One Way, Miles: 1.0

RATTLESNAKE CANYON

General Information
Location Map G5
Munds Mt. USGS Map
Coconino Forest Service Map

Driving Distance One Way: 23.0 miles *36.8 km* (Time 45 minutes)
Access Road: All cars, Last 1.0 miles *1.6 km* medium gravel
Hiking Distance One Way: 0.75 miles *1.2 km* (Time 30 minutes)
How Strenuous: Moderate
Features: Remote scenic canyon

NUTSHELL: This trail takes you to the bottom of Rattlesnake Canyon, a little known beautiful spot.

DIRECTIONS:
From the Sedona Y Go:
    South on Highway 179 (toward Phoenix) for 14.7 miles *23.6 km*, to the I-17 Interchange. Turn north and head toward Flagstaff on I-17. At the 22.0 mile *35.2 km* spot you will see Exit 306 "Stoneman Lake" (MP 306.1). Make this exit. Go under I-17 into the lane marked south, to Phoenix, but look for a dirt road to your right (west), FR 647, just beyond the underpass. Turn off onto FR 647. For the first 0.75 miles *1.2 km* it is in good condition except for one gully. At the 22.75 mile *36.4 km* point you reach a T. Turn right here. The road becomes much worse, bare dirt with lots of ruts and rocks. Most cars should be able to make it to the 23.0 mile *36.8 km* point, beyond which the road is too rough. Pull off the road and park.

TRAILHEAD: There are no signs. You walk the road to the canyon rim and then hike down to the bottom.

DESCRIPTION: If you park at the 23.0 mile *36.8 km* point as we recommend, then you must walk about 0.25 miles *0.4 km* to the canyon.
    You won't have to ask *what* canyon. As you near the rim you can see it plainly. This is one of those hidden canyons that you don't see from anywhere unless you fly over it. But it is a deep and interesting canyon. The walls are quite sheer and are made of successive layers of columnar-jointed basalt. There are many such canyons in northern Arizona, but this one has more color and character than most.
    At the canyon rim you will see that the road goes down into the canyon but that no one drives it. Walk down the road. The road will disappear in about 0.10 miles *0.16 km.*

Beyond this point you will find a footpath in good condition. It is a real walking path, with erosion control and other improvements and you can see that a lot of work has been done on it. It is not a recreational trail, but is used to provide access to the gaging station that you will find at the bottom.

We think the rock walls you pass by are interesting and have some beautiful markings, including accents made by lichens and mosses.

At the bottom is a cable strung across the canyon and the gaging station, which is a sort of tall corrugated tube with a box on top. There is a depth gauge on the front of the tube showing depths as high as ten feet.

Beyond this there is a waterfall with a thirty foot drop. Water was running over it while we were there and it seemed dangerous to climb. Other sources indicate that one can climb down it, but we do not recommend dangerous climbing. From this point, Rattlesnake Canyon joins **Woods Canyon** in about 2.25 miles *3.6 km*. It is a satisfying hike just to sit at the waterfall. If you want to explore the canyon, go upstream.

RED CANYON (PALATKI) RUINS

General Information
Location Map C2
Loy Butte and Page Springs USGS Maps
Coconino Forest Service Map

Driving Distance One Way: 17.4 miles *28 km* (Time 30 minutes)
Access Road: All cars, Last 7.8 miles *12.5 km* good dirt road
Hiking Distance: Trail #1 is a 0.6 mile *1.0 km* loop; *Trail #2* is 0.3 miles *0.48 km* one way
How Strenuous: Easy
Features: Indian ruins, Pictographs, Caves

NUTSHELL:
  This adventure takes you to the Palatki Indian Ruins 17.4 miles *28 km* northwest of Sedona for a short jaunt to cliff dwellings and a meander along the base of Bear Mountain to see pictographs and caves.

DIRECTIONS:
From the Sedona Y Go:
          Southwest on Highway 89A (toward Cottonwood) a distance of 9.6 miles *15.4 km* (MP 364.5) to the Red Canyon Road. Turn right on Red Canyon Road, (FR 525) and follow it to the 12.4 mile *20 km* point where FR 525C branches to the left. Stay on FR 525, the road to the right. Follow FR 525 to the 15.4 mile *24.7 km* point, where it intersects the Boynton Pass Road, FR 152C. Stay on FR 525, the road to the left. At 15.6 miles *25 km* you will reach an intersection with FR 795. Turn right here on FR 795. At 17.4 miles *28 km* you will come to the parking area.

TRAILHEAD: There are two trails, with signs for both at the north end of the parking area.

DESCRIPTION: TRAIL NO. 1, COMPLETE LOOP 0.6 MILES *1.0 KM*. This trail, to the right of the driveway, is the one to the Palatki ruins, and it is paved. In about 0.20 miles *0.32 km* you will reach the left turn to the main ruins, requiring a short steep climb. The ruins are in two shallow caves. The first (east) ruin is the larger one, with a two story structure that contained eight rooms. The walls of the ruins are well preserved even to the juniper poles that supported doors and windows. The second ruin is smaller and also contained eight chambers, but its walls have collapsed. Date of construction is about 1200 A.D. and the site housed about 100 people. From the ruins, you will enjoy the view to the south across the Verde Valley and over to the

Black Hills and Jerome. Retrace your path to the bottom and finish the loop back to the parking lot.

TRAIL NO. 2, ONE WAY 0.30 MILES *0.48 km*. This trail is to the left (west) of the first, starting at a point across the driveway. It zigzags up to the base of a tall red butte to the left of and above the ranch house. It takes you to a series of caves at the base of the butte. Behind (north of) the first cave you will find what appears to be an ancient ruin but is really a 1920s dwelling which was a temporary residence before the ranch house was built. The string of caves continues to the west. These caves contain the largest collection of rock art in the Verde Valley, ranging from art of the ancient Sinagua to the more modern Apaches. They also contain inscriptions by Anglo pioneers. The caves end at the 0.3 mile *0.48 km* point in a black cave that has the inscription "M. F. Farrell 1900" written high on its wall.

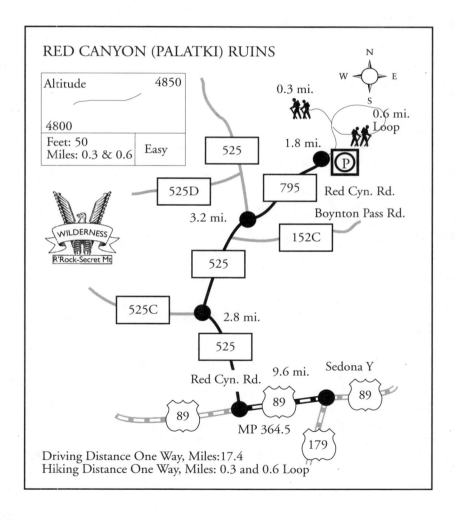

RED TANK DRAW

General Information
Location Map G6
Apache Maid and Casner Butte. USGS Maps
Coconino Forest Service Map

Driving Distance One Way: 16.1 miles *25.8 km* (Time 30 minutes)
Access Road: All cars, All paved
Hiking Distance One Way: 0.9 miles *1.5 km* (Time 1 hour)
How Strenuous: Moderate
Features: Intermittent stream, Picturesque cliffs

NUTSHELL: This hike follows the course of Red Tank Draw, 16.1 miles *25.8 km* southeast of Sedona, in the Wet Beaver Creek country. You walk along the streambed enjoying a beautiful little canyon.

DIRECTIONS:
From the Sedona Y Go:
        South on Highway 179 (toward Phoenix) for 14.7 miles *23.6 km*, to the I-17 Interchange. Instead of going onto I-17, go underneath it onto the paved road. At 15.2 miles *24.5 km*, you will come to a junction. The right fork goes to Montezuma Castle. Take the left fork (FR 618), staying on the paved road. At 16.1 miles *25.8 km*, you will see a sign reading, "Red Tank Draw" located just in front of a small bridge. There is a dirt road to the left here. Pull in on it and park.

TRAILHEAD: There is no designated or marked trail. You go down into the streambed and walk the canyon upstream (north).

DESCRIPTION: From the parking place, you simply walk down to the streambed at any place you choose. It is easy to enter it anywhere in this area because the canyon walls are low. Farther upstream the walls become higher.
        The best time we found for this hike was in late April, when the stream was carrying just enough water to be interesting. We tried it in early April and the runoff waters were too high for hiking. You can hike it when it is dry also, which is most of the year, but we think a little running water adds interest.
        At the place where you go into the canyon there are two forks. It doesn't much matter which fork you choose to hike, as they will merge upstream. This is a rock hopping hike, as the bottom of the draw is boulder strewn. Such hikes can be fun but they are hard on the feet.

As you move upstream, the canyon will deepen. At about 0.6 miles *1.0 km* you come to a narrow spot with sheer red walls, not tremendously high as Northern Arizona canyons go, about thirty feet, but very pleasing to the eye. The area is one of geologic uplifts, the result of which has been to twist the rock into some very interesting angles. Look for swallows' nests throughout this area. The birds make their nests by cementing countless beakfuls of mud into globular nests that hang from the underside of rock shelves. They are about the size of a baseball.

You will move out of the most scenic part of Red Tank Draw soon afterwards. At 0.9 miles *1.5 km* you will come to an old barbed wire fence with a gate. We think this is a good stopping place for the hike, though we have gone much farther.

RED TANK DRAW

Altitude   4100

4000

Feet: 100
Miles: 0.9   Mod.

Sedona Y

89

89

179

14.7 mi.

I-17

0.9 mi.

I-17

618

1.4 mi.

Bridge

Driving Distance One Way, Miles: 16.1
Hiking Distance One Way, Miles: 0.9

ROBBERS ROOST

General Information
Location Map C1
Loy Butte and Page Springs USGS Maps
Coconino Forest Service Map

Driving Distance One Way: 19.2 miles *30.1 km* (Time 30 minutes)
Access Road: All cars, Last 9.6 miles *15.4 km* good dirt road
Hiking Distance One Way: 1.5 miles *2.4 km* (Time 45 minutes)
How Strenuous: Easy
Features: Fascinating cave with unique window

NUTSHELL: This is a short hike to an interesting cave in a red butte located 19.2 miles *30.1 km* northwest of Sedona.

DIRECTIONS:
From the Sedona Y Go:
      Southwest on Highway 89A (toward Cottonwood) a distance of 9.6 miles *15.4 km* (MP 364.5) to the Red Canyon Road. Turn right on Red Canyon Road, also known as FR 525, and follow it to the 12.4 mile *20 km* point where FR 525C branches to the left. Turn left on FR 525C and follow it to the 19.2 miles *30.1 km* point. There you will see a rough road branching to the right marked FR 9530. Take this but drive it only a short distance to the top of the hill, where you will park.

TRAILHEAD: You walk up the road, FR 9530, for 1.1 miles *1.8 km*. There you will see the trail going down into a ravine to your right. It is not signed.

DESCRIPTION: If you have a high clearance vehicle and tough tires you can drive right up to the trailhead and save a mile of walking, but don't try to make it in an ordinary passenger car.
      As you walk up the road you approach Casner Mountain. Your target is the muffin shaped red butte just in front of and on the right hand side of the mountain. Robbers Roost is located on the far side of that butte.
      At the trailhead you will see an area to your left where the vegetation is matted down because of cars parking there. Look for the trail to your right. Usually there are cairns marking the beginning of the trail. The trail goes straight downhill into the bottom of a ravine, then goes up the other side.
      The trail, after rising from the bottom of the ravine, curls around to the north side of the butte and climbs about two-thirds of the way to the top of it. At 0.35 miles *0.56 km* from the beginning of the trail, the trail forks.

The right fork goes to the top. Ignore it for now and take the left fork. This will require that you walk out on the face of the butte on the slickrock (a misnomer, as the rock actually gives very good traction, like sandpaper). As you go around the bend of the rock you will see two metal rods five feet high sticking vertically out of the rock face.

After that you will see the cave. Rock walls have been built at the mouth of the cave to support dirt fill that was placed there to make the floor of the cave level. There are even steps to the "door" of the cave.

The cave looks out to the northeast, toward Bear Mountain and Maroon Mountain. Down below it there is a cattle tank.

There is a circular window in the cave that looks more to the south. This window is unique. There is nothing else like it in the Sedona area. The cave gets its name, Robbers Roost, from the fanciful notion that this would be a good hideout for robbers, who could use the window as a lookout. It was used by a moonshiner during Prohibition.

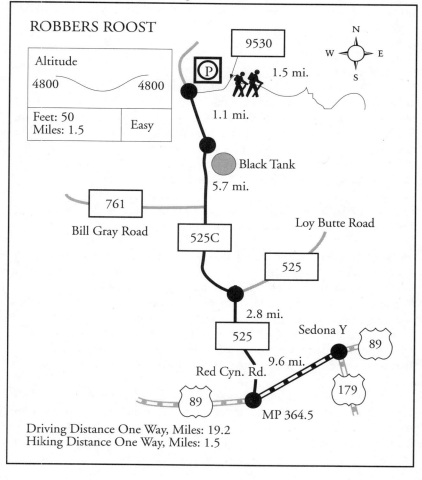

ROBBERS ROOST

Altitude

4800   4800

Feet: 50
Miles: 1.5   Easy

9530
1.5 mi.

1.1 mi.

Black Tank

5.7 mi.

761

Bill Gray Road

525C

Loy Butte Road

525

2.8 mi.

525

Sedona Y

89

179

9.6 mi.

Red Cyn. Rd.

89

MP 364.5

Driving Distance One Way, Miles: 19.2
Hiking Distance One Way, Miles: 1.5

SACRED MOUNTAIN

General Information
Location Map G6
Casner Butte USGS Map
Coconino Forest Service Map

Driving Distance One Way: 18.0 miles *29 km* (Time 30 minutes)
Access Road: All cars, Last 0.8 miles *1.3 km* good dirt road
Hiking Distance One Way: 0.35 miles *0.56 km* (Time 30 minutes)
How Strenuous: Moderate
Features: Indian ruins, Views

NUTSHELL: Located 18.0 miles *29 km* southeast of Sedona, this special mountain takes moderate effort to climb. At the top are pueblo ruins and fine views.

DIRECTIONS:
From the Sedona Y Go:
      South on Highway 179 (toward Phoenix) for 14.7 miles *23.6 km*, to the I-17 Interchange. Instead of going onto I-17, go underneath it onto a paved road, FR 618. Stay on FR 618. The paving ends at the bridges at the Beaver Creek Campground. Half a mile beyond, at 17.9 miles *29 km*, as the road is curving right, you will see a dirt road, FR 9201A, to your left. Pull off on this. You will see that the road leads to a fence. Try to get as close to the fence as you can (it's about 0.2 miles *0.32 km*) and park.

TRAILHEAD: You will not see a trail sign. Go through the gate and turn right and walk parallel to the fence. The path is obvious.

DESCRIPTION: The mountains that are constantly on the northern horizon as you drive through the Beaver Creek area are all part of the Mogollon Rim, a giant uplift that runs from Silver City, New Mexico to Ashfork, Arizona. As you come around a curve in the road, Sacred Mountain comes into sight. It is really more of a butte than a mountain in this country full of mountains, and it stands alone in front of the rim. It is set apart by its color—white—against the darker colors of the rim, which are gray, black and red. At times, when the low evening sun hits Sacred Mountain, the mountain seems to glow.

      We saw a beautiful example of this one March evening when we were at the nearby Montezuma's Well (a recommended visit). From the top of the well we looked northwest and saw Sacred Mountain as if it were isolated by a spotlight—magic. One can well understand why the ancient

Indians thought that the mountain was sacred.

At the fence surrounding Sacred Mountain there is a small sign indicating that the ruins are protected by Federal law. Go through the gate and immediately turn right, walking along parallel to the fence. You will pick up the trail there and will see it going up the toe of the mountain that faces the road. The trail will take you to a sign with a register to add your name to. At the top of the mountain you will find extensive ruins that have been partially excavated. They have also been thoroughly pot hunted, more's the pity. Please do not disturb them.

The site has not been restored, just investigated. The remains of many walls have been uncovered so that you can see the outline of the pueblo. It was a fairly large site, perhaps as large as Tuzigoot.

SCHNEBLY HILL BUTTES

General Information
Location Map E5
Munds Mt. and Munds Park USGS Maps
Coconino Forest Service Map

Driving Distance One Way: 5.5 miles *8.8 km* (Time 20 minutes)
Access Road: All cars, Last 4.7 miles *7.5 km* good gravel road
Hiking Distance One Way: 0.60 miles *1.0 km* (Time 45 minutes)
How Strenuous: Moderate
Features: Views, Fascinating rock formations and sculptures

NUTSHELL: This is a scrambling, bushwhacking experience just off the Schnebly Hill Road, only a mile east of Sedona as the crow flies.

DIRECTIONS:
From the Sedona Y Go:
    South on Highway 179 (toward Phoenix) for a distance of 0.3 miles *0.48 km* (MP 313.1) to the Schnebly Hill Road. It is just across the bridge past Tlaquepaque. Turn left onto the Schnebly Hill Road. It is paved for the first half mile and then turns into a gravel road that is all right for any car unless the road is muddy. At the 5.0 mile *8.0 km* point, you will see a gate. At 5.5 miles *8.8 km* is a knoll to your left fronted by an apron big enough to hold three or four cars. Park on this apron.

TRAILHEAD: At the parking place.

DESCRIPTION: You park at the foot of a knoll. There you will see a footpath going straight up to the top of the knoll. Take it. On top you will see some fine views and you will find several paths heading toward the cliffs to the west.
    Look straight ahead to the west and you will see a tall butte across the valley. Pick out the main trail going toward the butte. As you reach the base of the butte, one trail will go to your left (south) skirting the base, while the other goes up. Go up. The trail is pretty easy except for one place where you must climb up a red stone ledge. You need to find the gap that makes this climb easy.
    You will top out on a saddle. To your left (south) you can go to a point jutting out into Bear Wallow Canyon. The right hand trail goes up to a taller butte.
    Try the south trail first. The point is narrow and has several stages or landings. You can walk around it for magnificent views. This is a real

"Ah!" experience.

If you are afraid of heights, adjust your comfort level as to how far out on the point you want to go. Daredevils can walk right out to the cantilevered tip of a "diving board" where it's 1200 feet straight down to join Elvis. Sissies can stay well back on solid footing and still get great views.

It's fun to watch cars coming up the Schnebly Hill Road from this point. If they see you they will wonder how you got there and why you're foolishly risking your neck.

From the diving board it's on to the higher butte. It is an easier climb than you would expect from its appearance. The main path is quite distinct and gentle. The views are not as good as you would hope because another butte to the west partially blocks southward sights. You do have good views to the north.

Coming down is easy. The only trick is to find an easy-to-descend crevice in the sandstone ledge about halfway down.

SCHNEBLY HILL BUTTES

Altitude   5600

5500
Feet: 100
Miles: 0.6   Mod.

0.6 mi.

89   Sedona Y   89

0.3 mi. 179   Schnebly Hill Road

MP 313.1   5.2 mi.

179

Driving Distance One Way, Miles: 5.5
Hiking Distance One Way, Miles: 0.6

SCHNEBLY HILL TRAIL #158

General Information
Location Map E5
Munds Mt. and Munds Park USGS Maps
Coconino Forest Service Map

Driving Distance One Way: 5.5 miles *9.0 km* (Time 30 minutes)
Access Road: All cars, Last 4.7 miles *7.5 km* good gravel road
Hiking Distance One Way: 2.4 miles *3.9 km* (Time 1.5 hours)
How Strenuous: Moderate
Features: Historic road, Views

NUTSHELL: This trail climbs to the top of Schnebly Hill, on an old road, then swings south and follows the edge of the rim to join the **Munds Mountain Trail**.

DIRECTIONS:
From the Sedona Y Go:
        South on Highway 179 (toward Phoenix) for a distance of 0.3 miles *0.5 km* (MP 313.1) to the Schnebly Hill Road. It is just across the bridge past Tlaquepaque. Turn left onto the Schnebly Hill Road. It is paved for the first half mile and then turns into a dirt road that is all right for any car unless the road is muddy. At 5.0 miles *8.0 km* you will see a gate made of very thick steel pipes used to close the road in winter. At 5.5 miles *8.8 km*, you will see a low redrock butte to your left with a parking area big enough for four cars. Park there.

TRAILHEAD: Walk down the road about twenty yards from where you have parked. You will see the trailhead marker to your left, on the uphill side.

DESCRIPTION: The first half of the trail is the original 1902 alignment of the Schnebly Hill Road, and as you walk along it, you will have fascinating and ever changing views. First you will look down into the Bear Wallow-Mitten Ridge area. As you move farther south (uphill) you will begin to see around the south end of the ridge into Sedona. At the top you can see right through a natural corridor into the Verde Valley. There are many superb vista points.
        At the 1.2 miles *1.92 km* point look to your right just as you come to the top of the grade, at a hairpin curve. Here you will see a footpath going to your right (south), into the trees. Follow it. This is the new leg of the trail. It is marked by cairns and takes you south along the rim. In some places you

are right on the rim and have choice views into colorful country. At others you go inland a bit. You will pass through two gates. The second gate is at Committee Tank, located to your left (east), a favorite spot for wildlife.

Soon after, the trail reaches a thin ridge connecting to Munds Mountain. This ridge is a wonderful and unusual land feature. From the ridge you can see to the north into the Schnebly Hill area and south into Jacks Canyon, a great double-header. You are high enough to have sweeping views out over the landscape on top of the Mogollon Rim. The San Francisco Peaks stand out and are very attractive from here. The ridge then dips down to join the **Munds Mountain Trail** at the 2.4 miles *3.9 km* point, a place marked by a super cairn. The **Jacks Canyon Trail** terminates here, coming up from the bottom of Jacks Canyon.

The Munds Mountain Trail is steep, climbing 500 feet in half a mile to the top.

SCHNEBLY HILL TRAIL #158

Altitude 6340

5490

Feets: 850
Miles: 2.4

Mod.

Sedona Y

89 89

0.3 mi. 179 Schnebly Hill Road

MP 313.1 5.2 mi.

179

1.2 mi.

1.2 mi.

Driving Distance One Way, Miles: 5.5
Hiking Distance One Way, Miles: 2.4

SCHNEBLY TO-MARG'S DRAW

General Information
Location Map E5
Sedona and Munds Mt. USGS Maps
Coconino Forest Service Map

Driving Distance One Way: 0.9 miles *1.4 km* (Time 5 minutes)
Access Road: All cars, All paved
Hiking Distance One Way: 1.3 miles *2.1 km* (Time 40 minutes)
How Strenuous: Easy
Features: Views

NUTSHELL: Marg's Draw is a beautiful area in Sedona's backyard, being a bowl surrounded by the Crimson Cliffs, Munds Mountain, Lee Mountain and Twin Buttes. This short hike takes you around the base of the Crimson Cliffs and out on the Schnebly Hill Road.

DIRECTIONS:
From the Sedona Y Go:
      South on Highway 179 (toward Phoenix) for a distance of 0.7 miles *1.2 km* (MP 312.8) to Sombart Lane, which is just beyond a Circle K store. Turn left onto Sombart Lane and follow it to the 0.9 mile *1.4 km* point, where there is an unpaved parking area to the right. Park there.

TRAILHEAD: You will see no trail signs. You will see a footpath going uphill through a wooden gate framed by high steel pipe fence posts.

DESCRIPTION: You will hike uphill a bit to get through the wooden gate and then you will reach a flat. There are several paths and trails through the flat area, so follow these directions carefully. At 0.27 miles *0.44 km* you will reach a fork with two trails. Take the left fork. At 0.35 miles *0.56 km* the trail splits three ways. Take the left trail. At 0.375 miles *0.6 km* the **Marg's Draw Trail** goes to the right along a redrock shelf. The Schnebly-Marg's Connection forks to the left and takes you around the base of the Crimson Cliffs and to the north, linking up with the Schnebly Hill Road. The **Snoopy Rock Trail** is the middle fork. It heads straight for the cliff. You want to take the left fork.
      Once you get the trails sorted out and get started on the Schnebly-Marg's Connection, this trail is easy to follow. It proceeds along the contour of the Crimson Cliffs, not too close to the base, and heads north toward the Schnebly Hill Road. The Crimson Cliffs are beautiful and walking along so near to them is a wonderful experience. At 0.48 miles *0.77 km* you will reach

another fork. Take the path to the right. A few paces beyond that a trail comes in from the right. Ignore it.

At 0.53 miles *0.85 km* a trail to the left takes off downhill. Ignore it. Just beyond that is a trail to the right. Ignore it.

At this point you are at a place where you can look to your left (west) and see into uptown Sedona. This is an unusual vantage point from which to see the town. Beyond this place a trail goes left. Ignore it. You are a little closer to the cliffs here but never get right up to them.

At 0.73 miles *1.2 km* the forest begins to change to a cypress forest and the trail crosses several drainages coming down from the cliffs.

At 1.2 miles *1.9 km* a faint trail to the left goes down into a gully and then it goes up to join the Schnebly Hill Road. The main path goes on a bit farther, then branches left to join the road. The place is marked by a small cairn. The point where you come onto the Schnebly Hill Road is about 0.80 miles *1.3 km* from the stop sign.

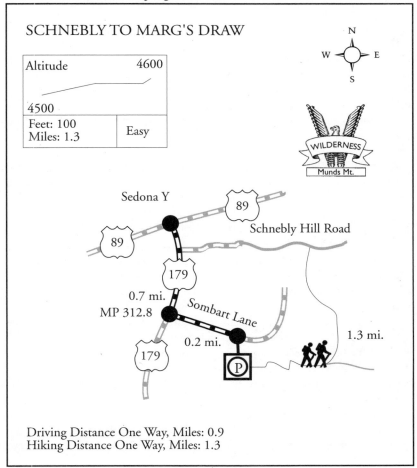

SCHNEBLY TO MARG'S DRAW

Altitude	4600
4500	
Feet: 100 Miles: 1.3	Easy

Sedona Y

89

Schnebly Hill Road

89

179

0.7 mi.

MP 312.8

Sombart Lane

0.2 mi.

179

1.3 mi.

Driving Distance One Way, Miles: 0.9
Hiking Distance One Way, Miles: 1.3

SCHUERMAN MOUNTAIN #56

General Information
Location Map E3
Sedona USGS Map
Coconino Forest Service Map

Driving Distance One Way: 7.3 miles *11.7 km* (Time 15 minutes)
Access Road: All vehicles, All paved
Hiking Distance One Way: 3.0 miles *4.8 km* (Time 1.5 hours)
How Strenuous: Moderate
Features: Views

NUTSHELL: This sprawling mountain southwest of Sedona is rather drab but is a platform for great views.

DIRECTIONS:
From the Sedona Y Go:
    Southwest on Highway 89 (toward Cottonwood) for a distance of 5.5 miles 9.0 *km* (MP 368.6) to the Lower Red Rock Loop Road. Turn left on the Lower Red Rock Loop Road and follow it to the 7.3 miles *11.7 km* point, where you will see a parking apron to your right big enough for four cars.

TRAILHEAD: Walk across the road and go back the way you came for several hundred feet, looking for a horse trail going off to your right (east). There is a lath marker for the trail.

DESCRIPTION: Schuerman Mountain is a shallow but wide mountain located southwest of Sedona. The trail zigzags up to a saddle on the low southwest side of the mountain. It is a good trail, winding its way uphill so that the climb is gradual. Almost immediately you are rewarded with good views.
    You will come to a saddle, then turn north and begin climbing the higher parts of the mountain, with many excellent views. Once you have reached the 0.66 miles *1.1 km* point, the slope becomes more level and the hike is relatively easy. Soon after, you will see to your right (east), a steep canyon with interesting lava formations, a good example of columnar jointing in the thick lava.
    When you reach the 1.5 mile point *2.4 km*, the trail dips down into a basin where a pond is located (though it is often dry). From here you make another climb to the highest saddle, which you reach at the 2.4 mile point

3.6 km. Here the trail forks. We recommend that you take the right trail. It goes out onto an overlook that gives you good views of **Cathedral Rock** and Oak Creek. This viewpoint is about 0.20 miles *0.32 km* from the saddle. The left fork goes to the highest point on the mountain, about one hundred feet of climbing in 0.4 miles *0.64 km.*

Schuerman Mountain is a shield volcano like **House Mountain, Windmill Mountain** and others in the area. This means it is rather shallow and sprawling with a center that is not very deep.   The mountain's name comes from Sedona pioneer Henry Schuerman, a German immigrant who spelled his name Schürman. The standard way to Americanize that spelling is to place an e after the ü, so that the correct spelling would be Schuerman. For some unknown reasons the persons who prepared the government map spelled the name Scheurman and changed the name.

SECRET CANYON #121

General Information
Location Map C4
Loy Butte and Wilson Mt. USGS Maps
Coconino Forest Service Map

Driving Distance One Way: 8.6 miles *13.8 km* (Time 30 minutes)
Access Road: Most cars, Last 3.4 miles *5.5 km* medium dirt
Hiking Distance One Way: 2.5 miles *4.0 km* (Time 90 minutes)
How Strenuous: Moderate
Features: Views, Remote canyon

NUTSHELL: This beautiful canyon, 8.6 miles *13.8 km* northwest of uptown Sedona, provides a delightful hike along a streambed through the redrocks. **A Personal Favorite.**

DIRECTIONS:
From the Sedona Y Go:
Southwest on Highway 89A (toward Cottonwood) for 3.2 miles *5.2 km* (MP 371) to Dry Creek Road. Turn right on Dry Creek Road (FR 152C) and proceed to the 5.2 mile *8.4 km* point. Turn right on FR 152, the Vultee Arch Road, and follow it to the 8.6 mile *13.8 km* point. You will see a road sign pointing to the trail turnoff. Make a sharp turn to your left into the parking area.

TRAILHEAD: There is a rusty sign at the roadside where you turn in reading, "Secret Canyon #121."

DESCRIPTION: The access road to this hike, FR 152, is rough but has been improved since the first edition of this book. We frequently see people in ordinary passenger cars driving this road, but be on the lookout for ruts and rocks.
Watch carefully for the turnoff to the Secret Canyon trailhead. The road in this area is lined with a screen of brush and trees and the entry is a brief opening in this screen. A large sign has been installed, making this trailhead easier to find.
The parking space is limited. It can hold only about five cars.
From the parking area the trail goes immediately to Dry Creek and then turns right and runs along the bottom of Dry Creek, going up toward its headwater. If water is running in Dry Creek you may not be able to make this hike, as the trail winds back and forth across the creek several times.
The trail takes you through some beautiful back country, passing

through impressive redrocks. At 0.60 miles *1.0 km* you will see the **H S Canyon** trail taking off to the left.

We like this part of the Secret Canyon hike the best, where you are going through the redrocks. There are several side canyons that are fun to explore, and are recommended.

At about 2.25 miles *3.6 km* you come up out of the canyon bottom and walk along the side of the canyon. At 2.5 miles *4.0 km* you will enter a pine forest. Up to this forest, the hike has been unshaded, but from this point the pines provide ample shade.

For the purposes of this book, which features day hikes, we have you stop here in the cool pines at 2.5 miles *4.0 km*. The trail goes farther.

SHOOTING RANGE RIDGE EAST

General Information
Location Map D4
Wilson Mountain USGS Map
Coconino Forest Service Map

Driving Distance One Way: 1.5 miles *2.4 km* (Time 10 minutes)
Access Road: All cars. Last 0.40 miles *0.65 km* medium gravel
Hiking Distance One Way: 0.7 miles *1.2 km* (Time 40 minutes)
How Strenuous: Moderate
Features: Easy to reach, Good views

NUTSHELL: You climb to the top of a 300 foot high ridge for excellent views.

DIRECTIONS:
From the Y in Sedona Go:
        North on Highway on 89A (toward Flagstaff) for 0.30 miles to Jordan Road, which is in the middle of uptown Sedona. Turn left (north) and take Jordan Road to its end, where the paving stops. Keep going on the unpaved road. Your goal is the former Shooting Range. At 1.1 miles *1.8 km*, you will intersect a private road. Turn left here. You will reach the Shooting Range gate at 1.5 miles *2.4 km*. Park outside.

TRAILHEAD: This is not a signed trail. The trail starts on a side road located just in front of the gate to the old shooting range.

DESCRIPTION: Just before you reach the gate to the old shooting range you will see a road to your left (west). Park and walk back to this road, then follow it. You will find that it is a jeep trail. Keep following it uphill as far as it goes. It soon ends and a foot path starts. This path was marked by cairns when we hiked it and was easy to follow.
        On the way up you will begin to enjoy views that are even better at the top. You will reach a well-defined trail on the top of the ridge at 0.46 miles *0.75 km*. From here turn to the left and follow the trail out to its end, which is on the toe of the ridge. Along the way you will enter an area where there are steep redrock cliffs to either side. We enjoy looking down on these. The trail ends at a great viewpoint where you look down on upper Sedona. To your left you have fine views of Wilson Mountain. To your right you see into the Capitol Butte and Coffee Pot Rock areas.
        After you have had your fill of the views you can go back the way you came or you can check out the balance of the ridge. From the point

where you came up to the ridgetop trail, you walk along the top for a short distance. Then the trail dips down to a saddle, and rises again, taking you to a fence at 0.1 miles *0.16 km*. From there the trail generally follows the fence line. You will come to a gate at 0.23 miles *0.37 km*, where the **Shooting Range Ridge West Trail** takes off downhill to your left.

Go beyond this point about five paces, where you will see a trail in a deep groove going downhill to your right. This is the trail to take on the way back. It intersects the Brins Mesa Trail at 0.4 miles *0.65 km*, at a point that is only 0.05 miles *0.08 km* from the gate.

If you want to go on out to the far end of the ridge, you will get to it at 0.5 miles *0.8 km*. From there you will have exceptionally fine views of Brins Mesa and Wilson Mountain.

This is a nice little hike, a good choice when the backroads are too muddy or you don't have time to drive far out into the country.

SHOOTING RANGE RIDGE EAST

Altitude	4700
4500	

Feet: 200 Miles: 0.7	Mod.

N
W — E
S

Old Shooting Range

Brins Mesa Trailhead

P

0.7 mi.

1.2 mi.

WILDERNESS
R'Rock-Secret Mt

Jordan Road

Sedona Y

89

0.3 mi.

89

179

Driving Distance One Way, Miles: 1.5
Hiking Distance One Way, Miles: 0.7

SHOOTING RANGE RIDGE WEST

General Information
Location Map D4
Sedona and Wilson Mt. USGS Maps
Coconino Forest Service Map

Driving Distance One Way: 3.0 miles *5.0 km* (Time 10 minutes)
Access Road: All cars, All paved
Hiking Distance One Way: 1.35 miles *2.2 km* (Time 45 minutes)
How Strenuous: Moderate
Features: Views

NUTSHELL: Starting from Devil's Kitchen in the Soldier Pass area, this moderate hike takes you to a scenic ridge dividing Soldier Pass from the upper Jordan Road area of Sedona.

DIRECTIONS:
From the Sedona Y Go:
Southwest on Highway 89A (toward Cottonwood) for a distance of 1.25 miles *2.4 km* (MP 372.8) to Soldier Pass Road. Turn right onto Soldier Pass Road and follow it to the 2.75 mile *4.4 km* point, where it intersects Rim Shadows Drive, where you turn right. Follow Rim Shadows a short distance, to a three-way intersection. Go straight onto Canyon Shadows and follow it to the 3.0 miles *5.0 km* point. There you will see a sign saying "National Forest Access." Take the road to your left there and park in the parking area. This is well defined and spacious.

TRAILHEAD: You will see a rusty sign at the parking area reading, "Soldier Pass Trail #66."

DESCRIPTION: This trail is an old jeep road and is still used by jeep tours. Walk down the road 0.10 miles *0.16 km*, where you will see a road branching off to your right marked FR 904B. Take this road. You will climb uphill a short distance, reaching **Devil's Kitchen** at 0.35 miles *0.6 km*. See the entry for Devil's Kitchen for information about it. It is the largest sinkhole in the Sedona area.

The jeep road to Devil's Kitchen appears to continue around the sinkhole. Follow it to the point where the road ends, which is about two hundred yards beyond the sinkhole.

Keep walking at roughly the same level as the road, staying near the base of the cliff. As you come to the end of a slickrock ledge you will see some cairns marking the trail you are to take. Look carefully for them, as the trail is rather faint and you need the cairns to guide you. Farther along, two cairn-marked trails fork to the right. The second trail that you will reach is better than the first one. Here you will go to the right, down into a gully. You will walk up out of the gully on the other side, then cross a second ravine. From there you will turn left and walk up a small canyon.

At 0.60 miles *1.0 km* you will join another trail. Take the fork to the left. At 0.70 miles *1.2 km* another trail joins in. Here you are walking along a streambed. You will see a path to your right going up the ridge. Take it. You will reach an intermediate top at 0.90 miles *1.5 km*. There is a fence at this point. Uphill a few feet from this place there is a gate in the fence. Go through the gate, then turn right and follow the fence to the true top of the ridge.

You will come out onto red slickrock, where you get great views.

SHOOTING RANGE RIDGE WEST

Altitude 4600

4400

Feet: 200
Miles: 1.35 | Mod.

Devil's Kitchen

0.1 mi. / 0.25 mi.

1.0 mi.

Rim Shadows

1.5 mi.

0.25 mi.

Cyn. Shadows

WILDERNESS
R'Rock-Secret Mt

Soldier Pass Road

1.25 mi.

Sedona Y

89

MP 372.8

89

89

179

Driving Distance One Way, Miles: 3.0
Hiking Distance One Way, Miles: 1.35

SLIDE ROCK

General Information
Location Map C5
Wilson Mt. USGS Map
Coconino Forest Service Map

Driving Distance One Way: 6.9 miles *11.1 km* (Time 15 minutes)
Access Road: All cars, All paved
Hiking Distance One Way: 0.5 miles *0.8 km* (Time 30 minutes)
How Strenuous: Moderate
Features: Slide Rock State Park

NUTSHELL: You enjoy two hiking trails in Slide Rock State Park 6.9 miles *11.1 km* north of Sedona, one at water's edge and the other on the cliffs above Oak Creek.

DIRECTIONS:
From The Y in Sedona Go:
 North on Highway 89A (toward Flagstaff) a distance of 6.9 miles *11.1 km* (MP 381.1) to the entrance to Slide Rock State Park. The park is well marked and signed and you will have no trouble finding it. Pull in to the park (there is an entry fee) and park on the large lot.

TRAILHEAD: From the parking lot, walk upstream along a paved walkway. When you get to the Apple Packing Shed, you will be at the place where the two hiking trails start.

DESCRIPTION: (1) **Creekside Trail**: At the Packing Shed you will see a flight of steps going down to Oak Creek. Take the steps. You will emerge onto a long redrock ledge going upstream. It is easy and fun to walk along the ledge, enjoying the water and the redrock cliffs on either side. This is a favorite place for visitors and is likely to be crowded. You will see a place in the creek where the water has cut a channel into the bedrock. This is the slide of Slide Rock and you will probably see people using it, as they sit in the water at the beginning of the channel and let the current sweep them down to its end in a deep pool.
 There are well-worn trails at the base of the cliffs and also at the edge of the water. When the water is low, you can walk across the creek on a duckboard bridge, but we think the best sights are on the west bank, the side you start on. The trails end at an interesting old shed built of rock in front of an irrigation flume at about 0.5 miles *0.8 km*. From there you can rock hop upstream for a considerable distance depending on the depth of the

water and your desire to explore.

(2) **Clifftop Trail**: Now go back to the top of the stairs. There you will see a sign for the Cliff Top Trail. The trail runs along the top of the cliffs parallel to the creek, providing several places where you can step off the trail and go over to the cliff tops to look down on Slide Rock. The Cliff Top Trail ends at about 0.10 mile *0.16 km* at the ruins of a concrete gatehouse that controlled the flow of water in the irrigation ditch. You can go a few paces beyond this for a view of the irrigation flume winding its way around the face of cliffs, but can go no farther due to a *No Trespassing* sign.

Slide Rock has been a popular spot for years, but its use soared when the state bought it and improved the access and parking. In the height of the tourist season, it can be so crowded as to be annoying. We like to visit it in the off season in order to avoid the throngs.

SLIDE ROCK

5000	Altitude
	4950
Feet: 50 Miles: 0.5	Mod.

0.5 mi.

89

Slide Rock

MP 381.1

P

6.9 mi. 89

Sedona Y

179

89

Driving Distance One Way, Miles: 6.9
Hiking Distance One Way, Miles: 0.5

SMOKE TRAIL

General Information
Location Map F3
Sedona USGS Map
Coconino Forest Service Map

Driving Distance One Way: 8.8 miles *14.1 km* (Time 15 minutes)
Access Road: All vehicles, All paved
Hiking Distance One Way: 0.40 miles *0.64 km* (Time 15 minutes)
How Strenuous: Easy
Features: Creekside shady nature walk

NUTSHELL: This easy trail, located in Red Rock State Park 8.8 miles *14.1 km* southwest of Sedona, takes you from the Visitor Center down to the creek bank, where you take a leisurely creekside walk to the Cottonwood Picnic Area, using a booklet to enjoy a self-guided tour.

DIRECTIONS:
From the Sedona Y Go:
Southwest on Highway 89A (toward Cottonwood) for a distance of 5.5 miles *8.8 km* (MP 368.6) to the Lower Red Rock Loop Road. Turn left on the Lower Red Rock Loop Road and follow it to the 8.5 miles *13.6 km* point, where you will see the entry to Red Rock State Park. Turn right into the park. You will come to a toll booth where an admission is charged. From that point, drive to the Visitor Center and park there, at 8.8 miles *14.1 km.*

TRAILHEAD: This is a marked and maintained trail, part of the network of trails in the park. Go down through the Visitor Center. Though the center is not marked as the trailhead for this hike, it is the starting point for it.

DESCRIPTION: Enjoy the Visitor Center and then walk through it, turning right on the paved trail. At 0.08 miles *0.13 km* you will come to the first trail junction. Here the Smoke Trail forks to the right, where Sentinel Crossing is located. Turn right here and go down to the creek. At creekside you will find a small lecture area, where a few seats have been set up around a lectern. There is a nice bench facing the creek where you can sit and watch the water. You will also find the Sentinel Trail crossing, which is not really a trail in its own right, just a low bridge across the creek to give the hiker trail access. Where the Smoke Trail turns to the right, you will find a metal box attached to a pole. Take a trail guide from it, then follow the trail downstream along the creek bank.

A lot of work has been done on this trail to define it and make it comfortable. It is easy to walk and very relaxing with its shade and the water of Oak Creek sliding by. The booklet makes the walk even more enjoyable. Be sure to sit on the bench and look for the petroglyphs high on the cliffs above you.

In 0.3 miles *0.48 km* the trail swings away (to your right) from the creek and goes up to the Cottonwood Picnic Area. From the Visitor Center to the Cottonwood Picnic Area is 0.35 miles *0.6 km.*

On the way back, you have an option. You will see a side trail going uphill to your left less than one-tenth of a mile from the Cottonwood Picnic Area. This trail winds up to the parking lot at the Visitor Center. It is about 130 yards to the top, at the parking lot.

The dedicated hiker may find this trail too short and simple to be of much interest but we noted a number of elderly people who were obviously enjoying it, and it is informative.

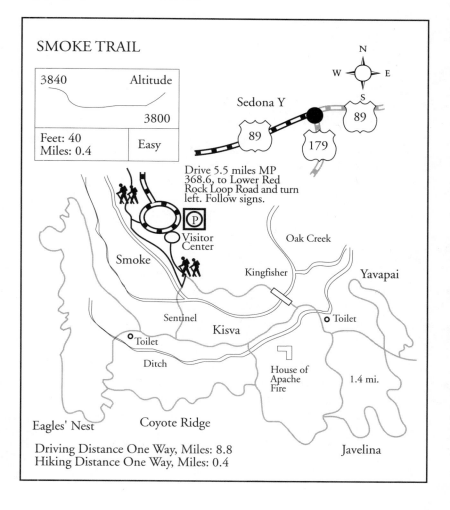

SMOKE TRAIL

3840	Altitude
	3800
Feet: 40 Miles: 0.4	Easy

Sedona Y

89

89

179

N
W E
S

Drive 5.5 miles MP 368.6, to Lower Red Rock Loop Road and turn left. Follow signs.

P

Visitor Center

Smoke

Oak Creek

Kingfisher

Yavapai

Sentinel

Kisva

o Toilet

o Toilet

Ditch

House of Apache Fire

1.4 mi.

Eagles' Nest

Coyote Ridge

Javelina

Driving Distance One Way, Miles: 8.8
Hiking Distance One Way, Miles: 0.4

SNOOPY ROCK

General Information
Location Map E5
Sedona and Munds Mt. USGS Maps
Coconino Forest Service Map

Driving Distance One Way: 0.9 miles *1.4 km 1.8 km* (Time 5 minutes)
Access Road: All cars, All paved
Hiking Distance One Way: 1.1 miles *1.8 km* (Time 60 minutes)
How Strenuous: Moderate
Features: Views, Favorite rock formation

NUTSHELL: A very nice, very accessible hike that takes you to Snoopy Rock, which is located on the Crimson Cliffs at the north end of Marg's Draw, only 0.9 miles *1.4 km* from the Y. This hike is fun, a good one when you don't have much time or the roads are muddy.

DIRECTIONS:
From the Sedona Y Go:
    South on Highway 179 (toward Phoenix) for a distance of 0.7 miles *1.2 km* (MP 312.8) to Sombart Lane, which is just beyond a Circle K store. Turn left onto Sombart Lane and follow it 0.2 miles *0.32 km* to a point that is 0.9 miles *1.4 km,* from the Y, where there is an unpaved parking area to your right, where the paved road curves left. Park in the unpaved lot.

TRAILHEAD: You will see no trail signs. You will see a footpath going uphill through a gate framed by high steel pipe fence posts.

DESCRIPTION: Go through the gate. The trail will take you uphill to a flat area where you will see several other trails. Follow the directions carefully so that you do not get off on the wrong trail.
    The easiest way to stay on the right trail is to know what your objective is. If you know Snoopy Rock, then it is simple. If not, look to your left (north). You will see large red cliffs. To your farthest left is a lower formation with a couple of comparatively short red columns rising from it. This is your goal.
    At 0.27 miles *0.44 km* you will reach a well-defined fork. Take the left fork. At 0.35 miles *0.56 km* the trail splits again. Go left (north). In a few feet there is a third fork, where you go right (NE). You will know you have the correct trail if it brings you closer to the cliff. Once we got the trails sorted out, the Snoopy Rock trail became evident, well-traveled and marked with cairns.

From about 0.40 miles *0.65 km* you can see how Snoopy Rock gets its name. If you use your imagination you can see Snoopy sleeping on top of his doghouse. The column to your left is his feet, while the column to the right is his nose. Sometimes it is one main feature about a rock formation that gives it its name. In this case it is the bulb on the end of Snoopy's nose. Otherwise you have to use a lot of imagination to see Snoopy. There is a distinct mauve rock on the top of the nose, making the bulb. The stomach is caved in instead of bulging out as it should be with a well-fed Snoopy.

At about 0.50 miles *0.8 km* the trail begins to climb the cliff. It is a good trail, zigzagging its way up to make an easy climb. The trail tops out at 1.1 miles *1.8 km*, at a saddle just above Snoopy's head. You can see over the other side of the saddle into uptown Sedona. Behind you are glorious views of the Marg's Draw area.

Back in Sedona, look at Snoopy Rock and congratulate yourself. From there it looks unclimbable.

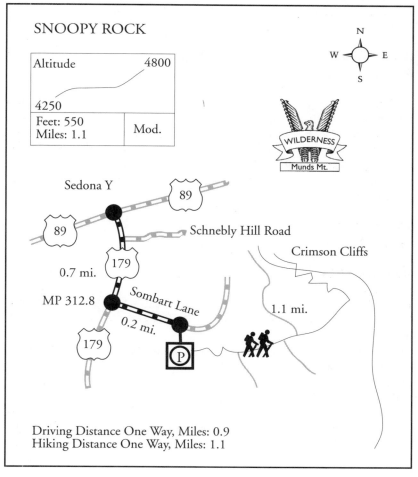

SNOOPY ROCK

Altitude	4800
4250	
Feet: 550 Miles: 1.1	Mod.

WILDERNESS
Munds Mt.

Sedona Y

89

89

Schnebly Hill Road

Crimson Cliffs

179

0.7 mi.

MP 312.8

Sombart Lane

0.2 mi.

1.1 mi.

179

P

Driving Distance One Way, Miles: 0.9
Hiking Distance One Way, Miles: 1.1

SOLDIER PASS ARCHES

General Information
Location Map D4
Sedona and Wilson Mt. USGS Maps
Coconino Forest Service Map

Driving Distance One Way: 3.0 miles *5.0 km* (Time 10 minutes)
Access Road: All cars, All paved
Hiking Distance One Way: 1.1 miles *1.8 km* (Time 60 minutes)
How Strenuous: Moderate
Features: Views, Arches

NUTSHELL: Located off of Soldier Pass Road, the trailhead for this hike is only 3.0 miles *5.0 km* from the Y. The hike follows an old jeep road most of its way, then climbs up to a trio of interesting arches.

DIRECTIONS:
From the Sedona Y Go:
   Southwest on Highway 89A (toward Cottonwood) for a distance of 1.25 miles *2.4 km* (MP 372.8) to Soldier Pass Road. Turn right onto Soldier Pass Road and follow it to the 2.75 mile *4.4 km* point, where it intersects Rim Shadows Drive, where you turn right. Follow Rim Shadows a short distance, to a three-way intersection. Go straight onto Canyon Shadows and follow it to the 3.0 miles *5.0 km* point. There you will see a sign saying "National Forest Access." Take the road to your left there and park in the parking area. This is well defined and spacious.

TRAILHEAD: You will see a rusty sign at the parking area reading "Soldier Pass Trail #66."

DESCRIPTION: This trail is an old jeep road. As you walk up the road you will see a sideroad at 0.10 miles *0.16 km* going off to the right. It is marked FR 904B. This is the way to the **Devil's Kitchen**, which is not part of this hike but if you haven't seen it, it is only 0.25 miles *0.4 km* away and is worth a detour.
   Keep walking up the main road. You will see some side paths forking off here and there but don't take them. At 0.85 miles *1.4 km* you will reach a stone barrier where there is a sign reading, "Road Closed. Wilderness Boundary Ahead."
   The road forks here. Do not take the left fork. Instead, step over the stones. Walk up the larger wash. You will see the that the road follows the wash, comes out of it and then goes back down into the wash. Soon after that

you come out of the wash for good. Beyond the wash you will come out onto a large red slickrock ledge, which provides good views in all directions. You are in a box canyon at this point, with interesting and colorful cliffs on all sides except east (toward Sedona). Walk up to the left edge of the ledge. If you look up at the cliffs to your left from this spot you will see one arch.

From there the trail is narrow and steep up to the arch, but it is a short climb. When you arrive you will see two arches. You can walk under the first one. It is fun to explore, as it forms a sort of cave. There is a third arch that you can't see. You can reach it by walking along the cliff face on a faint trail. The third arch is the smallest and least interesting. Just above you on top of the rim is the **Brins Mesa Trail**.

This is a good hike to take when the roads are muddy because the access road is all paved and it is near town.

SOLDIER PASS ARCHES

Altitude 4800

4400

Feet: 400
Miles: 1.1

Mod.

1.1 mi.

N
W — E
S

Devil's Kitchen

Rim Shadows →

1.5 mi.

0.25 mi.

Cyn. Shadows

WILDERNESS
R'Rock-Secret Mt

Soldier Pass Road

1.25 mi.

Sedona Y

89

89

MP 372.8

89

179

Driving Distance One Way, Miles: 3.0
Hiking Distance One Way, Miles: 1.1

SOLDIER PASS TRAIL #66

General Information
Location Map D4
Sedona and Wilson Mt. USGS Maps
Coconino Forest Service Map

Driving Distance One Way: 3.0 miles *5.0 km* (Time 10 minutes)
Access Road: All cars, All paved
Hiking Distance One Way: 1.5 miles *2.4 km* (Time 60 minutes)
How Strenuous: Moderate
Features: Views

NUTSHELL: Located off Soldier Pass Road, the trailhead for this hike is easily reached. The hike follows an old jeep road most of its way, then climbs to the top of Brins Mesa, a Sedona landmark.

DIRECTIONS:
From the Sedona Y Go:
Southwest on Highway 89A (toward Cottonwood) for a distance of 1.25 miles *2.4 km* (MP 372.8) to Soldier Pass Road. Turn right onto Soldier Pass Road and follow it to the 2.75 mile *4.4 km* point, where it intersects Rim Shadows Drive, where you turn right. Follow Rim Shadows a short distance, to a three-way intersection. Go straight onto Canyon Shadows and follow it to the 3.0 miles *5.0 km* point. There you will see a sign saying "National Forest Access." Take the road to your left there and park in the parking area. This is well defined and spacious.

TRAILHEAD: You will see a rusty sign at the parking area reading, "Soldier Pass Trail #66."

DESCRIPTION: This trail is an old jeep road. As you walk up the road you will see a sideroad to your right at the 0.10 mile *0.16 km* point. This is marked FR 904B. This fork goes to **Devil's Kitchen**, which is only 0.25 miles *0.4 km* away and is well worth a detour if you haven't seen it.
Keep walking up the main road. You will see some side paths forking off but don't take them. At 0.85 miles *1.4 km* you will reach a stone barrier where there is a sign reading, "Road Closed, Wilderness Boundary Ahead."
The road forks at this point. Do not take the left fork, as it ends in a loop about 0.20 miles *0.32 km* from here. Instead, step over the stones. Walk up the larger wash. You will see the road follow the wash, come out of the wash, then dip into it again. Soon after that, it splits, with the right

hand fork going up to the **Soldier Pass Arches**.

Stay on the lower trail, which goes into the wash for the third time. Look for a sign to your left that reads, "National Forest Wilderness. Closed to Vehicles and Motorized Equipment." This sign marks the path that you want to take. This is at 0.90 miles *1.5 km*.

At about 1.0 miles *1.6 km*, look to your right and you will see the three Soldier Pass Arches clearly. The trail from here follows along the top of a low ridge in the canyon bottom. At 1.25 miles *2.0 km* the trail begins a fairly steep ascent up to **Brins Mesa**. You are high enough there to get some great views.

At 1.3 miles *2.2 km* you will reach a gate in a barbed wire fence. You top out at 1.4 miles *2.3 km*. From this point you can follow the trail to link up with the Brins Mesa Trail at 1.5 miles *2.4 km*.

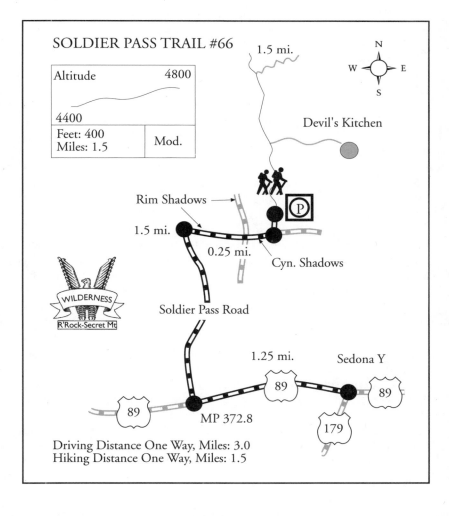

STEAMBOAT ROCK

Drive Distance One Way: 1.1 miles *1.8 km* (Time 5 minutes)
Access Road: All cars, All paved
Hiking Distance One Way: 1.5 miles *2.4 km* (Time 1.5 hours)
How Strenuous: Hard
Features: Views

NUTSHELL: Located 1.1 miles *1.8 km* north of Sedona, Steamboat Rock is one of the area's most famous landmarks. This hike takes you near the top, just below the "funnel" for breathtaking views and an unforgettable adventure. *For experienced hikers only.*

DIRECTIONS:
From the Sedona Y Go:
         North on Highway 89A (toward Flagstaff) for a distance of 1.1 miles *1.8 km* (MP 375.9). Go just across Midgley Bridge and turn left into the parking area.

TRAILHEAD: You will see a rusty sign at the parking lot. It reads, "Wilson Canyon #49." Start this hike by taking the **Wilson Canyon Trail** for 0.5 miles *0.8 km* .

DESCRIPTION: The trailhead is as easy as pie to locate. Just walk toward the picnic tables at the end of the parking lot. There you will find the Wilson Monument, a bronze plaque set in stone, and two rusty signs. The sign to the left marks **Wilson Canyon #49** and is the one you want for this hike. The other sign marks an uphill trail, Wilson Mountain #10, which is called **Wilson Mountain South** in this book.
         Take note of how far it is to the first point where the trail crosses the streambed (0.25 mi. *0.4 km*), which is just beyond the old bridge abutment. Walk another 0.25 miles *0.4 km* along the trail to a point where you will see an old road coming down from your left. This road is badly eroded, with rocks sticking out everywhere. It is a piece of the **Old Jim Thompson Road.** Turn left (west) here and go uphill on the old road.
         You will top out at 0.75 miles *1.2 km*. Go left on the road you find here. In about 20 yards you will reach another intersection. Avoid both of the wide trails here and instead take the narrow footpath going right, uphill

toward the nearest red butte. Look carefully for the trail, as it is rather faint and you must follow it to take advantage of the only two approaches on the face of the butte that allow you to go to the top.

As you come onto the slickrock, look for cairns. They lead you up the east face of Steamboat Rock. After a short stretch of scrambling, you'll be on top of the butte, where walking is easy and the trail is wide. Ahead is the towering "funnel" of the "steamboat." Near it you will find a talus slope going up to a band of mauve Ft. Apache sandstone forming a ledge (the "deck") at the funnel's base. If you are afraid of heights, stop here. If not, scale the slope; it is steep but short. You will find that the Apache layer is too thick to climb. Work your way west (to your right) and you will find a four-rung ladder made of rebar going to the top. The ladder is not perfectly stable. There is danger in climbing it. If you do climb it, you will be rewarded with sublime views. If it breaks off with you. . .well, this is a beautiful place to die. Once up you can walk almost all the way around the "deck."

STEAMBOAT ROCK

Altitude	5250
4600	

| Feet: 650 Miles: 1.5 | Hard |

N
W — E
S

1.5 mi.

89

WILDERNESS
R'Rock-Secret Mt

P

MP 375.9

1.1 mi.

Midgley Bridge

89

Sedona Y

89

179

Driving Distance One Way, Miles: 1.1
Hiking Distance One Way, Miles: 1.5

STERLING PASS #46

General Information
Location Map C5
Munds Park and Wilson Mt. USGS Maps
Coconino Forest Service Map

Driving Distance One Way: 6.2 miles *10.0 km* (Time 10 minutes)
Access Road: All cars, All paved
Hiking Distance One Way: 1.65 miles *2.7 km* (Time 60 minutes)
How Strenuous: Hard
Features: Views, Great rock formations

NUTSHELL: Located 6.2 miles *10.0 km* north of Sedona, just above the north end of Manzanita Campground, and just below Slide Rock Lodge, this steep but beautiful hike climbs through a heavy forest to a mountain pass.

DIRECTIONS:
From the Sedona Y Go:
　　　　North on Highway 89A (toward Flagstaff) for a distance of 6.2 miles *10.0 km* (MP 380.4). Park anywhere you can along the roadside in this area.

TRAILHEAD: There is a rusty sign in a little alcove marking this maintained trail. The sign reads, "Sterling Pass #46."

DESCRIPTION: There is very little parking at the roadside near the trailhead. You have to pick out a wide spot on the shoulder and do your best.
　　　　This trail rises steeply, climbing all the way. For the first portion you parallel a little side canyon, which may contain running water during spring thaw. When it does, it creates a charming waterfall near the highway. The trail wanders back and forth over the streambed four times.
　　　　For those who think of the Oak Creek area as sun swept expanses of redrock dotted with cactus, this trail will be an eye-opener. It goes through a cool pine forest. While you will cross over a bit of red slickrock at the beginning and will see some gorgeous red cliffs and buttes as you progress, the soil underfoot will be a rich brown loam. The forest is heavy. In addition to the familiar ponderosa pine you will see some Douglas fir and a few spruces. After about the first quarter mile you are far enough away from the road so that you can no longer hear its sounds and can see no signs of human activity. The area feels primeval and is truly delightful.
　　　　Because the forest is so heavy, you can't see much until you have gone about 1.25 miles *2.0 km*. Until then you get glimpses of giant white

cliffs ahead of you (west) and red cliffs on your right and left. Then you rise above the trees and get great views across Oak Creek Canyon and nearby. The cliffs here are a treat to the eye, highly sculptured, with many interesting lines and angles. You will find a viewpoint at a bend of the trail where you can look over into an adjacent canyon to your left for views of soaring white cliffs.

The crest is at about 1.65 miles *2.7 km*, where you come onto a saddle. There is a heavy stand of trees here with oaks on the east side and oaks and maples on the west wide. Because of these trees the views are not as good at the top as they are just below the top. This is a true mountain pass, there being a decided gap in the cliffs here.

The trail continues down the other side, another 0.75 miles *1.2 km*, to intersect the **Vultee Arch Trail.** If you do go down the west side you might as well go on to Vultee Arch, which is only 0.20 miles *0.32 km* from the trail junction. Many hikers will stop at the saddle.

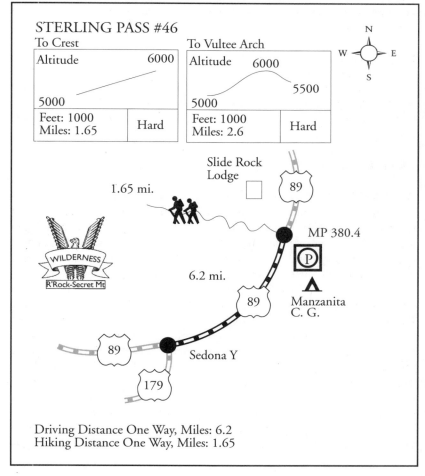

STERLING PASS #46

To Crest

Altitude		6000
5000		
Feet: 1000 Miles: 1.65		Hard

To Vultee Arch

Altitude	6000	
		5500
5000		
Feet: 1000 Miles: 2.6		Hard

N
W ✦ E
S

Slide Rock Lodge

1.65 mi.

89

MP 380.4

P

WILDERNESS
R'Rock-Secret Mt

6.2 mi.

89

Manzanita C. G.

89

Sedona Y

179

Driving Distance One Way, Miles: 6.2
Hiking Distance One Way, Miles: 1.65

SUBMARINE ROCK

General Information
Location Map E5
Sedona USGS Map
Coconino Forest Service Map

Driving Distance One Way: 2.0 miles *3.2 km* (Time 10 minutes)
Access Road: All cars, All paved
Hiking Distance One Way: 1.0 miles *1.6 km* (Time 30 minutes)
How Strenuous: Easy
Features: Rock formation, Views

NUTSHELL: Located only a couple of miles southeast of uptown Sedona, this interesting rock formation is fun to climb and pretend that you are Captain Nemo.

DIRECTIONS:
From the Sedona Y Go:
> South on Highway 179 (toward Phoenix) for 1.4 miles *2.3 km* (MP 312.1) to Morgan Road in the Broken Arrow Subdivision. Turn left (east) on Morgan Road and follow it to its end, at 2.0 miles *3.2 km*, where you park just beyond the cattle guard.

TRAILHEAD: The jeep road, FR 179F, is the trail.

DESCRIPTION: Walk down the jeep road. You will see a sign at the cattle guard reading "Trail Walk-Through." We suggest that you disregard the walkthrough and just stay on the road. The road is widely used by the jeep tours that have proliferated in Sedona, so the road is well maintained, although you may have to share it with motor vehicles, which detracts from the back-to-nature qualities of the experience.

As you walk the road, you will reach a spot at 0.34 miles *0.6 km* where a sunken road goes off to the right (south). This is the trail to the **Devil's Dining Room**, a large sinkhole. It is a short jaunt and worth seeing. At 0.42 miles *0.7 km*, the road splits but it doesn't matter which fork you take, as the roads converge on the other side of a hill. The high road gives better views. At 0.67 miles *1.1 km* you reach a T fork. Go straight here. The right fork goes up to a nice viewpoint, again worth a short detour. At 0.71 miles *1.2 km* you come to a Y fork. The left branch goes down into a gully and up to Submarine Rock. The right fork goes to **Chicken Point**.

Submarine Rock is well named. It looks like a submarine lying on the floor of the valley. It is a low rounded redrock formation that stands alone.

The jeep tours love to drive the tourists up the face of Submarine Rock and in doing so they have unfortunately left unsightly black tire marks behind them. The marks make it easy to follow the path, however.

Submarine Rock is easy to climb and once you are on top of it you can have great fun walking around it, getting the views and clambering up to the top of the "conning tower."

When you are at Submarine Rock you are only about three-quarters of a mile from **Chicken Point** and may want to take that hike on the same trip.

Submarine Rock is located at the south end of **Marg's Draw**, a scenic bowl formed by the Crimson Cliffs on the north, Munds Mountain and Lee Mountain on the east and **Twin Buttes** on the south. This is a beautiful natural area and the home of several good hikes. Marg's Draw is remarkable, being unspoiled and yet close to developed parts of Sedona.

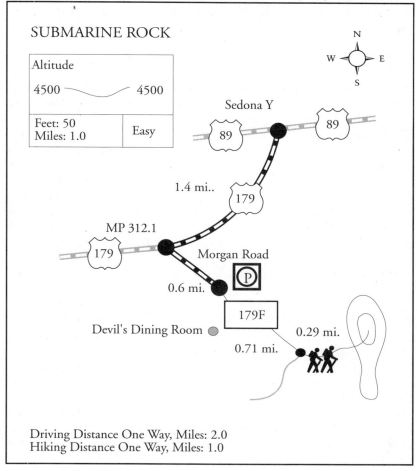

SUBMARINE ROCK

N
W — E
S

Altitude

4500 — 4500

Feet: 50
Miles: 1.0   Easy

Sedona Y

89   89

1.4 mi..   179

MP 312.1

179   Morgan Road

P

0.6 mi.

179F

Devil's Dining Room   0.29 mi.

0.71 mi.

Driving Distance One Way, Miles: 2.0
Hiking Distance One Way, Miles: 1.0

SUGARLOAF AT BLACK MT.

General Information
Location Map C1
Page Springs and Sycamore Basin USGS Maps
Coconino Forest Service Map

Driving Distance One Way: 29.8 miles *48 km* (Time 60 minutes)
Access Road: High clearance vehicles, Very rough roads
Hiking Distance One Way: 0.33 miles *0.6 km* (Time 30 minutes)
How Strenuous: Moderate
Features: Ruins, Views

NUTSHELL: Located 29.8 miles *48 km* southwest of Sedona, this small mountain is moderately easy to climb. There are Indian ruins at the top. Great views.

DIRECTIONS:
From the Sedona Y Go:
    Southwest on Highway 89A (toward Cottonwood) a distance of 16.0 miles *25.6 km* (MP 358) to FR 761, the unpaved Bill Gray Road. Turn right and take FR 761 to the 25.5 miles *41 km* point, which is the junction of FR 761 and FR 258A, the Buckboard Road. Go right here, staying on FR 761. At 26.2 miles *42 km*, you will see a road to your left marked FR 761A. Turn left onto this road. Up to this point, the road has been good, but now it gets quite rough. A high clearance vehicle with sturdy tires is recommended, and you should drive it only when the road is dry. At 27.6 miles *44.2 km*, you reach a Y fork, with FR 761A going right and FR 761C going left. Drive FR 761A, to the right. This is a very rough but spectacular road. Pick a good parking place in the area of the 29.8 mile *48 km* point and park.

TRAILHEAD: No trail. You bushwhack up the mountain.

DESCRIPTION: Although this Sugarloaf (there are two others near Sedona) is a small mountain, the south face is not easy to climb because of some thick eroded ledges there. On the east face, where we have had you park, the access to the top is much easier.
    You will have to contend with two ledges here, one of redrock and the other of buff colored stone, but they both narrow down on this face and it is easy to get around them.
    At the top you will find a small ruin, just a short wall about three feet high filled with sand. Hikers have also built a cairn at the top. Add a stone to the cairn to show you've been here. There is another ruin on the

west side of the crest, downhill a bit.

    The area at the top is small, so you can easily walk around it and get good views in all directions. The views to the north, east and south are terrific.

    Since you are so close to it, you should also visit the **Black Mountain Mystery House** while you are here.

    The early settlers in Sedona were hard pressed to come up with names for the multitude of hills, mountains, rock formations and other land features they found and they used the name Sugarloaf three times. See **Sugarloaf in Sedona** for an explanation of what a sugarloaf is..

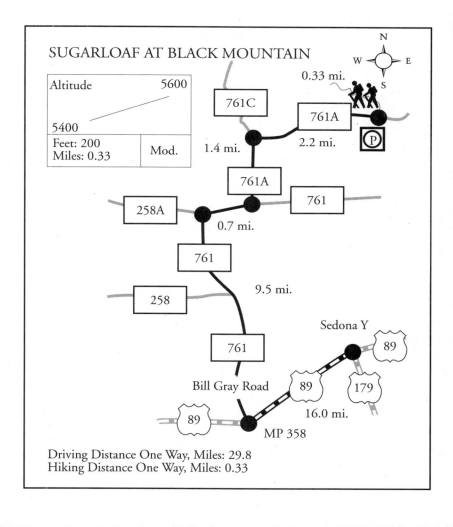

SUGARLOAF IN SEDONA

General Information
Location Map D4
Sedona and Wilson Mt. USGS Maps
Coconino Forest Service Map

Driving Distance One Way: 2.6 miles *4.2 km* (Time 10 minutes)
Access Road: All cars, All paved
Hiking Distance One Way: 0.70 miles *1.2 km* (Time 30 minutes)
How Strenuous: Moderate
Features: Rock formation, Views

NUTSHELL: This ramp-shaped landmark located a couple of miles west of uptown Sedona can be climbed with moderate effort for great views.

DIRECTIONS:
From the Sedona Y Go:
        Southwest on Highway 89A (toward Cottonwood) for a distance of 1.7 miles *2.8 km* (MP 372.5), to Mt. Shadows Street. Turn right onto Mt. Shadows Street. Follow it to the 2.6 mile *4.2 km* point where you will find a large water storage tank and a transmitter inside a chain link fence. The road intersects Fabulous Texan Way here (the streets in this area were named after movies filmed in Sedona). Drive across the street onto the dirt apron around the fenced area and park there.

TRAILHEAD: At the parking area. There are no signs, but you will see a crawl-through in the fence; it looks like a picture frame.

DESCRIPTION: Squeeze through the crawl-through and walk uphill along the fence. The path forks just past the fence. Take the left fork (west), which goes uphill. It circles the base of Sugarloaf and takes you around to the north side, where you will find the low point of the "ramp," which is the obvious place to begin the ascent to the top. You will find this in a clearing where the old road ended. There is a line of flat red rocks blocking the entrance to a road going up Sugarloaf. You want to walk this "ramp."
        It is as if Sugarloaf was created to be a viewpoint, because you have the ramp to allow easy hiking to the top, and natural forces have sheared off the east face of the butte to give you unobstructed views once you reach the crest.
        There is another Sugarloaf in the Sedona area, which we call **Sugarloaf at Black Mountain** in this book to distinguish the two. It is also a good hike.

The early settlers in Sedona were hard pressed to come up with names for the multitude of hills, mountains, rock formations and other land features they found and they can be forgiven for using the name Sugarloaf more than once. There is yet a third Sugarloaf adjacent to the **Airport Hill Vortex** hike.

One hundred years ago, when these pioneers came, people didn't buy granulated sugar as we know it today. In those days molasses was boiled down until it began to crystallize and was poured into cone-shaped molds, where it hardened. These "loaves" of sugar, about the size of a golf ball, were their sugar. The loaves became very hard as they aged and it was usually the job of the children in a family to break up the loaves with a hammer so that the sugar could be measured and used in cooking. Eating a bit of the sugar was their reward. A sugarloaf was a blunt-tipped cone, a shape that aptly describes these buttes.

SUGARLOAF IN SEDONA

Altitude 5000
4800
Feet: 200
Miles: 0.70   Mod.

Sugarloaf   0.7 mi.

Fabulous Texan Way

0.9 mi.

Mt. Shadows St.

Sedona Y

1.7 mi.

89

89

MP 372.5

179

Driving Distance One Way, Miles: 2.6
Hiking Distance One Way, Miles: 0.7

TELEPHONE TRAIL #72

General Information
Location Map B5
Munds Park USGS Map
Coconino Forest Service Map

Driving Distance One Way: 10.9 miles *17.5 km* (Time 20 minutes)
Access Road: All cars, All paved
Hiking Distance One Way: 1.25 miles *2.0 km* (Time 2.0 Hours)
How Strenuous: Hard (Very steep)
Features: Interesting rock formations, Views

NUTSHELL: This is a marked and posted trail in upper Oak Creek. It climbs northerly to a ridge top and then turns east to reach the rim.

DIRECTIONS:
From the Sedona Y Go:
North on Highway 89A (toward Flagstaff) for a distance of 10.9 miles *17.5 km* (MP 385.1). Here you will see a wide apron on the right side of the highway under a twenty foot high cliff. Park here.

TRAILHEAD: From the parking place, walk up Highway 89A on the right shoulder about one hundred yards. You will see the typical rusty metal trailhead sign off the highway a few feet to your right. The sign reads, "Trail 72, Telephone."

DESCRIPTION: From the sign look sharp and you will see cairns marking the trail. The trail itself is hard to see because it is covered with pine needles. The trail runs along parallel to the highway for about 0.05 mile *0.1 km*, then swings to the right. You are walking along an old road bed, probably a construction road that was created while the old telephone line was being installed.
At 0.1 miles *0.16 km* you will walk under the new phone line. The trail up to here is obvious and easy to follow. From this point on, the trail is difficult to find, and even with markers, we think this hike is for experienced hikers only.
The next leg of the hike takes you sharply uphill, to your left (north). You will zigzag your way up to the top of a finger ridge that runs west from the East Rim, reaching the first top at about 0.5 miles *0.8 km*. Turn right (east). You are in a zone of white sandstone studded with fossils. You stay on top of the ridge for a while and then dip below it. At 0.6 miles *0.96 km*, you will be on top again, and will come to a fascinating little reef about

thirty feet long and twelve feet high that contains several windows. It is called the Peep Holes.

There is a rough spot beyond this, where the trail dips again and gets difficult. There are several confusing game trails. Be sure to follow the flags and cairns. You will find one of the old phone pole stubs, with guy wire and support sleeve where the trail turns back to the top. Hard scrambling in here.

When you get back to the ridge top, the trail becomes more obvious. At about 0.75 miles *1.2 km*, you move along another intermediate top. Soon after that, you begin the very steep climb to the top of the rim. This is in a beautiful fir forest, which lasts all the way to the top. Along the way here you will see the remains of several old phone poles.

The trail ends at the top at 1.25 miles *2.0 km*, at a large cairn. You can walk out to the rim in several places here for wonderful views out toward the cliffs of West Fork.

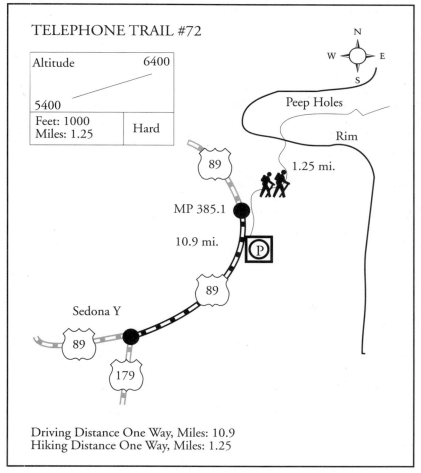

THOMAS POINT #142

General Information
Location Map B5
Munds Park USGS Map
Coconino Forest Service Map

Driving Distance One Way: 10.5 miles *17 km* (Time 20 minutes)
Access Road: All cars, All paved
Hiking Distance One Way: 1.0 miles *1.6 km* (Time 60 minutes)
How Strenuous: Hard
Features: Views

NUTSHELL: This is a marked and posted trail that climbs the east wall of upper Oak Creek Canyon 10.5 miles *17 km* north of Sedona.

DIRECTIONS:
From the Sedona Y Go:
   North on Highway 89A (toward Flagstaff) for a distance of 10.5 miles *17 km* (MP 384.7) You will see a road sign for the parking area, which requires a sharp turn to your left (west).

TRAILHEAD: The parking area driveway forms a loop. Park at the farthest point, the south end of the loop. Walk the trail you will see heading south, parallel to the highway and not very far from it. The trail will fork soon. Take the left (southeast) fork and head toward the paved road. You will approach some houses. There is a fence protecting them. Just before the fence the path turns left (east) and goes up to the highway. Cross over the paving, turn right (south) and walk along the east shoulder of Highway 89A about 100 yards. You will find the trailhead to your left, uphill a bit from the road.

DESCRIPTION: The start of the trail looks like a groove worn into the soil bank with the trailhead sign at the beginning of the groove. Look sharp, for the sign is hard to see.
   Like the other trails that climb the east wall of the canyon, this trail goes nearly straight up, with little finesse. You start the hike in a pine and spruce forest. The trail zigzags in such a way that it isn't a killer trail like the **Purtymun Trail** or Thompson's Ladder.
   After hiking a short distance you will climb high enough to get good views of the sheer white cliffs of the West Fork and East Pocket areas across the canyon to the west. You can see the path of Oak Creek and glimpse bits of the highway.

At about the half mile point the trail winds around onto an unshaded south face of the canyon wall. Here the pines disappear and you enter the chaparral and juniper life zone. These plants are small compared to the pines so you have better views along this part of the trail. Near the top you come back into the pine and spruce forest.

At the top, pine needles may cover the trail and make it indistinct, so look for cairns. They mark an extension of the trail to a viewpoint to the left (north), where Thomas Point is located. Thomas Point is well named, for it is a peninsula or tongue pointing west. Standing at the tip of the point you will have good views north, west and south. Particularly good are the views of the San Francisco Peaks and the head of Oak Creek Canyon. As long as you are at the top of the rim, you might enjoy walking along the rim in both directions to find different viewpoints and places of interest.

This hike and the **Harding Spring** trail are our favorites for climbing the east wall of Oak Creek Canyon.

THOMAS POINT #142

Altitude   6000

5100

Feet: 900
Miles: 1.0   Hard

West Fork Trail

P

89

MP 384.7

1.0 mi.

89

10.5 mi.

89   Sedona Y

179

Driving Distance One Way, Miles: 10.5
Hiking Distance One Way, Miles: 1.0

TURKEY CREEK TRAIL #92

General Information
Location Map F3
Sedona USGS Map
Coconino Forest Service Map

Driving Distance One Way: 11.7 miles *19.0 km* (Time 30 minutes)
Access Road: High clearance, Last 1.5 mile *2.4 km* medium dirt road
Hiking Distance One Way: 3.5 miles *5.6 km* (Time 2.0 hours)
How Strenuous: Moderate
Features: Rock formations, Views

NUTSHELL: Located 11.7 miles *19.0 km* southwest of Sedona, behind the
Verde Valley School, this moderate hike has you climb 1000 feet in about a
mile through interesting redrocks to the top of House Mountain.

DIRECTIONS:
From the Sedona Y Go:
South on Highway 179 (toward Phoenix) for 7.2 miles *11.5 km*
(MP 306.1), to the Verde Valley School Road, where there is a stoplight.
Turn right (west) onto Verde Valley School Road. The first 3.0 miles *4.8 km*
of this road are paved. Follow it to the 10.7 mile *17.2 km* point where you
will see a sign marking the **Turkey Creek Trail**. Just beyond the sign you
will see FR 9216B, a dirt road to your left. Turn onto FR 9216B. Any vehicle with medium clearance can handle the road. At 11.3 miles *18.1 km* you
will reach a fork where a lath marks FR 9891 to the right. Don't take that
fork; stay on FR 9216B. At 11.7 miles *18.8 km* you will come to another
fork. Here you will find a sign showing Turkey Creek Trail to the left and
State Park to the right. Park here. Walk the left road for 0.1 mile *0.16 km*,
where you will come to a barrier of rocks. Beyond this another 0.2 miles
0.32 km you will reach a junction. Turn right (west). You will soon come to
another junction, where you go straight. Keep following this road for 1.2
miles *2.0 km*, to Turkey Creek Tank. In other words, from where you park,
it is a 1.5 mile *2.4 km* hike to Turkey Creek Tank.

TRAILHEAD: At Turkey Creek Tank. It is marked with a rusty sign.

DESCRIPTION: Access to this fine hike has been improved since the first
edition of this book. Signs have been erected and the road has been graded
up to the parking place. The "State Park" referred to on the sign is Red Rock
State Park, and the road to the right goes to its rear entrance. We highly recommend Red Rock State Park, though we urge you to go through the front

entrance, described in our entry for the **Apache Fire Trail.**

When you get near Turkey Creek Tank you will recognize its presence because it is encircled by cottonwood trees. It is a pleasant oasis, though it goes dry in summer. The hiking trail starts at its farthest edge and goes along a former jeep road, winding through some fine redrocks. It changes to a footpath in about half a mile.

Soon after this you begin to climb House Mountain. The path is fairly steep but the footing is good. The path is an old stock trail. It zigzags to a saddle on the top, where you crest out on the rim of an extinct volcanic crater, a rather flat and shallow one. From that point you can take the trail down into the bowl of the crater, though there isn't much to see there. We prefer to bushwhack along the rim to the north for the fine views of Sedona, which are magnificent from there. The mountain's high point is to the north, a basalt tower worth scaling.

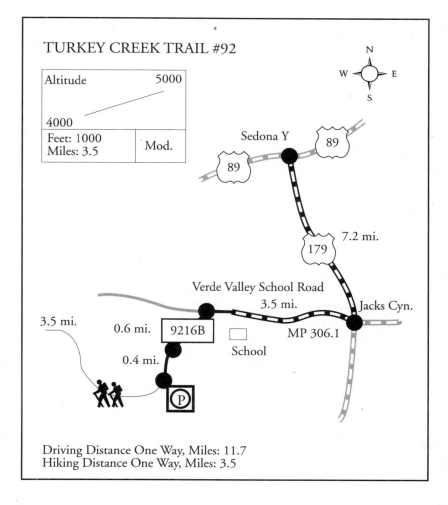

TURKEY CREEK TRAIL #92

Altitude   5000

4000

Feet: 1000
Miles: 3.5   Mod.

N
W — E
S

Sedona Y   89

89

7.2 mi.
179

Verde Valley School Road
3.5 mi.
Jacks Cyn.

3.5 mi.

0.6 mi.   9216B   MP 306.1

School

0.4 mi.

P

Driving Distance One Way, Miles: 11.7
Hiking Distance One Way, Miles: 3.5

TWIN BUTTES

General Information
Location Map E5
Sedona USGS Map
Coconino Forest Service Map

Driving Distance One Way: 2.0 miles *3.2 km* (Time 10 minutes)
Access Road: All cars, All paved
Hiking Distance One Way: 1.5 miles *2.4 km* (Time 1.25 hours)
How Strenuous: Hard
Features: Views

NUTSHELL: The Twin Buttes formation is located a couple of miles south of the Sedona Y. The famous Chapel of the Holy Cross was built near its south face. It is a hard haul to the top of the north face over an unmaintained trail but once there you will enjoy superb views.

DIRECTIONS:
From the Sedona Y Go:
    South on Highway 179 (toward Phoenix) for 1.4 miles *2.3 km* (MP 312.1) to Morgan Road in the Broken Arrow Subdivision. Turn left (east) on Morgan Road and follow it to its end, at 2.0 miles *3.2 km*, where you park just beyond the cattle guard.

TRAILHEAD: You will see no trail signs. Walk the road, which is FR 179F.

DESCRIPTION: At the cattle guard you will see a sign indicating a "Trail Walk-through." We have tried this and see no reason to use it. It is better to walk right down the middle of the road.
    This road is used by the jeep tours that abound in Sedona and you are likely to meet some of them on this hike in good weather. They act as if they own the road, and in a certain sense they do, as they have a maintenance agreement for it with the Forest Service.
    At 0.26 miles *0.42 km* turn right, going up on a red sandstone ledge. The jeeps go up there to thrill the dudes, so the trail is easy to follow. You stay on the lower part of the ledge and walk across it, where the dirt road resumes.
    At 0.34 miles *0.55 km* go to the right on a sunken road. This will lead you to a sinkhole called the **Devil's Dining Room** at 0.42 miles *0.7 km*. At this site, you will come out into a small clearing where you will see a line of boulders and a barbed wire fence. These mark the sinkhole.

This sinkhole isn't nearly as big as **Devil's Kitchen** but it is impressive. Sinkholes develop when underground cavities undermine a ledge of rock to the point where it collapses into the void. Some geologists speculate that this sinkhole and Devil's Kitchen were both caused by the same underground river that removed the supporting subsoil from both places.

Behind the sinkhole is a hill. You will see a path going up this hill. This is the path you want to follow. At 0.65 miles *1.1 km* you will come out onto a redrock ledge. In a little over 100 feet you will see a trail going left marked by cairns. Take this trail.

At 1.0 miles *1.6 km* you will come out onto a saddle, which is a point on the **Battlement Mesa** hike. Just as you top out, look for a trail going left, uphill, marked by cairns. This is the trail you want. Moderately steep up to now, the trail gets much steeper. Your target is the big saddle in the Twin Buttes to your left, and you have a half mile of hard hiking to get there.

Once you top out, we think you will not regret your effort.

TWIN PILLARS

General Information
Location Map F4
Sedona USGS Map
Coconino Forest Service Map

Driving Distance One Way: 11.7 miles *19.0 km* (Time 30 minutes)
Access Road: High clearance, Last 1.5 miles *2.4 km* medium dirt road
Hiking Distance One Way: 1.0 miles *1.6 km* (Time 45 minutes)
How Strenuous: Moderate
Features: Rock formations, Views

NUTSHELL: Located 11.7 miles *19.0 km* southwest of Sedona, behind the Verde Valley School, this moderate hike has you climb through interesting redrocks to the top of a ridge overlooking the school.

DIRECTIONS:
From the Sedona Y Go:

South on Highway 179 (toward Phoenix) for 7.2 miles *11.5 km* (MP 306.1), to the Verde Valley School Road, where there is a stoplight. Turn right (west) onto Verde Valley School Road. The first 3.0 miles *4.8 km* of this road are paved. Follow it to the 10.7 mile *17.2 km* point where you will see a sign marking the **Turkey Creek Trail**. Just beyond the sign you will see FR 9216B, a dirt road to your left. Turn onto FR 9216B. Any vehicle with medium clearance can handle the road. At 11.3 miles *18.1 km* you will reach a fork where a lath marks FR 9891 to the right. Don't take that fork; stay on FR 9216B. At 11.7 miles *18.8 km* you will come to another fork. Here you will find a sign showing Turkey Creek Trail to the left and State Park to the right. Park here.

TRAILHEAD: Not marked. The trail begins where you park.

DESCRIPTION: The access road for this hike is the same up to a point as that for the **Turkey Creek Trail**, which is a very good hike.

From the parking place, walk on the road to the left. At 0.1 mile *0.16 km*, you will come to a barrier of stone. In 0.2 miles *0.32 km* beyond that you will reach a junction. Turn left (S). Walk along this closed road for another 0.2 miles *0.32 km*, where the road ends in a little loop. In other words, you will walk 0.5 miles *0.8 km* from the parking spot.

At this point where the road ends, you will be looking up at a saddle. The hiking path is to your left, and it moves over toward the red cliff and climbs up along the north side of a wash. The hike is about 0.5 miles *0.8 km* long from here.

There are always hoof prints on this trail and we would guess that the trail was created as a horse path for the students at Verde Valley School, which is on the other (east) side of the butte. It makes a good hiking trail.

Though the trail was not marked, we had no trouble following it. The path winds around in such a fashion that it makes good use of the terrain to climb the butte gradually. It is not very steep, rising 200 feet in 0.35 miles *0.6 km.* As you climb you rise high enough to get good views of some pretty country.

At the top you come onto the saddle. The Twin Pillars for which we named the hike are to your right (south). We could find no name for this place on any map, so we christened it after these prominent redrock pillars. From the saddle you look down onto the school, white buildings with red roofs in a beautiful setting.

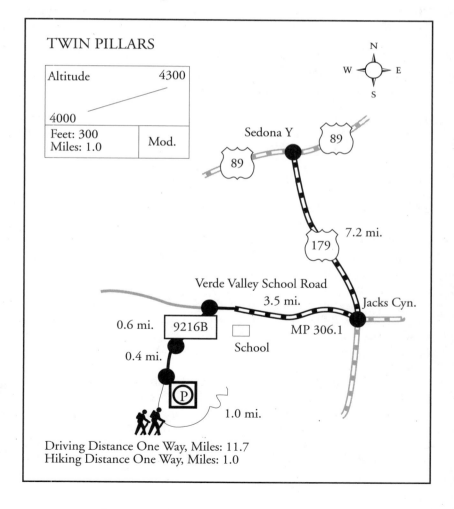

TWIN PILLARS

Altitude	4300
4000	
Feet: 300 Miles: 1.0	Mod.

N
W — E
S

Sedona Y   89
89

7.2 mi.
179

Verde Valley School Road
3.5 mi.

Jacks Cyn.

0.6 mi.   9216B   MP 306.1

School

0.4 mi.

P

1.0 mi.

Driving Distance One Way, Miles: 11.7
Hiking Distance One Way, Miles: 1.0

VAN DEREN CABIN

General Information
Location Map C4
Wilson Mt. USGS Map
Coconino Forest Service Map

Driving Distance One Way: 7.6 miles *12.2 km* (Time 30 minutes)
Access Road: Most cars, Last 2.4 miles *3.9 km* medium dirt road
Hiking Distance One Way: 0.30 miles *0.5 km* (Time 15 minutes)
How Strenuous: Easy
Features: Historic cabin, Views

NUTSHELL: This is a short easy hike to a historic cabin located off the road to Vultee Arch, 7.6 miles *12.2 km* northwest of Sedona.

DIRECTIONS:
From the Sedona Y Go:
      Southwest on Highway 89A (toward Cottonwood) a distance of 3.2 miles *5.2 km* (MP 371) to the Dry Creek Road. Turn right on Dry Creek Road, also known as FR 152C, and follow it to the 5.2 mile *8.4 km* point where FR 152 branches to the right. Take FR 152. You will see a sign for Vultee Arch on this road. Follow the road to the 7.6 miles *12.2 km* point, where you will see an unmarked road to your left. Turn left on this road and park as soon as you can.

TRAILHEAD: There are no trail signs. Walk the road, which is FR 9917.

DESCRIPTION: Jeep tours regularly come here and drive FR 9917 all the way to the cabin. However, we recommend that you park just off the main road and walk to the cabin because the road is uneven and rough and this is a book of hikes.
      At 0.16 miles *2.6 km* you will come to the place where the road fords Dry Creek. If the water is high you might want to wait for another day. Upstream to your right there is a broad redrock ledge cut by the action of the creek into charming sculptures. It is well worth a short detour to walk along it and enjoy the shapes.
      When you cross the creek the road goes to the top of the bank on the other side. The road forks there. Take the left fork and follow it to its end. From there you will see the cabin. The old homestead was composed of several acres. The Forest Service purchased the cabin site only and devotes it to public use, while the remainder of the old ranch is private property. The private property has been enclosed by a fence that is garlanded with No

Trespassing signs. Don't worry about these, because access to the cabin site is guaranteed.

The cabin was built by pioneer Earl Van Deren in the 1890s. The oldest part is nearest to the new fence. Later Earl fell in love but his fiancee refused to marry him until he expanded the cabin. He added the second unit, connected the two with a roof forming a breezeway, satisfying his fiancee, and they married.

Earl ranched and made some money as a movie extra. In the 1940s he bought acreage in what turned out later to be uptown Sedona, where there is a Van Deren Road honoring him. At the back of the cabin site, you can see the remains of Earl's root cellar. Legend says that the cellar was used by a bootlegger after Earl moved to town and that the bootlegger was murdered there.

VAN DEREN CABIN

Altitude	4900
4800	
Feet: 100 Miles: 0.3	Easy

0.3 mi.

9917

2.4 mi.

152

2.0 mi.

152C

Dry Creek Road

Sedona Y

3.2 mi.

89

89

MP 371

179

Driving Distance One Way, Miles: 7.6
Hiking Distance One Way, Miles: 0.3

VERDE HOT SPRINGS

General Information
Location Map G6
Strawberry USGS Map
Coconino Forest Service Map

Driving Distance One Way: 55.8 miles *90 km* (Time 1.5 hours)
Access Road: All cars, Last 20.4 miles *32.7 km* good dirt road
Hiking Distance One Way: 1.25 miles *2.0 km* (Time 40 minutes)
How Strenuous: Easy, but you have to wade across the Verde River
Features: Historic site, Permanent river, Wide easy trail, Views, Hot springs

NUTSHELL: This adventure is worth making for the sake of the drive alone, but is spiced by the addition of wild country, an historic electrical power plant and flume, a hot spring, a river and the ruins of a former resort. NOTE: You must be equipped with wading shoes and shorts to go to the springs.

DIRECTIONS:
From the Sedona Y Go:
      South on Highway 179 (toward Phoenix) for 14.7 miles *23.6 km*, to the I-17 Interchange. Turn south on I-17 and go to the 23.6 miles *37.8 km* point, where you take Exit 289 for Camp Verde. Go into Camp Verde, where you will come to a stop sign at 27.3 miles *43.6 km*. Turn left here and go east on Highway 260 to the 35.4 mile *56.6 km* point (MP 228.5), where you turn right (south) on unpaved FR 708. It is signed. Follow this narrow winding mountain road to the 49.5 mile *79.2 km* point, where it meets FR 502. Turn right (SW), toward Childs. You will drive a very winding road down to the 55.8 mile *90 km* point, where the road splits, with the right hand road going into the power plant. You want to go left down to the campground here, but washouts have made the last 0.15 mile *0.24 km* stretch very rough. High clearance is necessary. You may want to park here and walk down.

TRAILHEAD: At the campground by the Verde River bank, you will see a trail sign.

DESCRIPTION: The trail moves up to the historic power plant, built in 1916 to serve Jerome, Prescott and Phoenix. You pass over a catwalk in front of the power house, where the waters of Fossil Creek (channeled into the seven mile flume you saw while driving in) come surging through hydro-electric turbines and discharge into the Verde. Then the trail goes down to the river bank. Soon after, it climbs away from the river and goes up on a ridge to meet a road. You turn left and follow this road down to its end, where it joins the river. There is a campground here.

You will see a ranch house to your right on the opposite bank. The rancher drives across the river here, so it is usually the best place to wade across, but be careful. At normal levels, the river will be from knee to waist deep, but when it is high, it may be dangerous to cross. Once over, you climb up onto a trail and turn left, going back downstream. You will soon come onto a bench that was created as the site for a resort that flourished here decades ago, before burning down in 1962. Keep following the trail. You will see a number of white pillars marking the trail as it dips down to the river. At the end of the trail is the main spring.

The spring water is contained in a green pool sitting atop a rock bath house. It is open to public use and is an interesting place. Be aware that many people who use the spring like nudity. That explains the anti-nudity signs you saw on the trail earlier.

VERDE HOT SPRINGS

Altitude 2900

2800

Feet: 100
Miles: 1.25 | Easy

Sedona Y

89   89

14.7 mi.   179   I-17

8.9 mi.

I-17

Exit 289
Camp Verde   3.7 mi.

I-17

Camp Verde   260   8.1 mi.

260

708

14.1 mi.

1.25 mi.   708

Verde R.   6.3 mi.   502

Childs

Hot Spring   P

Driving Distance One Way, Miles: 55.8
Hiking Distance One Way, Miles: 1.25

VULTEE ARCH #22

General Information
Location Map C4
Loy Butte and Wilson Mt. USGS Maps
Coconino Forest Service Map

Driving Distance One Way: 9.6 miles *15.4 km* (Time 45 minutes)
Access Road: Last 4.4 miles *7.0 km* rough, Most cars
Hiking Distance One Way: 1.6 miles *2.6 km* (Time 1 hour)
How Strenuous: Moderate
Features: Arch, Historic marker, Scenic canyon

NUTSHELL: Located 9.6 miles *15.4 km* north of Sedona, this hike takes you to a natural arch and a commemorative plaque in a beautiful box canyon. **A personal favorite**.

DIRECTIONS:
From the Sedona Y Go:
      Southwest on Highway 89A (toward Cottonwood) for 3.2 miles *5.2 km* (MP 371) to Dry Creek Road. Turn right on Dry Creek Road (FR 152C) and proceed to the 5.2 mile *8.4 km* point. Turn right on FR 152, the Vultee Arch Road, and follow it to the 9.6 mile *15.4 km* point. Here there is a parking loop, with the **Vultee Arch** Trailhead at the tip. Parking is provided at the trailhead.

TRAILHEAD: This is a marked and maintained trail. You will see a rusty sign at the parking place reading, "Vultee Arch #22."

DESCRIPTION: FR 152 has been improved since the first edition of this book was issued. We feel that almost any passenger car, except one that is very low slung, can make this trip now. Even so, keep your eyes open for ruts and rocks, as this situation changes with every storm.
      The hiking trail is sandy and gives nice soft footing. The trail climbs as it progresses, passing through several life zones, which leads to interesting changes in the vegetation surrounding the trail. When you begin the trail you are in a forest of Arizona cypress. After that you will go through oak and pine and finally you will find Douglas fir. The route is shaded the entire way, which makes it a good choice in hot weather.
      The trail crosses a creekbed several times, so don't try to hike it when a lot of water is running in the creek. The creek is dry except for a few weeks in the spring, generally in March and April or after a hard summer rain.

At 1.4 miles *2.3 km* you will reach the junction of this trail and the **Sterling Pass Trail**, which forks to the right.

At the end of the trail you will break out into a clearing in a box canyon and the trail will climb onto redrock ledges. You will see Vultee Arch against a far wall of the box canyon. There is a trail leading to it that you can easily pick up. It is possible to walk right up to the arch and even to climb on top of it.

The historical plaque is cast in bronze and fastened to the face of a redrock ledge, the second ledge above you as you enter the box canyon. The plaque commemorates the airplane crash that killed Gerald Vultee, an aviation pioneer, and his wife in 1938. They did not crash here, but on nearby East Pocket, when they were caught in a storm at night. Had Vultee been flying one of today's planes with modern instruments, he probably would have brought it in safely.

WALKER BASIN TRAIL

General Information
Location Map G6
Walker Mtn. USGS Map
Coconino Forest Service Map

Driving Distance One Way: 31.8 miles *51 km* (Time 1.25 hours)
Access Road: All cars, Last 14.6 miles *24 km* good dirt road
Hiking Distance One Way: 8.0 miles *13 km* (Time 4.5 hours)
How Strenuous: Hard
Features: Views

NUTSHELL: This trail runs from a point 6200 feet high on the Mogollon Rim to the bottom, a 2000 foot drop in 8.0 miles *13 km.*

DIRECTIONS:
From the Sedona Y Go:
　　　　South on Highway 179 (toward Phoenix) for 14.7 miles *23.6 km,* to the I-17 Interchange. Go underneath onto FR 618 (paved for 2.5 miles *4.0 km*) and follow it. At the 19.7 mile *31.6 km* point you will see a sign for the Walker Basin Trail and a road going left. Pass by. At the 24.5 mile *40 km* point, will take a road left, FR 214, "Cedar Flat." FR 214 takes you to the top of the Mogollon Rim, a 2000 foot climb. You will come to the high point at about 30.0 miles *48 km,* then go downhill. Just past a cattle guard, at the 31.8 mile *51 km* point, you will see a dirt road to your left (west) marked 214B. Pull in and park. Do not try to drive 214B.

TRAILHEAD: There is a sign where you park.

DESCRIPTION: This is a hard hike. We recommend doing this hike with two cars, in which case it is still pretty strenuous, but is an enjoyable experience instead of an ordeal. The way to do this is to take two cars in to the lower trailhead, at the 19.7 mile *31.6 km* point on FR 618, mentioned above. You can drive in about 0.9 miles *1.5 km,* to the parking place. Leave one car there and take the other to the top.
　　　　There is one trick at the top, and an important one. After you have hiked about 0.1 miles *0.16 km,* you will come to a gate. Go *inside* the gate. There is a path outside as well, but it is not your trail. The gate is not signed, so be sure to follow these instructions.
　　　　The first leg of the hike is on a mesa top. The area has been cleared, giving fine views in all directions. At 1.75 miles *2.8 km* you come to a drop-off where you descend to a lower bench. As you drop, you will see a pond

down to your right. This is Walker Basin.

You reach the pond at 2.5 miles *4.0 km*, where the trail gets a little tricky, not well marked. Up to now it has been a jeep road, but here it becomes a footpath. Walk around the right shoulder of the pond, and take the trail to the right, at the end of the fence. You will see cairns and limbs cut from trees. The path goes north from the pond.

From here you climb to the 3.3 mile *5.3 km* point, then walk across a fairly level stretch. At 4.2 miles *6.8 km* you come upon a mysterious trail-less sign, "Jacobs Tank 1/4 mi." At 4.75 miles *7.6 km* you come to another drop-off, where you have great views west. As you wind down from here, the views to the south open, to the Verde Valley.

At 5.4 miles *8.7 km* you reach the final drop-off where you enter an area of beautiful sandstone ledges with impressive sights both near at hand and far away. You reach the bottom at 7.25 miles *11.6 km* and walk across level country to get back to your waiting car at 8.0 miles *13 km*.

WALKER BASIN TRAIL

Sedona Y

89

89

179   I-17

14.7 mi.

I-17

6200   Altitude

4200

Feet: 2000
Miles: 8.0   Hard

618

(5.0 mi.)

2d Car
Here

8.0 mi.

9.8 mi.

P

7.3 mi.

214

618

Driving Distance One Way, Miles: 31.8
Hiking Distance One Way, Miles: 8.0

WEIR TRAIL #85

Driving Distance One Way: 17.2 miles *27.6 km* (Time 30 minutes)
Access Road: All cars, Last 0.3 miles *0.5 km* good dirt road
Hiking Distance One Way: 2.5 miles *4.0 km* (Time 90 minutes)
How Strenuous: Moderate
Features: Views, Creek

NUTSHELL: Located in Wet Beaver Creek country, some 17.2 miles *27.6 km* southeast of Sedona. You hike for two miles on the Bell Trail then dip down to the creek to a pool formed by a weir.

DIRECTIONS:
From the Sedona Y Go:
　　　　South on Highway 179 (toward Phoenix) for 14.7 Miles *23.5 km* (MP 298.9), to the I-17 intersection. Go straight here rather than getting on I-17. Follow paved road FR 618 until you see a sign for Beaver Creek Ranger Station and trailheads at 16.9 miles *27.1 km*. Turn left. Parking is at 17.2 miles *27.6 km*.

TRAILHEAD: This is a marked and maintained trail. There is a sign at the parking lot for the **Bell Trail**. Take this trail.

DESCRIPTION: From the trailhead the trail goes up the canyon along the course of Wet Beaver Creek, sometimes near it, sometimes away from it, but always following its path. There is also a Dry Beaver Creek in the area. "Wet" means that the creek you will follow on this hike flows year around. Even when you are not near the creek you can hear water running, a pleasant sound in desert country. The waterway is lined with typical riparian vegetation, tall sycamores and cottonwoods.
　　　　The trail is broad and easy to walk, as it was a road. You will cross through an active cattle ranch. Don't be startled if you run into some cows. As you walk along the trail pay attention to the canyon walls. You will note that they contain the same redrock as in Sedona in the lower layers but that the top is covered with a thick cap of lava. If it weren't for that top layer of hard rock, this country would be just as eroded and colorful as Sedona.
　　　　At about 0.60 miles *1.0 km* look for a large boulder on the left side of the trail. On the side that faces away from you are a number of interest-

ing petroglyphs. At 1.5 miles *2.4 km*, you will find the **Casner Mt. South** trail to the left. At the 2.0 mile *3.2 km* point you will reach the **Apache Maid Trail, #15** branching to the left. Soon after this fork you will find a signboard. Just beyond the signboard is a trail going off to the right, down to the water. This is the Weir Trail, your objective. It is 0.50 miles *0.8 km* from the fork to the water.

A weir is a low dam used to regulate the flow of water. You will see the weir, complete with a gaging station that is used to measure water depth and runoff. When the water is high, the pool formed by the weir is a good swimming hole. Upstream from the pool is an interesting cable car and a dense blackberry bramble.

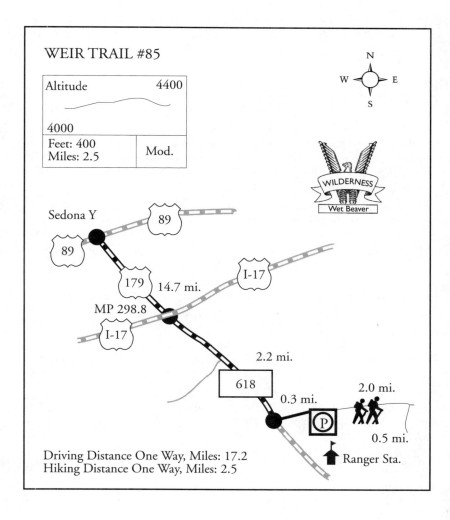

WEST CLEAR CREEK TRAIL #17

General Information
Location Map G6
Buckhorn Mtn., Walker Mtn. USGS Maps
Coconino Forest Service Map

Driving Distance One Way: 29.5 miles *47.2 km* (Time 1 hour)
Access Road: All cars, Last 12.3 miles *20 km* good dirt road
Hiking Distance One Way: 1.0 miles *1.6 km* (Time 30 minutes)
How Strenuous: Easy
Features: Historic ranch, Permanent creek, Wide easy trail, Views

NUTSHELL: This easy trail starts from the West Clear Creek Campground 29.5 miles *47.2 km* south of Sedona and takes you through an interesting old ranch to a lovely creek in a deep scenic canyon.

DIRECTIONS:
From the Sedona Y Go:
    South on Highway 179 (toward Phoenix) for 14.7 miles *23.6 km*, to the I-17 Interchange. Instead of going onto I-17, go underneath it onto paved road FR 618. The paving ends at the Beaver Creek bridge. Follow FR 618. At the 24.5 mile *39.2 km* point, you will see a dirt road branching left to Cedar Flat. Keep going south on FR 618. At 26.5 miles *42.4 km* you will come to a road to the left (FR 215) to the West Clear Creek Campground. Turn left on FR 215 and go to the 29.5 mile *47.2 km* point, all the way to the end of the road. Parking for the trail is located there and signed.

TRAILHEAD: At the parking area you will see trail signs for the West Clear Creek Trail #17, and the **Blodgett Basin Trail.**

DESCRIPTION: When we visited this trail in March 1992, it was still routed up the side of a hill to avoid crossing the old Bull Pen Ranch. (This trail is also called the Bull Pen Trail.) The ranch is now public property, so, for an easy enjoyable hike, ignore the official trail and just walk the ranch road The first part of the road is lovely, as it is quite close to the creek and passes through a lush riparian forest. Farther on it moves away from Clear Creek and opens up into typical scrub and cactus habitat.
    At 0.66 miles *1.1 km* you will come out into an open field, where you see a sight that sticks in the mind of every visitor to this place, a rock house with cactus growing on its roof. When you inspect this small structure, which is about 20 x 12 feet, you will see that the builders heaped dirt on the roof, an old trick in the Southwest. Prickly pears got established in

235

this dirt and have grown there for years. Behind the rock house, on the north side of the canyon, there is a hill composed of exposed red sandstone adding a welcome touch of color to the landscape. The ranch site is very beautiful.

You will continue along the road to the 1.0 mile *1.6 km* point where the fields end and the road dips down to the creek. There you will find some redrock ledges just above the water that seem to have been placed there by nature as places to sit and take the sun and watch the creek gurgle by.

When the water is low enough, you can wade across the creek here and hike upstream on the opposite bank for another mile with relative ease. Beyond that point the hike gets pretty tough. There is a place at about 3.0 miles *4.8 km* where the trail lifts out of the canyon on the north wall, requiring a strenuous 2000 foot climb to a point on FR 214 about 1.2 miles *2.0 km* above the Blodgett Basin trail terminus.

For an easy day hike we recommend stopping at the 1.0 mile *1.6 km* point.

WEST FORK #108

General Information
Location Map B5
Dutton Hill and Munds Park USGS Maps
Coconino Forest Service Map

Driving Distance One Way: 10.5 miles *17 km* (Time 20 minutes)
Access Road: All cars, All paved
Hiking Distance One Way: 3.0 miles *4.8 km* (Time 90 minutes)
How Strenuous: Moderate
Features: Gorgeous canyon with stream

NUTSHELL: One of the best, most popular hikes in Arizona. The trailhead is located 10.5 miles *17 km* north of Sedona. **A personal favorite.**

DIRECTIONS:
From the Sedona Y Go:
North on Highway 89A (toward Flagstaff) for a distance of 10.5 miles *17 km* (MP 384.7.) You will see a road sign for the parking area, which requires a sharp turn to your left (west).

TRAILHEAD: On the west side of the parking area loop, you will see a sign board. This marks the trailhead.

DESCRIPTION: Since the first edition of this book, a parking area has been added and a new trailhead installed. From the new trailhead at the new parking area, the trail goes west, to Oak Creek. You must climb down the east bank and cross the creek on some stepping stones. This can be a bit dicey when the stones are wet, and we have seen several people have trouble with this crossing. You then climb up the opposite bank and turn left (south) on a wide sandy track. Soon you will draw abreast of houses across the creek. Just beyond the last house, you will enter the ruins of Mayhews Lodge, where there are a few brick structures still standing. This point is 0.3 miles *0.48 km* from the beginning.

Mayhews Lodge was built as a hunting and fishing lodge in the early 1900s by the Thomas family. Zane Grey immortalized the location in *The Call of the Canyon*. The owners of the lodge tried to raise as much of their own food as they could for guests. You can see areas where they had orchards and vegetable gardens and you will see the remains of their chicken coop set into a shallow cave. The Forest Service bought the lodge two decades ago only to have it burn shortly afterward.

As you enter the West Fork canyon you become immediately aware of the charm of this place, with the gentle stream flowing through a lush habitat framed by tremendously high and colorful canyon walls. It is a magic place.

The path follows along the streambed, crossing back and forth over the water. At the crossings you will usually find stepping stones that allow you to get across without getting wet, but these are not foolproof. You should count on getting your feet wet. Some hikers prefer to wear old tennies or jungle boots and wade. You will find distance markers every half mile.

The canyon is narrow, so you are often right next to the cliffs. The stream has undercut them in many places, creating interesting overhangs. You really feel the majesty of the canyon on this hike, for the cliffs dwarf you.

The canyon is 12.0 miles *19.2 km* long. We have you stop at 3.0 miles, a distance that allows you to see some of the finest parts.

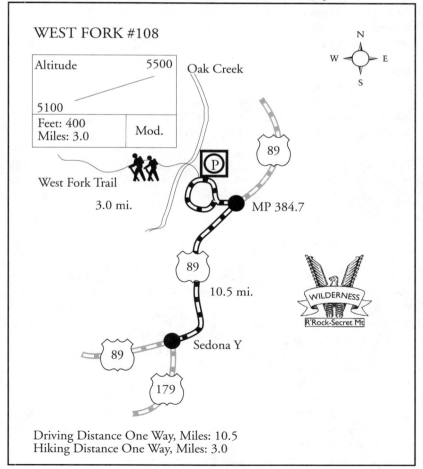

WEST FORK #108

Altitude	5500
5100	
Feet: 400 Miles: 3.0	Mod.

Oak Creek

N
W — E
S

89

P

West Fork Trail
3.0 mi.

MP 384.7

89

10.5 mi.

WILDERNESS
R'Rock-Secret Mt

89

Sedona Y

179

Driving Distance One Way, Miles: 10.5
Hiking Distance One Way, Miles: 3.0

WILD HORSE CONNECTOR

General Information
Location Map F5
Munds Mountain and Sedona USGS Maps
Coconino Forest Service Map

Driving Distance One Way: 9.3 miles *15 km* (Time 15 minutes)
Access Road: All cars, All paved
Hiking Distance One Way: 1.75 miles *2.8 km* (Time One hour)
How Strenuous: Moderate
Features: Views

NUTSHELL: Located 9.3 miles *15 km* south of the Sedona Y, this horse trail starts at a corral on the Jack's Canyon Road, then skirts a subdivision, climbs to a low saddle on a ridge, then joins the Hot Loop Trail halfway up Wild Horse Mesa.

DIRECTIONS:
From the Sedona Y Go:
      South on Highway 179 (toward Phoenix) for a distance of 7.2 miles *11.5 km* (MP 306.2) to Jack's Canyon Road. There is a stoplight at the junction. Turn left (east) onto Jack's Canyon Road and follow it. It is paved all the way. Drive to the 9.3 miles *15 km* point, where there is a road to your right going to a corral. If you see tall green steel poles where a horse trail crosses the road, you have gone too far. Go through the gate and drive to the end of the gray gravel driveway. Park by the corrals but don't block the loading chute.

TRAILHEAD: Not marked. Start at the corrals.

DESCRIPTION: From the corrals, you will see a set of jeep tracks running south, parallel to the corral fences. This is the main horse trail, and is the trail that you will follow. For the first 0.6 miles *1.0 km*, the trail moves around a subdivision. Do not take any of the branch trails to your right, as they lead to private corrals. Keep moving uphill, toward the mountain.
      As the trail passes the last house, it begins to rise significantly. You can see a low saddle on the ridge ahead of you. This is your first target. Look behind you as you climb, and you will have good views into the Jack's Canyon, Pine Valley areas.
      The climb is not terribly hard and the trail is a good one, easy to follow. You will reach the top of the saddle in about 1.1 miles *1.76 km*. From this vantage point you will have excellent views to the north, into the Village

of Oak Creek area and its surroundings. A particularly nice feature about this hike is that just over the other side of the ridge, the landscape will change entirely. In just a few steps, you will change from views of an urban scene to views of wild undeveloped country.

The trail dips down below the ridge and moves east. You will pass through some nice redrocks, with thrilling views. The big canyon you can see here is Woods Canyon. Your trail winds down and comes to a side canyon where you cross a slickrock face. On the other side of this you will intersect a larger trail. This is the **Hot Loop Trail**, coming up from its base on the **Woods Canyon Trail**. From this point you can turn left and climb to the top of Wild Horse Mesa. (When the first settlers came into Sedona, starting in 1876, they found herds of wild horses in the area, and some of the men caught and sold them. There was a large band of horses on top of this mesa, hence its name). It is a steep climb of 700' in about 0.75 miles *1.2 km*. The Hot Loop Trail then goes some seven miles to Jack's Point.

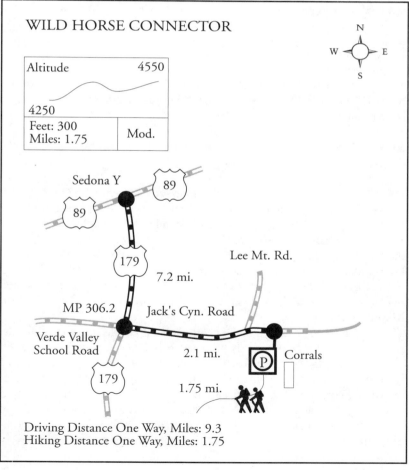

WILD HORSE CONNECTOR

Altitude	4550
4250	

| Feet: 300 Miles: 1.75 | Mod. |

Sedona Y — 89 — 89

179

Lee Mt. Rd.

7.2 mi.

MP 306.2   Jack's Cyn. Road

Verde Valley School Road

2.1 mi.   Corrals

179

1.75 mi.

Driving Distance One Way, Miles: 9.3
Hiking Distance One Way, Miles: 1.75

WILSON CANYON #49

General Information
Location Map D5
Munds Park USGS Map
Coconino Forest Service Map

Driving Distance One Way: 1.1 miles *1.8 km* (Time 5 minutes)
Access Road: All cars, All paved
Hiking Distance One Way: 1.5 miles *2.4 km* (Time 1 hour)
How Strenuous: Moderate
Features: Views

NUTSHELL: Just 1.1 miles *1.8 km* north of Sedona, Wilson Canyon is spanned by Midgley Bridge. You can take a short easy stroll along the rim of the canyon or a longer hike up the canyon.

DIRECTIONS:
From the Sedona Y Go:
North on Highway 89A (toward Flagstaff) for a distance of 1.1 miles *1.8 km* (MP 375.9). Go just across Midgley Bridge and turn left into the parking area.

TRAILHEAD: You will see a rusty sign at the parking lot. It reads, "Wilson Canyon #49."

DESCRIPTION: You will see the parking area just across the bridge. This is a very popular spot and you may not find a parking place open. If not, go up the road a bit. There are several wide shoulders for parking.
The trailhead is easy to locate. Just walk toward the picnic tables at the end of the parking lot. There you will find the Wilson Monument, a bronze plaque set in stone, and two rusty signs. The sign to the left marks Wilson Canyon #49 and is the one you want for this hike. The other sign marks an uphill trail, Wilson Mountain #10, which we call **Wilson Mountain South**.
The Wilson Canyon hike is little more than a leisurely stroll for the first 0.25 miles *0.4 km*. This may be as much of a hike as some readers want.
Up to the 0.25 mile *0.4 km* point, the trail is as broad and flat as a roadway. It was a road. Turn around and look at Midgley Bridge and imagine what the road would have been without it. Drivers had to make a sharp turn and go up the canyon to a point where it narrowed and a bridge could readily be installed, cross over the canyon, then go back out and make another sharp turn. Old-timers tell us that the sharp unexpected turns were very

dangerous. You will see the old bridge placements at the head of Wilson Canyon. This is the place to stop for the short hike.

For the longer hike, you keep walking up the canyon, which is sometimes wet. The trail meanders from bank to bank There are many intersecting paths, but it is easy to stay on course if you keep paralleling the canyon. At about 0.5 miles *0.8 km* you will see a footpath going uphill to your left. This is part of the **Old Jim Thompson Road**. A few yards beyond that you will see an alternate branch of the Old Jim Thompson Road coming down to intersect your path.

The trail is a gradual uphill climb, quite gentle. In a few places the trail will seem to scramble up a steep bank and go to the top. Ignore these side trails and keep following the canyon bottom.

The canyon encloses you so that you can't see much outside it. At 1.5 miles *2.4 km* you will reach a place where a side trail goes uphill to the right. This goes up to a viewpoint and is the place to quit.

WILSON CANYON #49

Altitude	4700
4600	
Feet: 100 Miles: 1.5	Mod.

N
W — E
S

1.5 mi.

89

MP 375.9

1.1 mi.

Midgley Bridge

89

Sedona Y

89

179

WILDERNESS
R'Rock-Secret Mt

Driving Distance One Way, Miles: 1.1
Hiking Distance One Way, Miles: 1.5

WILSON MOUNTAIN NORTH #123

General Information
Location Map C5
Munds Park and Wilson Mt. USGS Maps
Coconino Forest Service Map

Driving Distance One Way: 5.3 miles *8.5 km* (Time 10 minutes)
Access Road: All cars, All paved
Hiking Distance One Way: 3.4 miles *5.5 km* (Time 4.0 hours)
How Strenuous: Hard
Features: Views

NUTSHELL: Located just north of Sedona, Wilson is the highest mountain in the area. This trail, originating at Encinoso Picnic Area, climbs Wilson's north face.

DIRECTIONS:
From the Sedona Y Go:
North on Highway 89A (toward Flagstaff) for a distance of 5.3 miles *8.5 km* (MP 379.5), where you will see the Encinoso Picnic Area to your left. Park in the Encinoso parking lot.

TRAILHEAD: From the parking lot, walk up the canyon on the shoulder of the road about 100 yards. There you will see a trail sign reading, "Wilson Mt. #123" with the trail heading uphill.

DESCRIPTION: The trail climbs to the top of a small ridge at about 0.25 miles *0.4 km*, where you have a good vantage point to look across the canyon at the cliffs of the east wall. During spring runoff and after hard rains, the Encinoso Waterfall appears there and this is one of the best places from which to see it.

From this ridge the trail climbs gently for another 0.75 miles *1.2 km* along a refreshing, wooded side canyon through a lovely mixed forest of pine, fir, spruce, oak and maple. The streambed here seldom carries any water, but when it does, it is delightful. Best bet for this is in April and May.

At 1.0 miles *0.16 km* the serious work begins. Here the canyon pinches in and the trail begins a steep climb up the north face of Wilson. If you want an easy hike, the 1.0 mile point is the place to stop. The ascent beyond the 1.0 mile point is treacherous if the trail is slick with mud or snow. When dry, it is only strenuous. You will climb 1300 feet in 0.5 miles *0.8 km*.

After this hard haul, you top out on a flat flank of Wilson called

First Bench. You will have great views to the north from here. Across Oak Creek Canyon you will see a major tributary, Munds Canyon, which empties into Oak Creek at Indian Gardens.

Keep walking south along First Bench. At the 2.0 mile *3.2 km* point, at the edge of First Bench, you will intersect the Wilson Mt. South Trail coming up from Midgley Bridge. The junction is well marked with cairns. Take a look off the rim from here; it's great! You may want to quit here.

From this trail junction, you can go to the top of the mountain. See the **Wilson Mountain South** article for details. You will have to hike 0.60 miles *1.0 km* to Tool Shed, at the top of the mountain, climbing 800 feet, then hike a level trail 0.80 miles *1.3 km* to the North Rim viewpoint, 3.4 miles *5.5 km* total one way from Encinoso. This hike is 0.60 miles *1.0 km* longer than the Wilson Mountain South Trail because of the walk across First Bench from north to south.

WILSON MOUNTAIN SOUTH #10

General Information
Location Map D5
Munds Park and Wilson Mt. USGS Maps
Coconino Forest Service Map

Driving Distance One Way: 1.1 miles *1.8 km* (Time 5 minutes)
Access Road: All cars, All paved
Hiking Distance One Way: 2.8 miles *4.5 km* (Time 3.5 hours)
How Strenuous: Hard
Features: Views

NUTSHELL: This popular hike starts at Midgley Bridge, north of Sedona, and goes up Wilson Mountain to the highest point in the area, then crosses the mountain top to a fabulous lookout point.

DIRECTIONS:
From the Sedona Y Go:
North on Highway 89A (toward Flagstaff) for a distance of 1.1 miles *1.8 km* (MP 375.9). Just across Midgley Bridge is the parking area.

TRAILHEAD: You will see a rusty sign at the parking lot. It reads, "Wilson Mt. #10."

DESCRIPTION: The trailhead is easy to locate. Just walk toward the picnic tables. There you will find a bronze plaque set in stone, and two trail signs. The sign to the left is **Wilson Canyon**, #49. The other, uphill, is Wilson Mountain #10, which we call **Wilson Mountain South** in this book, and is the trail you want to take.
This hike is divided into three phases, each with a different feel:
Midgley Bridge to First Bench, 1.4 miles *2.3 km*, a 1700' climb;
First Bench to Tool Shed, 0.60 miles *1.0 km*, an 800' climb;
Tool Shed to North Rim, 0.80 miles *1.3 km*, fairly level.

Midgley Bridge to First Bench: This is a steep climb from the start. Ahead of you on the skyline you will see the saddle that is your destination. Along the way you have constantly enjoyable views of the formations of Wilson Mountain. You are in a high desert landscape, with juniper, manzanita and cactus. As you rise higher, you get into an area with little shade where you switchback to the top. This stretch would be murder on a hot sunny day. Finally you break over the top of First Bench, a long plateau running the length of the east side of the mountain. The views from here are very fine, though the bench itself is pretty drab and featureless.

First Bench to the Tool Shed: Take the path going left, toward the high cliffs. You will soon climb above First Bench and get into a heavy forest of pine and oak. This has a decidedly alpine feeling compared to the desert you have just been through. After a 500 foot climb you will come onto the top, where the land is pretty level, then make a modest 300 foot climb to the Tool Shed, where fire fighting tools are stored. The main trail goes ahead here, with a side trail to the left.

Tool Shed to North Rim: This is a delightful walk through a cool forest on nearly level ground, very easy compared to the first two phases of the hike. You are walking out to the mountain's north edge. When you come to a pond on the east side of the trail, you are almost at the end. Keep walking and you will come out onto a cliff face where you will find a soul-stirring view.

WILSON MOUNTAIN SOUTH #10

To North Rim

Altitude	7000

4500

Feet: 2500 Miles: 2.8	Hard

To Tool Shed

Altitude	7000

4500

Feet: 2500 Miles: 2.0	Hard

To First Bench

Altitude	6200

4500

Feet: 1700 Miles: 1.4	Hard

2.8 mi.

89

P

MP 375.9

Midgley Bridge

1.1 mi.

89

WILDERNESS
R'Rock-Secret Mt

Sedona Y

89

179

Driving Distance One Way, Miles: 1.1
Hiking Distance One Way, Miles: 2.8

WINDMILL MOUNTAIN

General Information
Location Map E2
Page Springs USGS Map
Coconino Forest Service Map

Driving Distance One Way: 9.5 miles *15.2 km* (Time 30 minutes)
Access Road: All vehicles, Last 1.3 miles *2.1 km* rough dirt road
Hiking Distance One Way: 1.0 miles *1.6 km* (Time 45 minutes)
How Strenuous: Moderate
Features: Views

NUTSHELL: This sprawling mountain 9.5 miles *15.2 km* southwest of Sedona is rather drab but is a platform for great views.

DIRECTIONS:
From the Sedona Y Go:
          Southwest on Highway 89A (toward Cottonwood) for a distance of 8.2 miles *13.2 km* (MP 365.9) to a place where you will see a dirt road, FR 9573C, going off to your right through a gate in a barbed wire fence. Go through the gate and follow FR 9573C. At 8.3 miles *13.3 km*, an unmarked road forks right. Ignore it. At 8.7 miles *14 km* FR 9573 branches to the left. Ignore it. At 8.9 miles *14.3 km* there is a fork. Take the right turn and begin to circle around the mountain headed north. At 9.3 miles *15 km* you will be on the north side and you will see a big power line. Turn left on FR 9573P. Drive up to the power line and park at 9.5 miles *15.2 km.*

TRAILHEAD: There are no signs. You will see a trail going uphill along the power line. Take that trail.

DESCRIPTION: As you drive to the trailhead, there are many roads in the area due to the wood cutting which was allowed there recently. The cutters went off in all directions, leaving tracks that sometimes look like roads but are not; so follow the map carefully. If you keep in mind that your destination is to curl around the north face of Windmill Mountain in counterclockwise direction, you will be able to pick out the correct path.
          From the parking place a jeep road goes up along the power line for 0.60 miles *1.0 km*, then it ends where the line dips down into a valley. From this point the way to the top of the mountain is obvious. You just bushwhack there. There is no trail and none is needed. The country is open and it is easy to see the way. The footing is not good, due to an abundance of rock and cactus. In fact, this place is a veritable cactus garden, so watch your step.

You will come out on the north rim of the mountain, from where you will get great views of beautiful redrock country. You will see **The Cockscomb**, **Doe Mountain**, **Bear Mountain** and **Loy Butte** very clearly. From where you will be standing, the rim of Windmill Mountain curves like a reverse C, with the opening to the east. It is plain to see that you are on a shield volcano like its cousins **Schuerman Mountain** and **House Mountain**.

Suit yourself in deciding how far you want to hike on the mountain top. Most hikers will want to make the whole circuit around the top. As you work west you will get views of **Casner Mountain, Black Mountain** and the Sycamore Pass country and you are high enough to enjoy grand panoramas of it all. The views to the south are dull.

WOODS CANYON TRAIL #93

General Information
Location Map G5
Munds Mt. and Sedona USGS Maps
Coconino Forest Service Map

Driving Distance One Way: 8.7 Miles *14 km* (Time 15 minutes)
Access Road: All cars, Paved except last 0.10 miles *0.16 km*
Hiking Distance One Way: 3.25 Miles *5.2 km* (Time 90 minutes)
How Strenuous: Moderate
Features: Views

NUTSHELL: South of the Sedona Y 8.7 miles *14 km*, this trail follows Woods Canyon, through which Dry Beaver Creek flows.

DIRECTIONS:
From the Sedona Y Go:
        South on Highway 179 (toward Phoenix) for 8.6 miles *13.8 km* (MP 304.8) to an unmarked dirt road to your left. Turn left on the road, follow it for 0.10 miles *0.2 km* and park.

TRAILHEAD: At the road you will see a gate and a rusty sign reading, "Woods Canyon #93."

DESCRIPTION: The gate is unlocked. Go through it. We recommend that you park just beyond the gate. You can drive farther but the road conditions are dicey, especially if the road is wet. We have driven in as far as a mile but do not recommend this unless you are sure you and your vehicle can handle it. If you park near the highway as we recommend then this is a 3.25 mile *5.2 km* hike each way.
        To follow the trail just walk along the main jeep road. At 2.0 miles *3.2 km* from the highway you will come to a fence. Just beyond the fence you will find a sign for the Hot Loop Trail, where the **Hot Loop Trail** branches off to the left, going uphill. It looks like a road. The Woods Canyon trail forks to the right here and turns into a footpath descending to the bottom of the canyon.
        We recommend going to about the 3.25 mile *5.2 km* point on the Woods Canyon Trail, where the trail goes onto a sloping redrock shelf above the water.
        Dry Beaver Creek usually is dry, living up to its name. During the spring thaw it can carry a lot of water and we have seen it at times when it was strong. This hike is more interesting when water is running. Your best

chance of hiking it when water is running is in March or April. There is another stream nearby called Wet Beaver Creek, which runs year around.

Woods Canyon goes all the way to Interstate-17 just south of the Pinewood Country Club in the Munds Park area. When you are driving on Interstate-17 you will see a sign for an exit marked "Fox Ranch" where the highway bridges Woods Canyon. Woods Canyon and Munds Canyon, which is located to the north, are major lateral canyons that cut into Oak Creek Canyon. You can see why Interstate-17 is located where it is: it crosses these canyons at their heads, where they are narrow. Even so, the highway department built high bridges at both places. These canyons were a major obstacle between Sedona and Flagstaff in the old days and detouring around them added miles to the trip.

The developed part of the trail ends at the 4.0 mile *6.4 km* point, but we think the best stopping place is at 3.25 miles *5.2 km*. To hike the entire length of the canyon would mean going a rough 12.0 miles *20 km* .

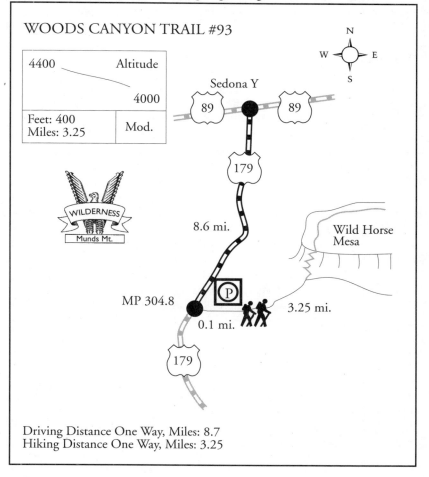

WOODS CANYON TRAIL #93

4400	Altitude
	4000
Feet: 400 Miles: 3.25	Mod.

N
W — E
S

Sedona Y

89   89

179

WILDERNESS
Munds Mt.

8.6 mi.

Wild Horse Mesa

MP 304.8

P

3.25 mi.

0.1 mi.

179

Driving Distance One Way, Miles: 8.7
Hiking Distance One Way, Miles: 3.25

YAVAPAI RIDGE TRAIL

General Information
Location Map F3
Sedona USGS Map
Coconino Forest Service Map

Drive Distance One Way: 8.8 miles *14.1 km* (Time 15 minutes)
Access Road: All vehicles, All paved
Hiking Distance, Complete Loop: 1.58 miles *2.5 km* (Time 1.0 hours)
How Strenuous: Moderate
Features: Oak Creek, Red Rock State Park, Views

NUTSHELL: This moderate trail is located in Red Rock State Park 8.8 miles *14.1 km* southwest of Sedona. It takes you through some scenic back country for interesting views.

DIRECTIONS:
From the Sedona Y Go:
    Southwest on Highway 89A (toward Cottonwood) for a distance of 5.5 miles *8.8 km* (MP 368.6) to the Lower Red Rock Loop Road. Turn left on the Lower Red Rock Loop Road and follow it to the 8.5 miles *13.6 km* point, where you will see the entry to Red Rock State Park. Turn right into the park. You will come to a toll booth where an admission is charged. From that point, drive to the Visitor Center and park there, at 8.8 miles *14.1 km*.

TRAILHEAD: This is a marked and maintained trail, part of the network of trails in the park. Go through the Visitor Center. Though the center is not marked as the trailhead for this hike, it is the starting point.

DESCRIPTION: Enjoy the Visitor Center and then walk through it, turning right on the paved trail. At 0.08 miles *0.13 km* you will come to the first trail junction. Here the **Smoke Trail** forks to the right, where Sentinel Crossing is located. Go straight here. The sign at this junction shows your destination as *"Kingfisher Crossing, House of Apache Fire."*
    Soon after this you will reach another junction. Turn right here, to Kingfisher Crossing, which is a major bridge across the creek. You will see the House of Apache Fire on a hilltop on the other side, a pueblo style structure of native rock.
    When you cross the bridge you will reach another trail junction, where the **Kisva** and **Eagles' Nest** trails go right. You will go left there, to the base of the knoll on which the House of Apache Fire is located. Turn left (SE) here, going uphill on the unpaved East Gate Road.

At the 0.6 mile *1.0 km* point, you will reach the beginning of the Yavapai Ridge Trail. It takes off to your left (north). At this same place, the Javelina Trail meets the road on the south.

The trail makes a 0.4 mile *0.64 km* loop around a point. Along the way you will find signs identifying some of the native plants that grow along the trail.

When you return to the East Gate Road, you turn right (NW) and follow the road down to the main path just across the Kingfisher Bridge, from where you cross the bridge and return to the Visitor Center.

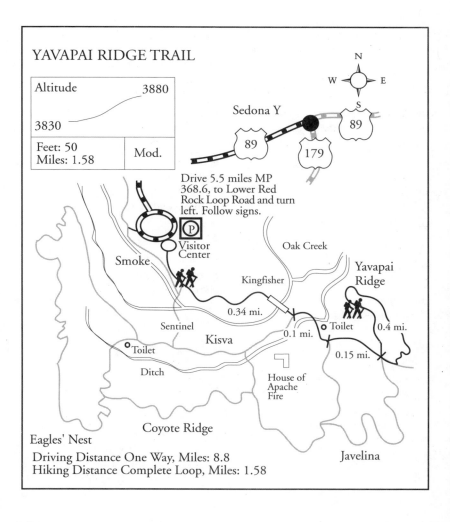

YAVAPAI RIDGE TRAIL

Altitude 3880

3830

Feet: 50
Miles: 1.58 Mod.

Sedona Y

89
179
89

Drive 5.5 miles MP 368.6, to Lower Red Rock Loop Road and turn left. Follow signs.

Visitor Center

Smoke

Oak Creek

Kingfisher

Yavapai Ridge

0.34 mi.

Sentinel

Kisva

0.1 mi.

Toilet

0.4 mi.

Toilet

0.15 mi.

Ditch

House of Apache Fire

Coyote Ridge

Eagles' Nest

Javelina

Driving Distance One Way, Miles: 8.8
Hiking Distance Complete Loop, Miles: 1.58

INDEX

Yesterday

AHS-PM

Sedona pioneers on the Harding Spring Trail

VORTEXES

Many persons claiming to be authorities have spoken about the Sedona Vortexes. Some of these people make very specific claims: that a particular Vortex is male, female, electric, magnetic, Yin, Yang, etc. These authorities don't always agree with each other.

We think it is a mistake to go to a Vortex expecting to find an anticipated experience. If you do, you may set up a self-fulfillment trap, where you deceive yourself into thinking that you have found what you were *told* you would find, rather than having your own authentic experience. We recommend that you approach a Vortex openly, seeking no pre-determined result.

The Vortexes are not hard to reach. You could easily visit all of them in a single day if you wish. Approach each one as a reverent seeker, open to what is there for you. Be quiet and unobtrusive so that you do not disturb others who are at the sites.

Experiences at the Vortexes range from negative, to neutral to cosmic. Each site is a place of beauty, worth visiting for aesthetic reasons; so your time will not be wasted even if you do not have a life-altering reaction. See the Index, page 254, for Vortexes that we recommend.

SCENIC DRIVES

Airport Hill: This is a very easy, short drive. The road is paved all the way. It takes you past one of the Sedona Vortex spots to the top of the hill where the Sedona Airport is located, an excellent viewpoint from which to see Sedona and some of its famous landmarks. When you get to the top, turn left and go toward the cross. You will find a fine lookout point there. See **Airport Hill Vortex,** page 12.

Boynton Canyon: If your time is limited and you want to see some of the redrock back country, this is a nice, short drive over paved roads. See **Boynton Canyon,** page 40.

Loy Butte: You will drive over ten miles of good unpaved roads through some unspoiled country, allowing you to get away from town and see some great redrocks. At the end of the trip you will be within an easy walk from the best Indian ruin in the area. See **Loy Butte,** page 138.

Oak Creek Vista: By taking this drive you will travel the length of Oak Creek Canyon, a beautiful scenic area. At the end of the drive you will be at a high point from which you can see the canyon, take a nature walk and learn about the area. See Oak Creek Canyon Recreation Map, page 8.

Schnebly Hill Road: This is a favorite six mile drive that takes you through some beautiful redrock country to the top of a hill from where you can enjoy sweeping views. The road is paved the first 0.5 miles. The unpaved portion can be traveled by an ordinary car unless the road is wet and slippery. See **Schnebly Hill Trail,** page 182.

RULES OF THE TRAIL

Artifacts: Leave potsherds, arrowheads, and other artifacts where you find them.

Bikes: Stay on roads and trails. You cannot ride a bike inside a Wilderness Area. Some people will go into an open area on a road and then sneak from it onto a wilderness trail. These scofflaws cause road and trail closures. Abuse it and lose it.

Cabins: Northern Arizona's climate is hard on cabins and they are scarce. Treat the few remaining ones gently. Don't climb on them, pry boards off, or go digging for buried treasure.

Dogs: If you take your dog along on a hike, it should be on a leash.

Garbage: Pack it in, pack it out.

Rock Art: Do not touch it. Skin oils cause deterioration. Professionals don't even apply chalk in order to photograph rock art today, because it causes damage.

Ruins: Just look, don't touch. Preserve them. Don't pot hunt, climb walls or do anything else that harm a ruin. Help them survive.

Trails: Stay on trails. They have been designed not only to provide access but also to bypass areas that can be harmed by people walking on them. Don't cut across switchbacks. It is disheartening to see how fast a trail can be destroyed by careless use.

Wilderness Areas: These are special places. The goal is to leave them unimpaired for future use and enjoyment. In the wilderness, the hiker is king. No mechanized travel is permitted in Wilderness Areas, not even bicycles. Horses are not allowed. Although Wilderness Areas may appear to be very rugged, they are quite fragile. Use them lightly. Leave no trace. They are a gift that we must all act to protect and preserve.

SEE YA ON THE TRAIL